How It Works®

Science and Technology

Third Edition

Marshall Cavendish
99 White Plains Road
Tarrytown, NY 10591

Website: www.marshallcavendish.com

Third edition updated by Brown Reference Group plc.

Library of Congress Cataloging-in-Publication Data
How it works: science and technology.—3rd ed.
p. cm.
Includes index.
ISBN 0-7614-7314-9 (set)   ISBN 0-7614-7322-X (Vol. 8)
1. Technology—Encyclopedias. 2. Science—Encyclopedias.
[1. Technology—Encyclopedias. 2. Science—Encyclopedias.]
T9 .H738 2003
603—dc21   2001028771

Consultant: Donald R. Franceschetti, Ph.D., University of Memphis

Brown Reference Group
Editor: Wendy Horobin
Associate Editors: Paul Thompson, Martin Clowes, Lis Stedman
Managing Editor: Tim Cooke
Design: Alison Gardner
Picture Research: Becky Cox
Illustrations: Mark Walker, Darren Awuah

Marshall Cavendish
Project Editor: Peter Mavrikis
Production Manager: Alan Tsai
Editorial Director: Paul Bernabeo

Printed in Malaysia
Bound in the United States of America
08 07 06 05 04   6 5 4 3 2

Title picture: The eye of the storm, see *Hurricane and Tornado*

How It Works®

Science and Technology

Volume 8

Gold
—————
Ink

Marshall Cavendish

New York • London • Toronto • Sydney

Contents

Volume 8

Gold

The story of gold and the history of humanity have been interwoven throughout recorded time. The reason for the preeminent position of gold can be traced to one particular chemical property of the metal: it will not oxidize under any naturally occurring conditions. Consequently, it is found in its free state rather than combined with other elements, like most metals. Gold can be fire refined, that is, melted and held at a temperature at which other less noble impurities will oxidize and float to the surface as dross to be discarded.

The fact that it is possible to obtain gold without advanced refining techniques meant that it was the earliest metal available. Its tarnish-free surface, attractive color, and very high density—1 cu. ft. (0.028 m³) of gold weighs over half a ton—as well as its rarity, make it highly prized.

Occurrence and extraction

Gold is widely distributed throughout the world, but only in a few localities is it present in sufficient quantities to make its recovery worthwhile. Some of the richer areas, such as California and Australia, have been pinpointed by the famous gold rushes of the 19th century, but the main producing region since the 1920s has been South Africa. In 1970, South Africa was responsible for almost 70 percent of the world's gold production, but by 1999 it had declined to 17.5 percent. However, South Africa is still the largest single producer in the world, followed by the United States with 13.2 percent and Australia with 11.7 percent.

The primary source of gold, in common with minerals of other metals, is quartz veins that have penetrated older rocks. With time, however, the veins are eroded and their remains are washed down to the sea by streams and rivers. The small particles of gold found in sand or silt are known as alluvial, or placer, deposits. In the Rand field in South Africa, the gold occurs in a quartz conglomerate rock thousands of feet underground. This gold at an earlier stage in its history had been an alluvial deposit in sand. Under the influence of pressure and heat at great depths, the sand formed a cement that bound the quartz pebbles of the conglomerate.

Alluvial gold is simpler to win, or recover, from the ore than vein or conglomerate gold. All that is required is a method of sifting through the silt and picking out the gold. Panning was the traditional technique of the prospector; a few pounds of silt were put in a pan and swilled away over the edge, leaving only the heavier gold particles behind. But since even in a fairly rich deposit,

◀ Gold nuggets encased in quartz. Gold is found in a pure form—not combined with other elements.

there may be little more than 1 oz. (28.3 g) of gold in every ton of silt or sand, commercial panning is now only of historical interest. Alluvial deposits are now worked on a much larger scale. They can be washed out of hillsides by powerful hydraulic jets similar to those used for mining china clay, although this method tends to add to the pollution of rivers, and for this reason, is forbidden in California. Alternatively, the deposits may be dredged up from the bottoms of lakes. In fact, it can be worthwhile to create a small artificial lake just to enable a dredger to operate. This method is known as paddocking, and it is possible, by moving the bounds of the lake, to cover large tracts of land and even dredge uphill.

Ore that has been mined from vein and conglomerate deposits must be crushed to release the gold. The amount of crushing required to liberate the gold depends on how finely it is dispersed

◀ Today, gold has important applications in space technology—such as providing a very thin film in this astronaut's helmet visor, and as a heat shield.

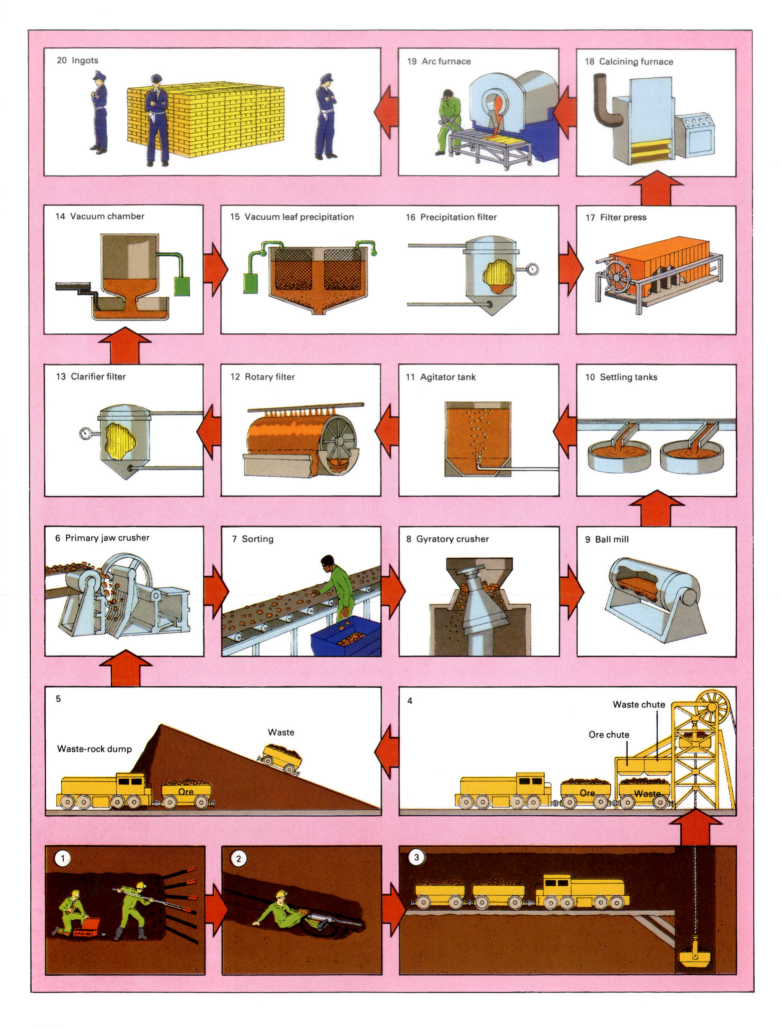

20 Ingots

19 Arc furnace

18 Calcining furnace

14 Vacuum chamber

15 Vacuum leaf precipitation

16 Precipitation filter

17 Filter press

13 Clarifier filter

12 Rotary filter

11 Agitator tank

10 Settling tanks

6 Primary jaw crusher

7 Sorting

8 Gyratory crusher

9 Ball mill

5

Waste-rock dump

Ore

Waste

4

Waste chute

Ore chute

Ore

Waste

1

2

3

◀ In gold production, miners blast out the waste rock (1). Ore is then extracted (2), taken to the shaft (3) then to the surface. There the waste is separated (4) and dumped (5). The ore is passed through a crusher (6) and more waste is removed by hand (7), mixed with water and pulped in a ball mill (9). This sludge is left to settle in tanks (10), then the thick residue is transferred to agitator tanks (11) where the gold is dissolved in a cyanide solution. A rotary filter (12) extracts the waste solids and the gold is passed through a clarifier filter (13) to be precipitated by the addition of zinc dust in a vacuum chamber (14). This process is completed in a vacuum leaf precipitation tank (15) or a precipitation filter (16). The gold slime produced is forced through a press (17), then roasted (18) to remove the zinc in vapor form. Finally, the gold is smelted (19) and poured into molds (20).

through the rock. If it is present only as fine, dispersed particles, the crushed ore must be reduced to a very fine powder by stamp, rod, or ball milling. The fine ore mixed with water is called a slime.

If the gold particles in alluvial deposits or crushed ore are sufficiently coarse (about 0.008 in., 200 μm, in diameter) they can be extracted by mechanical equipment such as rockers or strakes, which in principle amount to little more than scaled-up versions of the prospector's pan. A refinement of these techniques involves amalgamation. The gold is removed by washing the suitably crushed ore over slightly inclined copper plates coated with mercury. The gold alloys with the mercury to make an amalgam, which is periodically scraped from the plates and distilled in an iron retort to recover the gold.

Where gold is present in a slime as very small particles (about 0.0002 in., 5 μm, in diameter) that neither settle quickly nor have a good chance of amalgamation during their passage over the mercury-coated plates, it can normally be extracted economically only by cyanidation. In this process, which was invented by MacArthur and Forest in 1890, the slime is treated with a very dilute solution (about 0.05 percent) of sodium, potassium, or calcium cyanide in the presence of air. In large-scale practice calcium cyanide is used extensively.

The solution reaction (Eloner's reaction) can be written, in the case of sodium cyanide:

$$2Au + 4NaCN + O + H_2O \rightarrow 2NaAu(CN)_2 + 2NaOH$$
gold   sodium   oxygen   water   sodium   sodium
         cyanide   (from air)   cyanaurate   hydroxide

▼ The British Angel gold coin, official tender in the Isle of Man. The reverse of the coin shows the Archangel Michael slaying a dragon, a theme dating from medieval times, when it was first used in France. Made of gold from European sources, the Angel is popular with those wishing to invest in bullion.

After the gold plus any silver that may be associated with it have been dissolved in this manner, these metals can be recovered in various ways.

In the classical procedure, the gold-bearing solution is filtered from the leached ore particles, deaerated under vacuum, and the gold and silver precipitated by addition of zinc powder. The equation for the reaction in the case of sodium is

$$2NaAu(CN)_2 + Zn \rightarrow Na_2Zn(CN)_4 + 2Au$$
sodium cyanaurate   zinc   sodium zinc cyanide   gold

The precipitate is collected by filtration, and the excess zinc either dissolved away in acid or oxidized by heating the precipitate in air. A crude bullion can then be recovered from the material by smelting. It usually contains over 75 percent gold together with the silver that has been extracted with it plus small amounts of other metals.

This method for recovery of gold and silver from cyanide slimes is being replaced by a carbon-in-pulp (CIP) process in which activated carbon granules are added to the cyanided slime, or pulp. The gold and silver are strongly absorbed on these granules, which are separated by flotation and treated separately for recovery of the metals, either by burning off the carbon or by leaching with strong cyanide solutions.

The CIP process may itself be replaced by a resin-in-pulp (RIP) process in which the carbon granules are replaced by granules of ion-exchange resins characterized by their ability to take up gold and silver from cyanide solutions. An advantage of the CIP and RIP processes is that they do not involve the costly step of filtering barren ore.

Refining

The purity of gold is expressed in terms of its fineness. The totally pure metal is 1,000 fine, whereas an alloy containing, for example, 70 percent gold is 700 fine, and so on. Thus, gold extracted by the cyanide process (over 75 percent pure) normally has a fineness of over 750.

There are two important methods of further purification. In one, borax is put on top of the molten metal and chlorine gas is bubbled through. Most of the base metals present as impurities are turned into chlorides, which either come off as fumes or form a slag with the borax. The completion of the chlorination process is marked by the appearance of red-brown fumes of gold chloride. Chlorine-purified gold is usually 995 fine, depending on the nature of the impurities and the extent of the treatment. Purification by the Wohlwill electrolytic process yields gold better than 999 fine. The gold is deposited by electrolysis, using a technique comparable to that used for copper.

Applications

Although much of the gold won from the earth in the past is held for monetary purposes in bank vaults, the amount of this gold is not changing significantly, because the amounts of gold used for fabrication purposes in industry are now considerable. Moreover, significant quantities of gold are also purchased privately for investment purposes.

Gold jewelry

The production of jewelry creates the biggest demand for new gold. Since the pure metal is soft, it is rarely used in this form. Alloying with other metals, in particular, silver, copper, nickel, palladium, and zinc, yields a range of alloys with the required resistance to abrasion and corrosion. Moreover, such alloying permits the production of gold jewelry alloys in a range of shades—yellow, white, green, and red.

The quality and price of gold jewelry therefore depend greatly upon the content of gold in the metal used. Traditionally, this content is expressed in terms of the karats of the alloy—the number of parts by mass of the alloy. Thus pure gold is 24 karats, which is equivalent to 1,000 fine.

Only alloys of certain karats or fineness are permissible in most countries. The commonly accepted karats and corresponding finenesses are:

Karats	Fineness
22	916.6
18	750.0
14	583.3
10	416.6
9	375.0

Usually manufacturers stamp the karats or fineness on each article. In some countries, such stamping or hallmarking is compulsory and controlled. The term karat gold jewelry is reserved for jewelry made from an alloy of a recognized karat total. Such jewelry must be distinguished from gold-plated jewelry made from a cheap, nonprecious alloy and then decorated by electroplating a thin film of gold on it.

Karat gold jewelry must also be distinguished from rolled gold, gold-filled, or doublé jewelry, which are made from base metals that have been mechanically clad with a thin coating of gold. Rolled gold or gold-filled sheet is made by encasing a slab of base metal between gold or gold alloy sheets and rolling the composite to the required thickness.

Gold is used widely in the electronics industry because of its high electric conductivity, its low contact resistance, its resistance to tarnishing and corrosion, and its effect upon the electric properties of semiconductors. Its most important applications in this field are in the production of gold-plated connectors, thin-film gold circuitry, wire connectors to semiconductors, and contacts to semiconductors.

Gold is used with platinum, palladium, silver, copper, and other metals in dental prostheses and inlays. These metals are combined as alloys that have been developed especially for their mechanical properties, tarnish and corrosion resistance, biocompatibility, castability, ease of fabrication, and susceptibility to coating with porcelain.

Gold is extensively used for decoration of ceramics and of other metals. In the decoration of ceramics, the gold is applied in the form of solutions of certain of its complexes in organic media. On firing, the organic matter is burned off and the gold left as an adherent film on the ceramic base. In the decoration of metals, the gold is usually applied by electrodeposition or by cladding. Electrodeposition is usually carried out from solutions containing potassium gold cyanide. By codepositing other metals with the gold, gold-alloy coatings of different colors can be obtained.

Thin films of gold are used as heating elements in aircraft windows and very thin films of gold are applied to the window glass of air-conditioned buildings. Their function is to reflect radiant heat. Because of their ability to do this, they are also used as heat shields on spacecraft.

Alloys of gold also find use as high-temperature-brazing alloys in jet engines, as well as in temperature and high-pressure measuring instruments. Gold is also used in small amounts in the sensitization of photographic films and in the phosphors that create the images on television screens. It has many applications in medicine, and in particular, certain complexes of gold find application in the treatment of arthritis. The number of high-technology applications of gold is also increasing steadily.

▲ Golden windows in a high-rise London office. Applied in a very thin layer on glass, gold can cut out most infrared rays.

 SEE ALSO: Alloy • Coins and minting • Geology • Metal

Governor

A turbine hall in a power plant with four 500 MW turbogenerator units. Governors maintain the frequency of the AC supply.

A governor is an automatic control system used to regulate the rotational speed of a machine. The governor senses speed of rotation and compares this with the required value, correcting any error by altering the energy input to the machine.

In the simplest arrangement, the governor directly adjusts the energy flow, as with a centrifugal governor for a steam turbine. Here a shaft carrying weighted arms is rotated by a drive. Centrifugal force causes the weighted arms to pivot outward, and this movement is transferred through a linkage to provide the control action. Movement of the arms may be resisted by a spring so that if the speed rises above the required value, the force from the arms lifts the control linkage against the spring force to reduce the fuel supply. Conversely, if the speed falls below the set value, the spring force is greater than that from the arms and so moves the control linkage down to increase the fuel supply. This is a negative feedback system working in a closed loop.

This type of governor reacts only to a change in the sensed speed, and friction in the mechanism leads to a response lag. In addition, the amount of controlling action reduces as the set speed is approached, and these factors can lead to droop—a temporary or permanent change from the desired speed. An ideal governor that does not suffer from droop is known as isochronous.

Servomechanisms

The output from the governor can be amplified before being applied to work the control device, giving a servomechanism. Although mechanical means can be used to give the necessary ampli-fication, it is more usual for hydraulic power amplification to be used. Here, the governor action is used to control a valve that regulates the flow of oil to a power piston that operates the engine fuel control unit. The amplification available ensures that even a small output from the governor is sufficient to produce the required control action, so there is no droop.

In such an arrangement, however, the controlling force is not applied until the engine has speeded up enough for the governor to return to the set position. The inevitable lag in the system response means that the speed may continue to increase after it has reached the set level. In turn, this response leads to a further control action that reduces the speed to just below the set value, resulting in a control action to increase the speed, and so on. The result is that the engine speed oscillates around the set speed. These oscillations can be overcome by introducing a feedback path to link the governor mechanism to the output of the power unit. Then as the power unit starts to operate the engine control, it also acts to reduce the governor setting, so the engine speed rises smoothly to the required value without overshooting and oscillating.

Increasing use is being made of electronic speed-sensing systems—combining output signals with the output or load sensors— to give any required response in an automatic control system.

SEE ALSO:

HYDRAULICS • INTERNAL COMBUSTION ENGINE • SERVOMECHANISM • STEAM ENGINE • THERMODYNAMICS • TURBINE

Grass-Cutting Equipment

Until recent centuries, the principal grass-cutting tool was the scythe—a crescent-shaped metal blade, sharpened on the inner edge, fixed at one end to a wooden shaft. Land workers would clear rough grass and other vegetation using horizontal sweeps to catch stalks in the blade and cut them. Often, animals such as sheep and goats would be encouraged to graze on scythed land to complete the clearance and control regrowth.

In the late 18th century, a British landscape gardener, Lancelot "Capability" Brown, established a style of landscaping that included lawns cultivated to resemble natural grassland. He applied this so-called English style to the grounds of more than 100 country estates in Britain. The popularity of lawns spread through Europe and to other parts of the world, taking with it the need to maintain grass at a consistent height. Another 18th-century trend that stimulated the spread of finely maintained grassland was the growing popularity of the game of golf.

For many years, the only way to keep greens and lawns in peak condition was to employ teams of workers to cross the land in rows, using small sharp scythes to shave grass sometimes twice or three times a week. This practice gave rise to the description "shaven" for a well-trimmed lawn.

▲ This grass-cutting machine uses five cylinder mowers driven by the hydraulic system of the tractor. Such machines are cost-effective for cutting large expanses of grass.

Push mowers

The first mechanical device for trimming grass was patented in 1830 by the British inventor Edwin Beard Budding. His machine was of the cylinder type, similar to some modern machines, and incorporated helical cutting edges driven from a large rear roller via a chain drive.

A typical modern cylinder mower has a rotating cutting cylinder that consists of between five and ten helical blades mounted on a shaft so that their cutting edges lie on a cylindrical surface. The grass is cut by a scissor action between the helical cutting edges and a straight horizontal blade, parallel to the axis of the cylindrical blade, that lies close to the ground at the approximate cutting height. The fixed horizontal blade is made of a harder metal than that of the cylinder blades, which it sharpens as the mower cuts. From time to time, the position of the fixed blade must be adjusted to compensate for wear of the blades.

The twist of the helical blades is such that the leading end of each reaches the fixed blade just before the trailing end of the preceding blade leaves it. A chain-and-sprocket drive couples the cylinder to a large rear roller so that the cylinder rotates as the mower is pushed. The weight of the rear roller also helps level the ground surface.

Power mowers

The first motorized cylinder motors were built around 1920. They used two-stroke gasoline engines similar to those of motorcycles to drive the cutting cylinders. The main advantage of a motor-driven cutting cylinder lies in the greater rate of cuts (blade passes). A power mower can achieve 50 cuts per ft. (165 cuts/m) compared with 12 cuts per ft. (40 cuts/m) for a push mower, providing a better finish in less time.

A second advantage of motorized mowers is that the faster cutting action produces fine cuttings that fall to the roots of the grass and gradually decompose. In contrast, the longer cuttings from mechanical mowers would form an unsightly layer on top of the grass that would stifle its healthy growth. For this reason, clippings from mechanical mowers are caught in a bucket attachment as they are hurled from the cutting cylinder, or subsequently removed by raking.

Developments of the earliest powered mowers include electrically powered mowers and large ride-on mowers whose engines provide propulsion for the mower as well as drive for the cutting cylinder. Electric mowers are relatively quiet and produce no fumes; their cables can restrict motion and range, however, as well as presenting a risk of electrical shock if the cable is accidentally cut. Engine-driven mowers are relatively noisy and produce fumes, although these problems are rarer with four-stroke gasoline or propane engines than with noisier two-stroke engines that burn a mixture of gasoline and lubricating oil.

Rotary and hover mowers

These closely related types of mowers use a single blade that rotates in a horizontal plane to cut grass. The blade is covered from above by a squared-off dome of glass-reinforced or otherwise toughened plastic that contains any small stones that are struck by the rotating blade.

The difference between the two types of mowers is in their suspension. The casing of a simple rotary mower rests on two pairs of wheels that keep the blade at the required cutting height, while a hover mower has a blower that injects air into the casing so that the mower skims across lawns like an air-cushion vehicle. Hover mowers are lighter to move when in operation, and the fact that they dispense with wheels makes them more easy to maneuver and causes less damage to the surface of the mowed lawn.

The blades are made of toughened steel, which bends rather than shatters on high-speed impacts with stone. An electric motor or gasoline engine provides power for the blade and, in the case of hover mowers, for the blower.

The cutting height is adjusted by adjusting the wheel position, in the case of a rotary mower, or by adjusting the position of the blade within the casing. The latter is the only option for a hover mower, since the casing skims at a fixed height of around 0.25 in. (6 mm) above the ground. The quality of finish is generally rougher than that achieved with a cylinder mower.

String trimmers

Another type of device that uses the rotating-blade principal is the string trimmer. Instead of using rigid blades, however, a string trimmer uses a flexible nylon filament to cut through grass and other vegetation. The filament is typically between 0.05 and 0.15 in. (1.3–3.8 mm) thick.

The filament rotates at high speed on the end of a shaft driven by an electric motor or gasoline engine. A dome casing protects the user from flying debris, while a lens-shaped section cut from the dome allows the filament to attack stalks from the side and trim edges. Most models are light, handheld machines; others are wheel mounted, and their filaments can be inserted in the shaft at a variety of points to control cutting height. The finish is rougher than with other mowers.

Laser mowers

In 2000, a German company launched a prototype machine that cuts grass using a laser. At roughly the price of a family car, the initial versions are unlikely to find widespread acceptance. The use of lasers is nevertheless likely to be applied in cheaper models in the future.

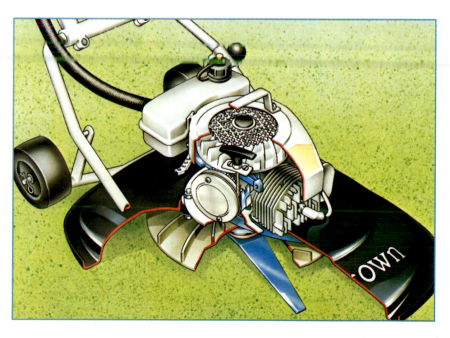

▼ This gasoline-driven hover mower has a cutting blade and blower unit driven from the same shaft. In operation, the mower floats on a cushion of air that also recirculates the cuttings until they turn to mulch, which settles at the roots of the grass. The rear wheels can be lowered for ease of movement when the motor is switched off.

SEE ALSO: AGRICULTURAL MACHINERY • AIR-CUSHION VEHICLE • LASER AND MASER

Gravity

The force that causes objects to fall to the ground (gravity) is also the force that keeps the planets moving around the Sun, but this fact was not realized until the end of the 17th century. The ancient Greeks thought that solid bodies fall because they are seeking their natural place (under the lighter elements, water, air, and fire), while the planets are moved by invisible crystalline spheres. Even the German astronomer Johannes Kepler, who proved in 1609 that the planets' orbits are ellipses around the Sun, thought that they must be moved by motions in the ether.

It was the English scientist and mathematician Isaac Newton who first realized, and proved in his *Principia* published in 1687, that the planets naturally move in ellipses because of an attractive force between the Sun and each of the planets. He showed that this force depends on the product of the masses of the two bodies divided by the square of the distance between them. He also showed that it was this same force that attracts an apple toward Earth by comparing the force on the apple with the force needed to keep the Moon in orbit about Earth. Since the distances from the center of Earth to the apple and to the Moon were known, he could demonstrate that these forces also depended on the inverse square of the distance—that is, the force decreases as the square of the distance increases. The real genius of Newton showed when he generalized his findings by stating that all bodies attract each other gravitationally, the force between them varying in the same way as it does between the Sun and the planets.

Measuring gravity

The force of gravity is actually extremely weak, and it is only because Earth is so massive that its gravitational effects are obvious. The attractive force between two 44 lb. (20 kg) objects 1 ft. (0.3 m) apart is only the same as the weight of one millionth of an ounce on Earth. The first measurement of gravitational force between two bodies of known mass was made in 1798 by the English natural philosopher and chemist Henry Cavendish.

His apparatus consisted of two lead balls 2 in. (50 mm) in diameter (each weighing 1.7 lbs., 0.8 kg) hung from the ends of a 6 ft. (2 m) long deal beam, which was supported at the center by a long wire, allowing the beam to swing horizontally. Two lead balls 1 ft. (0.3 m) in diameter (each weighing one-sixth of a ton) were placed near the small balls on opposite sides so that the gravitational attraction between each pair of large and small balls caused the beam carrying the latter to swing toward the large balls. The 1 ft. balls were

▲ The weightless conditions that astronauts experience as they orbit Earth affect their bodies in a number of ways. Within minutes of arriving in a weightless environment, their faces puff up and their noses and sinuses become congested as fluid is redistributed around the body. They also grow by around 2 in. (5 cm), as gravity no longer compresses the spine. Over longer periods, the wasting away of bone and muscle also become a problem.

then moved to the other side of the small balls, making the beam swing the other way. The total swing measured at the end of the beam was 0.3 in. (7.6 mm), and from this number, Cavendish calculated the force between the balls. He expressed his results as the gravitational force between two one-kilogram masses one meter apart, a quantity usually called G. Cavendish's value for G was the best for almost a century and is within 1 percent of the best modern value (6.673×10^{-11} N).

Newton's gravitational theory also explains the experimental results of the Italian scientist Galileo, who, in 1590, showed that all objects fall equally fast toward the center of Earth, irrespective of their masses (as long as there are no other forces acting on them, we have to add today for accuracy). The ancient Greeks, in particular Aristotle, had maintained that heavy bodies always fall faster than lighter ones, an assumption that is still intuitively felt to be true even today. Galileo disproved the Greeks' hypothesis, according to legend, by dropping two objects of different mass from the top of the Leaning Tower of Pisa in Italy, whence they hit the ground simultaneously. Newton showed that although the gravitational forces acting on the two masses are different, their accelerations, and hence speed of descent, are independent of their masses and depend only on the mass of Earth. The observation that a feather and a marble fall at different speeds is explained by air resistance.

Variations in gravity

The acceleration due to gravity at any place is called g and is about 32 ft. per second per second (9.8 m/s²). It changes slightly according to the altitude and latitude of the place where it is measured. Earth acts gravitationally as if all its mass were concentrated at the center. It is not a perfect sphere, so a change in either altitude or latitude means a change in the distance from the center of Earth, and thus a change in the gravitational force (according to the Inverse Square Law). There are also subtle variations in g depending on the density of the rock beneath where it is measured. Despite their apparent bulk, mountains are buoyed up by low-density rock 19 to 62 miles (30–100 km) below the surface. This low-density rock causes the gravitational force at the top of the mountain to be less than would be expected.

At a height of 100,000 ft. (30,500 m), g is 99 percent of its value at sea level. At the altitude of an orbiting spacecraft, about 200 miles (320 km), the gravitational force is still only 10 percent less than at the surface. However, a spacecraft has sufficient orbital velocity around Earth, so in any short space of time, its fall toward Earth is exactly

▶ This is the polar-ring galaxy NGC 4650A. Astronomers think that this type of galaxy is created by a colossal collision between two galaxies—one forming a ring that circles the other at an approximately 90 degree angle. Polar-ring galaxies provide a useful tool for studying dark matter. This is matter that cannot be seen and can be detected only by the gravitational pull it exerts on the stars and gas in galaxies. The unusual structure of polar-ring galaxies provides a useful tool for mapping the distribution and density of dark matter.

equal to the change in course it needs to continue in its circular orbit (if no forces acted, the spacecraft would fly off in a straight line, according to Newton's Second Law of Motion). As the spacecraft is forever falling, astronauts aboard experience a sensation of weightlessness, as they are falling at the same speed as the spacecraft.

Einstein's General Theory of Relativity (1915) introduced a more general theory of gravity, which for everyday purposes is the same as Newton's, but it explained a puzzling discrepancy in the motion of the planet Mercury. Einstein's theory also predicted that light is affected by gravity. Not only are light rays bent as they pass by massive objects, but incredibly dense objects are able to trap light in their powerful gravitational fields. These objects are called black holes, because, as no light can escape from them, they

are effectively invisible. Relativity also shows that time and space are inextricably linked in a four-dimensional space-time. Therefore, time can also be affected by gravity. It runs slower in a strong gravitational field and can even run backward inside a black hole.

The search for gravity waves

Another consequence of relativity theory is gravity waves. These are gravity disturbances that should be able to travel in waves, like ripples on a pond.

The effect of gravity waves on matter is similar to that of electromagnetic waves. A radio wave manifests itself by moving electric charges back and forth. Gravity waves also moves matter, but because gravity acts on everything, a detector of gravity waves could be anything at all—even a chunk of metal.

There are other crucial differences between gravitational and electromagnetic waves, however, particularly concerning their strength. Gravity is extremely weak compared with electricity. Even a battleship spinning once a second would generate less than a million billion billionth of a watt in the form of gravity wave.

For this reason, events that are powerful enough to cause measurable gravity waves are likely to involve masses of astronomical proportions. One possibility is two stars orbiting closely around each other, generating a traveling bump in space-time, which is dispatched into space. Another possibility is the explosion of a star in a supernova, which would generate great bursts of gravity waves. Supernovae are also believed to produce black holes, and immense quantities of gravity wave power would also be released by two holes colliding.

In principle, detecting gravity waves is simple. As the wave passes through matter, it will vibrate, and this vibration is all that need be measured. However, Earth is far removed from most violent cosmic events, and gravity waves spreading from the center of a disturbance become diluted with distance.

To detect tiny disturbances, two methods are used. The first is called a resonant mass detector and measures the energy that is deposited in a metal beam as the wave passes through it. The second, called an interferometer detector, uses lasers to measure the change in distance between two test masses as the wave causes them to move in relation to each other. NASA currently has plans to build interferometer detectors in space, where the low level of background disturbances increase the chances of spotting the waves. There is also virtually no limit on the size of the interferometer, allowing the test masses to be

placed thousands of kilometers apart—greatly increasing the accuracy of the measurements made between them.

A Theory of Everything

Even if gravitational waves are detected, the information gleaned from them will mainly be of use in providing further insights into relativity theory. The ultimate goal of physicists, however, is to combine the two currently accepted theories of matter in to a single "Theory of Everything."

At minute scales, matter is very successfully described by quantum theory, while massive objects conform to relativity theory. Unfortunately, these two theories are not compatible. On a quantum scale, there is not enough matter for gravity to have any noticeable effect, and at relativistic scales, tiny quantum effects are equally unnoticeable. Any viable theory will need to smoothly describe the functioning of everything in the Universe at all scales.

The current leading contenders for a Theory of Everything are "string theories," or "M-theory," as the latest formulation is called. These view all matter as being made of strings or membranes that vibrate in up to 10 dimensions. The complex vibrations give rise to all particles, including the graviton—a massless particle that is believed to carry the force of gravity. However, these theories are still incomplete and the subject of much discussion. It will be many more years before scientists have a framework to describe how everything in the Universe works at all scales.

▲ Gravitational forces cause Earth's tidal movements. At low tide (top left), the water's edge is far down on the beach, leaving room for people to stroll or make sand castles. When the tide comes in about six hours later (top right), the water washes away the castle and smoothes the beach again. At some points in orbits of the Moon and Earth, gravitational forces of attraction are stronger than usual, resulting in very high or low tides.

 SEE ALSO: AIR • ASTROPHYSICS • COSMOLOGY • EARTH • ENERGY, MASS, AND WEIGHT • RELATIVITY • TIDE

Gun

A gun is a weapon that uses rapidly expanding gases to accelerate a projectile—a bullet or shell —through a cylindrical barrel. Guns range in size from small handguns for close-range attack to enormous artillery guns that can fire projectiles over ranges of around 15 to 100 miles (around 25–160 km). Most guns use explosive charges to provide the expanding gases that impart energy to projectiles; some small weapons use the release of compressed air to the same effect.

Basic principles

The effectiveness of a gun is measured in terms of its ability to deliver an appropriate projectile to its target with sufficient kinetic energy to cause the required extent of damage. How this is achieved varies according to the intended range of fire.

For short-range weapons, the trajectories of projectiles are short enough for the effects of gravity to be minimal, and the projectile follows an essentially straight path along the line of the sights. An acceptable accuracy of fire is achieved through careful barrel design and high-precision manufacture. The design and choice of construction materials are intended to limit the extent of

barrel distortion and uneven wear caused by repeated firing. These measures help ensure that a weapon maintains a high degree of accuracy of aim throughout its projected working life.

Some guns have rifling—helical grooves in the inner surfaces of their barrels—that cause a projectile to spin around an axis that coincides with its line of flight. The gyroscopic effect of this spin contributes to stable flight and better accuracy.

Projectiles from long-range guns follow arch-shaped trajectories. The direction and speed of the projectile as it leaves the barrel and acceleration owing to gravity are the main factors that determine the flight path. Air resistance presents a force that retards the motion of the projectile, and atmospheric conditions, such as wind and rain, also have an influence on trajectory.

The greater the range of a gun, the more accurate must be the aim if the projectile is to stand a reasonable chance of hitting its target. Modern long-range guns use laser range finders and computerized aiming systems to ensure a high accuracy of fire; some of these systems take into account changes in barrel characteristics caused by wear and adjust the aim accordingly.

▲ These 15 in. (380 mm) weapons are examples of the naval guns of Royal Sovereign class battleships that served in the British Royal Navy in World Wars I and II. These guns fired shells that weighed around one ton (0.9 tonnes) each.

▶ This early percussion weapon used a tape of explosive pellets to fire the gunpowder in its barrel. Pulling the trigger released its hammer, shown here in the cocked position. The impact of the hammer would then cause the pellet to detonate, sending a stream of hot gases through a narrow bore in the nipple under the pellet to ignite the charge in the barrel.

Early guns

Around 1250 B.C.E., the Chinese developed the first weapons to launch projectiles using exploding gunpowder rather than a mechanical device, such as a bow or catapult. Instead of the bullets or balls used with later firearms, these devices launched arrows at their targets.

Historical reports indicate that forerunners of most types of modern guns developed in Europe during the early 14th century. Cannon that used gunpowder to launch stones and metal balls were reported in 1326, and there is some evidence for even earlier use of firearms.

Early guns and cannon were loaded through the muzzle with gunpowder, then a wad of paper, and then the projectile. Such weapons would be fired by igniting the gunpowder through a firelock—a narrow channel, filled with gunpowder, in the breech of the gun (the breech is at the opposite end of the barrel to the muzzle). The gunpowder in the firelock would be ignited by a hot wire or a slow-burning fuse of cord impregnated with potassium nitrate (KNO_3), which promoted combustion of the cord material.

Firing mechanisms

Handheld weapons became practical only with the invention of self-contained firing mechanisms. The first such weapon was the matchlock, invented in the mid-15th century. Matchlocks were muskets that were fired using an S-shaped trigger, called a serpentine, that had a central pivot. Pulling on the bottom of the trigger brought a slow-burning fuse into contact with gunpowder in a depression in the top of the weapon's barrel. The burning gunpowder then ignited the gun's charge through a firelock.

From the early 16th century to the early 19th century, the dominant firing mechanisms for handheld weapons used flints—actually lumps of iron pyrite (iron disulfide, FeS_2)—that showered sparks onto a flashpan and firelock when struck or rubbed by a hard surface. The first such device was the wheel lock, used in pistols from around 1515. Wheel locks consisted of a spring-loaded steel wheel that rotated against the flint when released by pulling on a trigger.

In the 17th century, wheel locks gave way to firing mechanisms that used a spring-loaded hammer to strike a flint against a roughened steel surface. The first such device was the snaphance, developed in the early 17th century; the second, introduced toward the end of the same century, was the flintlock. Flintlocks differed from snaphances by incorporating a plate that kept the powder in the flashpan dry until fired.

The next major development in firing mechanisms was the percussion lock, which was introduced in the 1820s. Percussion locks exploit the tendency of certain explosives to detonate under pressure. Mercury (II) isocyanate (or fulminate of mercury, $Hg(ONC)_2$) was the first such explosive to be used in this way. One of the advantages of the percussion lock was that the hammer that detonated the percussive priming charge also sealed the narrow channel through which the burning primer charge ignited the main charge in the barrel, thereby allowing a greater pressure to develop. Percussion locks were made more convenient by the introduction in 1845 of Maynard tape, which encapsulated slugs of fulminate of mercury powder between strips of paper or linen.

Cartridges and breech loading

Modern weapons use cartridges that contain the percussive priming charge in a metal cup that sits at the breech end of the barrel. The main explosive charge and projectile are the other main components of the cartridge. The first examples of such cartridges were first used in the 1860s in Britain and the United States.

The primer charge of a cartridge detonates when struck by a spring-loaded hammer that is released when the trigger is pulled. The primer then ignites the main charge, propelling the projectile through the barrel. This action leaves the metal cup in the breech, from which it is withdrawn before the next firing sequence.

The great advantage of cartridge ammunition is that firing causes the cup at the base of the cartridge to expand temporarily, sealing openings in the breech. This self-sealing action overcame the leakage problems of earlier breech-loading guns and made the design almost universal.

Multishot guns

Multishot guns are so called because they can be loaded and prepared for two or more shots before use and therefore give an advantage in combat and when shooting fast-moving animals. The 16th century saw the development of a bewildering array of multishot guns, ranging in size from pocket pistols to full-sized cannon.

Most early multishot guns had multiple barrels, either in line or mounted around an axis, and were fired by one or more locks. Some had a single barrel into which several sets of gunpowder, wad, and projectile were packed in succession. The charges would then be fired using multiple locks or a single lock that moved from the breech to the muzzle to fire the charges in order.

The predecessor of the modern double-barreled sporting gun developed in England about the middle of the 18th century as a flintlock. It became widely accepted as a sporting gun when modified with a percussion lock.

The introduction of cartridge ammunition, together with the associated shift from muzzle-loading to breech-loading guns in the 1860s, paved the way for semiautomatic and automatic weapons. These use some of the explosive energy of the charge to power the discharge of spent cartridges and reloading through the breech of the gun. The introduction of a new form of gunpowder, which left almost no residue in the barrel and developed far higher muzzle velocities than the original black gunpowder, made repeating and semiautomatic firearms a practical proposition.

Machine guns were introduced in the 1890s, and by the time of World War I, successful experiments had been made with semiautomatic rifles, which fired, discharged, and reloaded, ready for the next shot, with each press of the trigger. Fully automatic rifles appeared in the 1920s along with the submachine gun, but not until after World War II did the automatic rifle achieve general adoption by the world's armed forces.

Revolvers

The revolver is the principal multishot gun in current use by security forces and for personal protection. In general terms, a revolver is a pistol, shoulder gun, or machine gun that fires multiple charges either from a series of barrels mounted around a central axis or from a series of chambers mounted around an axis that rotates to align the chambers with a single barrel. In practice, the term *revolver* is usually reserved for single-barreled, multiple-chambered pistols.

Early firing mechanisms were ill suited for revolver designs, since they relied on a priming charge in a flashpan on the barrel to fire the main charge. Many inventors attempted to design a mechanism for filling each flashpan with powder as it aligned with the barrel: few were successful.

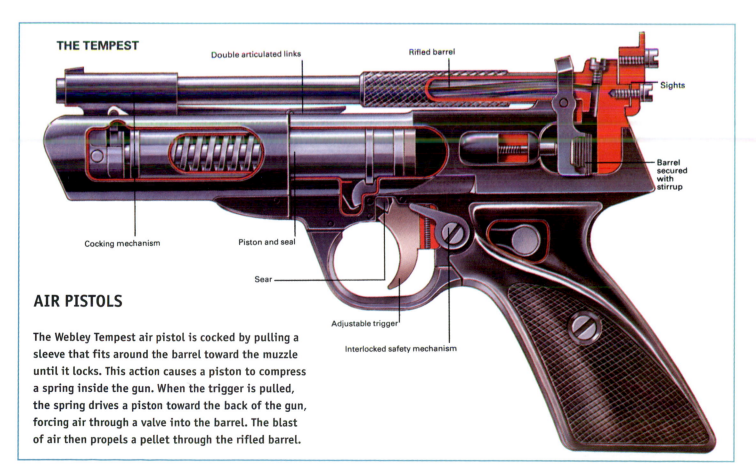

THE TEMPEST

Double articulated links

Rifled barrel

Sights

Barrel secured with stirrup

Cocking mechanism

Piston and seal

Sear

Adjustable trigger

Interlocked safety mechanism

AIR PISTOLS

The Webley Tempest air pistol is cocked by pulling a sleeve that fits around the barrel toward the muzzle until it locks. This action causes a piston to compress a spring inside the gun. When the trigger is pulled, the spring drives a piston toward the back of the gun, forcing air through a valve into the barrel. The blast of air then propels a pellet through the rifled barrel.

The only such design to achieve any degree of reliability was the Collier revolver of 1818. The development of percussion firing led to the invention of the multiple-barreled "pepperpot" revolver, so called because its rotating lock mechanism and bulky barrel assembly loosely resembled the handle and body of a peppermill. While pepperpot revolvers were technically straightforward, their bulk limited their popularity.

The forerunner of modern revolvers was patented in 1836 by the U.S. inventor Samuel Colt. The initial version of the Colt revolver had a cylinder that comprised six axial chambers. Each chamber would be loaded with a metal ball, a main charge, and a percussive cap. Pulling the spring-loaded percussive hammer into the cocked position advanced the cylinder by one chamber position and locked it in place. The charge of the aligned chamber would then be fired by pulling a trigger to release the hammer.

The introduction of cartridge bullets in the 1860s was readily integrated with Colt's design, and the resulting weapon became hugely popular with law enforcers and criminals alike. The second major development of the Colt revolver was the introduction of a double-action mechanism in 1873. Pulling the trigger of a double-action revolver releases the cylinder, rotates it by one chamber, locks the cylinder in position, and cocks the hammer before releasing it to fire the bullet. This series of actions requires a long, heavy trigger pull that makes accuracy of aim difficult to achieve. Consequently, most double-action revolvers can be set for single action with manual cocking for accurate fire at distant targets, reserving double action for rapid close fire.

Other modern gun formats

The overall size of a gun and its ratio of barrel length to barrel width depend on the type of ammunition that it is designed to fire and its intended range. A sporting scattergun has lightweight, wide-gauge barrels that achieve a spread of light shot, for example, whereas a handgun designed to fire solid shot in personal defense has a short, narrow barrel that allows a greater accuracy. Similarly, a high-caliber gun is used to fire stubby munitions that contain submunitions, whereas an antitank gun has a long, thin barrel that fires sleek armor-piercing shells at high muzzle velocities.

Long-range guns fire large munitions that have sufficient explosive power to cause the required damage even if they fail to score a direct hit. Consequently, such guns must have a sturdy construction in order to withstand the high pressures developed in accelerating heavy munitions to adequate muzzle velocities for the required range. As an example, a 6.1 in. (155 mm) weapon with a range of more than 15.5 miles (25 km) typically weighs more than 40 tons (36 tonnes).

Big guns of the 20th century

The grave international conflicts of the first half of the 20th century saw the development of big guns with ranges of 20 miles (32 km) or more. The first such guns were used in World War I. Their weight necessitated strong mountings that could cater for massive recoils in use, and they were best suited for installation on ships or in fortresses. When moved by road, the bulk of such guns impeded the movement of vehicles with stores, equipment, and troops. Accordingly, most long-range guns were railway mounted.

The French forces made considerable use of long-range railway guns in 1915 and 1918. Box mounts designed to support guns in naval or fortress service were placed directly on railway trucks, which recoiled along the track on firing. Curved spurs of track were built so that the guns could be aimed at targets by moving them until they pointed in the required direction. British forces used a mounting designed for the 9.2 in. (230 mm) naval gun. It had a ramp up which the gun recoiled then ran back to its original position for firing again. This method, however, allowed little gun elevation, and later guns were designed specifically for long-range railway firing.

The Germans undoubtedly produced the most effective guns, the most famous of which was the Paris gun. Developed from the Max E railway gun used in 1916 on Verdun, France, the Paris gun was of psychological value only, since the shells that fell on Paris caused little damage for the amount of effort expended.

▼ This early multiple-barreled revolver is of the "pepperbox" type—so called because of the appearance of its thick rotating cylinder.

GUN SILENCERS

The noise of gunfire is caused by the sudden release of compressed gases that happens when a bullet emerges from the barrel of a gun. The expanding gases form a pressure wave that spreads out from the muzzle. The pressure wave is perceived as a sharp cracking sound by an observer in its path.

A silencer reduces the sound of gunfire by breaking up the pressure wave so that it loses its power to be heard. As a bullet emerges from the muzzle of a gun fitted with a silencer, it passes through the central holes of a series of disk-shaped baffles. As gases emerge behind the bullet, part of the pressure wave rebounds off the first baffle, thus delaying its progress through the silencer. The same process occurs when the gases pass to the second chamber, and so on. By the time the gases from the exploding charge reach the exit of the silencer, the explosive expansion at the muzzle of the gun has transformed into a smooth and noiseless surge of gases.

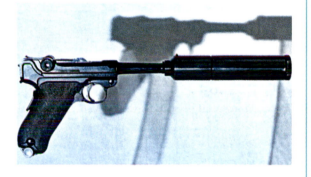

Pistol barrel

Bullet

Steel baffles

In addition to the gun silencer, the U.S. engineer Hiram Percy Maxim invented mufflers for air compressors and internal combustion engines that work in a similar way to gun silencers. Hiram Percy was the son of the British engineer Hiram Stevens Maxim, who invented an early form of machine gun that carried his name and was widely used by numerous forces in World War I.

◀ A silencer is a hollow metal cylinder divided into chambers by a series of baffles. Bullets pass through holes in the centers of the baffles.

▼ Detachable silencers fit snugly to the muzzles of guns. In this case, the silencer—the thick cylinder at right—is at least as long as the barrel of the gun that carries it.

During World War II, German forces continued their tradition of using long-range railway guns. The 8.3 in. (210 mm) K-12 gun of 1940 had a 105 ft. (32 m) long barrel, weighed 108 tons (98 tonnes), and had a range of 93 miles (150 km).

The most efficient German railway gun was arguably the 11 in. (280 mm) K-5. It fired a 560 lb. (254 kg) shell that was engraved to fit the rifling of the gun's barrel. At the apex of its trajectory, a rocket motor ignited to extend the range of the shell to 53 miles (85 km); the rocket assistance reduced target efficiency and was inconsistent, however. It was used to shell the Allied positions at Anzio, Italy, and was nicknamed Anzio Annie.

The biggest railroad gun was the 31.5 in. (800 mm) German Krupp gun of 1937. Weighing 1,488 tons (1,350 tonnes), it fired 4.4 ton (4 tonne) high-explosive shells over distances up to 29 miles (47 km). It had a team of 1,420 dedicated personnel, including its own track-laying crew. The gun was used on Sevastopol, Ukraine, and Warsaw, Poland, during the 1944 uprising.

Perhaps the most interesting of the German long-range gun systems was designed toward the end of World War II. Its construction site at Calais, France, was bombed out of existence before the gun could be built. Code-named V-3, it was to be a multichambered fixed gun.

The basic idea was simple: a primary charge would initiate the movement of the projectile through a 5.9 in. (150 mm) main bore with 28 secondary chambers on alternating sides of the main bore. The side chambers were to contain propellant charges that would boost the acceleration of the projectile as they ignited in the burning gases in its wake. The projected muzzle velocity of 5,000 ft. per sec. (1,520 m/s) would have produced a range of nearly 200 miles (322 km).

After World War II, the U.S. military built the first long-range gun designed to fire an atomic shell: the road-mounted 11 in. (280 mm) M-65. The development of free-flying guided rocket missiles in the 1950s then put an end to the use of guns for delivering warheads to distant targets.

SEE ALSO: AMMUNITION • ANTIAIRCRAFT GUN • AUTOMATIC WEAPON AND MACHINE GUN • BALLISTICS • BOMB-AIMING DEVICE • MISSILE • MORTAR, BAZOOKA, AND RECOILLESS GUN • RIFLE AND SHOTGUN

Gyrocompass

◀ A high-precision Sperry CL II directional gyroscope used in the compass systems of many aircraft. It is also used as part of the directional equipment of some rockets and submarines.

The gyrocompass is a true-north directional indicator used extensively in merchant and naval vessels. It is one of the most used navigational aids, as it provides a true-north indication regardless of any rolling, pitching, or yawing of the vessel and is entirely unaffected by any of the disturbances that commonly affect magnetic compasses. The gyrocompass is usually installed below deck, and its indication is relayed around the ship to operate ancillary equipment such as steering and bearing repeaters, course recorders, and gyropilots.

The basis of the gyrocompass is a gyroscope controlled in such a way that its spin axis is made to seek and maintain alignment with the geographic meridian (north–south line). This alignment is achieved by combining Earth's rotation and the force of gravity with inertia and precession (the regular movement of the axis of a rotating body as a result of an applied angular force, such that the axis describes a cone in space).

Theory of operation

Earth rotates about its polar axis from west to east with an angular velocity of one revolution in 24 hours, that is, 15 degrees per hour. At any point on Earth's surface, this angular velocity can be resolved into two components: a component aligned to the local vertical, known as the vertical Earth rate, and a horizontal component aligned to the meridian and known as the horizontal Earth rate.

The magnitude of these components varies with latitude. Vertical Earth rate varies as the sine of the angle of latitude and is 15 degrees per hour at the poles and zero at the equator, while the horizontal Earth rate varies as the cosine of the angle of latitude and is zero at the poles and 15 degrees per hour at the equator.

The gyroscope used in the gyrocompass is electrically driven and mounted in gimbals in such a way that it has freedom to move about both a vertical and a horizontal axis. The gyroscope can be considered as a space-stable element because its axes will remain pointed in the same direction with respect to inertial space unless acted upon by a force. Earth is not a part of inertial space but rotates within it. For this reason, the directions in which the axes of a gyroscope point, with respect to an observer stationary on Earth, will appear to change as Earth rotates, although they are in fact remaining constant with respect to inertial space.

Being a space-stable element, the gyroscope senses the rotation of Earth: the vertical axis senses the vertical Earth rate and the horizontal axis the horizontal Earth rate. Therefore, the effect of Earth's rotation on the axes of the gyroscope varies with the latitude. This idea can best be appreciated by considering the behavior of the gyroscope at various geographical locations.

If the gyro is located at the North Pole with its spin axis horizontal, the rotation of Earth will be measured entirely by the vertical axis, and to an observer using the spinning Earth as a refer-

▶ The apparent tilting of a gyrocompass in relation to Earth. Because of Earth's rotation, a gyrocompass that is freely mounted on Earth's surface appears to change axis. In the diagram, the axis of the gyrocompass at midnight is horizontal in relation to Earth but by 8 A.M. it has moved through 120 degrees.

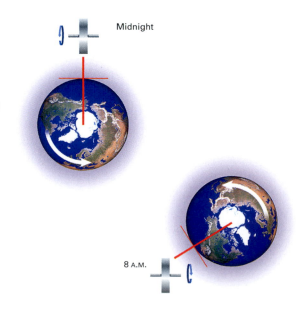

ence, the space-stable gyro appears to drift about its vertical axis at the Earth rate, that is 15 degrees per hour.

When the gyro is mounted at the equator with its spin axis pointing east to west, its horizontal axis is aligned with the meridian (the direction of horizontal Earth rate), and to an observer standing on Earth the space-stable gyro appears to rotate about its horizontal axis at Earth rate. This effect is referred to as tilting.

With the gyro still mounted at the equator but with its spin axis pointing north to south, the tilting effect, owing to the rotation of Earth, is zero, since the sensitive horizontal axis is displaced by 90 degrees from the meridian. With the spin axis pointing in an intermediate position, the horizontal Earth rate affects the horizontal axis by an amount proportional to the displacement of the spin axis from the meridian.

Practical gyrocompasses

It is the effect of the horizontal Earth rate that makes it possible to apply the force of gravity to convert the space-stable gyroscope into a north-seeking gyrocompass. When the gyro spin axis is aligned to the meridian there is no tilting effect about the horizontal axis. When the spin axis is east of meridian, the horizontal Earth rate causes the north end of the gyro to fall. The rate of tilt of the gyro is directly related to the value of the horizontal Earth rate (15 degrees per hour cosine latitude) and the misalignment of the spin axis from the meridian.

At points between the poles and the equator, the gyro appears to turn partly about its horizontal axis and partly about its vertical axis because it is affected by both horizontal and vertical Earth rates. In general, the horizontal Earth rate causes the gyroscope to tilt, whereas the vertical Earth rate causes it to rotate in azimuth (horizontally) with respect to the meridians.

A gravity reference system is used to measure any tilting of the gyro and produce torques (turning forces) to precess the gyro spin axis into alignment with the meridian. Early gyrocompasses used a weight to sense tilt and provide a north-seeking force; the weight, being secured to the bottom of the gyro case, forced the spin axis to remain level as a result of its reaction with gravity, and the resulting torque precessed the gyro toward the north. The principle was used by Dr. Elmer Sperry on his early gyrocompasses, one of which was successfully demonstrated aboard the USS *Delaware* in 1911 and is now on view at the Smithsonian Institution in Washington, D.C.

By the early 1920s, this weight arrangement had been replaced by a ballistic system compris-

ing two containers half filled with fluid, mounted on the north and south ends of the gyro, and interconnected by two small-diameter tubes. Any tilting of the gyro caused displacement of fluid from the higher to the lower container, and the resulting imbalance precessed the gyro toward the meridian. While improved versions of this system are still widely used today, electric devices are now extensively used in gyrocompass gravity reference systems because of their great flexibility. Such systems employ accelerometers and other devices to detect tilt, and the output of the device is amplified to drive the gyro torque motors to relay the action.

As already mentioned, it is the relatively slow rotation of Earth that provides the motive power for the north-seeking precessional movement of the gyrocompass. When a vessel is traveling over Earth's surface, however, and therefore about Earth's center, the vessel's movement is compounded with that of Earth and will impair the accuracy of the gyrocompass. Compensation systems have been designed to counteract these errors and leave the gyro accurately aligned with geographic north.

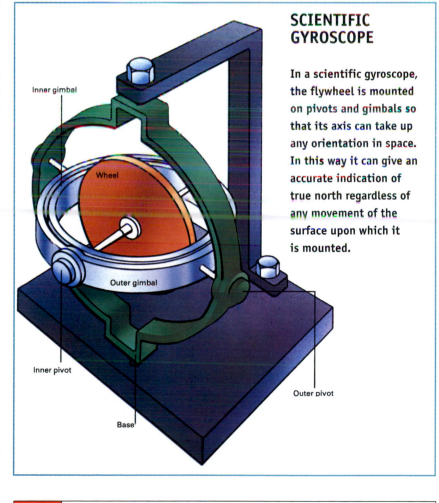

SCIENTIFIC GYROSCOPE

In a scientific gyroscope, the flywheel is mounted on pivots and gimbals so that its axis can take up any orientation in space. In this way it can give an accurate indication of true north regardless of any movement of the surface upon which it is mounted.

Inner gimbal

Wheel

Outer gimbal

Inner pivot

Outer pivot

Base

SEE ALSO: EARTH • GYROSCOPE • INERTIAL GUIDANCE • MAGNETISM • NAVIGATION

Gyroscope

▲ A toy gyroscope spinning precisely on the tip of a pencil. The flywheel is set spinning by pulling a string wound around the axis. This multiple-exposure shot shows the slow precessing of the gyroscope. Earth's precession takes 25,800 years.

A gyroscope is a spinning wheel mounted in such a way that its axis can tilt in any direction. Because of the property known as rotational inertia, a spinning wheel will tend to resist any change in the direction of the axis of rotation. It is this property that makes it easy to ride a bicycle in a straight line without tipping over, even though it is virtually impossible to balance a bicycle in the upright position when it is not moving. Similarly, to change the direction in which the bicycle is heading, and thus the direction in which the axles of the wheels are pointing, it is not enough to rotate the handlebar—the rider must also shift his or her weight to provide a significant torque on the wheels.

The relationship between torque and angular momentum requires some fairly complex mathematics to be described in full detail. Some basic insight, however, may be provided by a simple children's toy—the spinning top. A top that is not spinning will simply fall over when placed upright and released. If it is spinning, however, it will move, as it begins to tip over, so that its axis describes circles in space. The torque—produced by gravity pulling on its center of mass, which is a distance from the point of contact with the floor—now results in this circular motion, or precession instead of a simple falling over.

In a toy gyroscope, the wheel spins on an axis which turns with very low friction within a metal frame which is itself free to rotate about its base point. The low friction allows the wheel to spin at a higher rate than the toy top so the effect lasts longer and is more dramatic. If the frame, also known as a gimbal ring, is mounted inside a second frame and then a third, all with low friction bearings in mutually perpendicular directions, the gyroscope axis will be free to assume any direction in space. In addition, since both ends of the axis can move, the center of mass remains stationary, and since gravitational torques are balanced about this point, the axis direction can remain fixed in space no matter how the outer frame is moved.

In a good quality gyroscope, the axis of rotation will continue to point in the same direction in space, and, since Earth is rotating, it will appear to rotate or precess about a fixed line once a day. The effect is analogous to that exhibited by the famous Foucault pendulum, in which a large mass on the end of a long cord swings as a slow pendulum, and the plane of swing rotates by 360 degrees every 24 hours. To turn the gyroscope into a gyrocompass that always points towards geographic north a spring force or other source of torque is provided to counterbalance the precession due to Earth's motion.

Applications of gyroscopes

The most obvious application of gyroscopes is to use their property of being able to remember directions, so they are used in automatic pilots and compasses in aircraft for navigational guidance. They are also essential for the guidance and control of space vehicles.

In the design of wind generators of electricity, the collector fan blades are often made to follow the wind. If the wind speed is excessive, the gyroscopic torque may break the blades off the mounting shaft. Gyrodynamics had to be carefully studied in the design of flywheel-driven buses, tried in Europe in the 1950s. These flywheels were about 18 in. (46 cm) in diameter and reached speeds approaching 20,000 rpm. The smaller 2 to 3 in. (5–8 cm) brass wheels used in early autopilots for aircraft were spun at 85,000 rpm although modern autopilot gyros are much slower. The highest rotational speed achieved is 90 million rpm with a gyroscope designed by the American physicist Jesse W. Beams.

In 1933, the designers of the Italian ocean liner *Conte di Savoia*, recognizing the huge twist-

UPPER AND LOWER GYROSCOPES

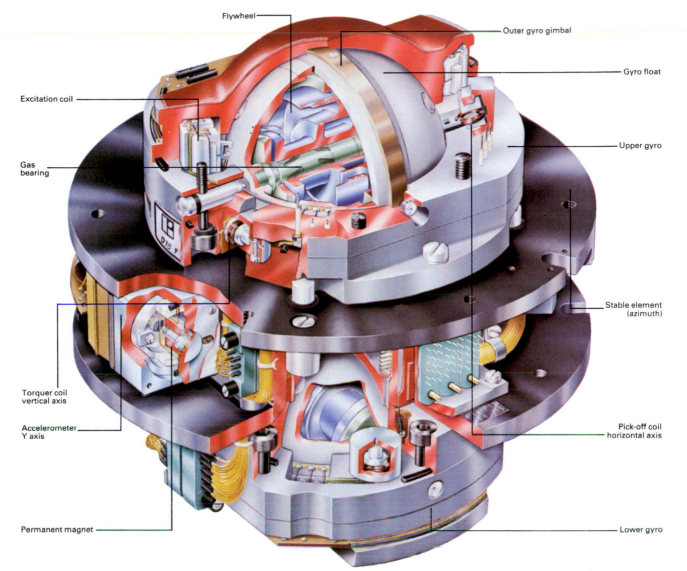

Flywheel

Outer gyro gimbal

Gyro float

Excitation coil

Upper gyro

Gas bearing

Stable element (azimuth)

Torquer coil vertical axis

Accelerometer Y axis

Pick-off coil horizontal axis

Permanent magnet

Lower gyro

▲ The PL-41's twin gas spin-bearing floated gyroscopes offer a high level of reliability. The precision of this system, designed originally for shipboard use, has resulted in its adoption by many naval forces.

▶ The platform unit of the PL-41 marine navigation system. The PL-41 has two other units consisting of a control and display and a power junction.

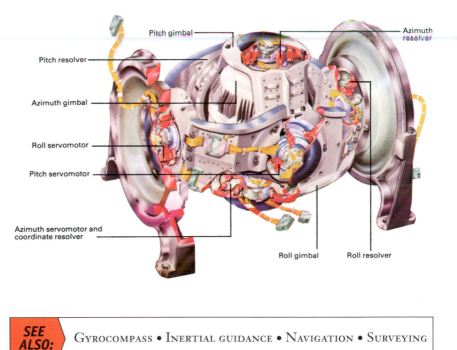

Pitch gimbal

Azimuth resolver

Pitch resolver

Azimuth gimbal

Roll servomotor

Pitch servomotor

Azimuth servomotor and coordinate resolver

Roll gimbal

Roll resolver

ing force that could be applied by large spinning wheels, fitted three giant gyroscope rotors on a vertical shaft in the bowels of the ship to act as stabilizers. Each wheel had a diameter of 13 ft. (4 m) and weighed 108 tons (97 tonnes).

Gyroscopes are also mounted on theodolites used in underground mine exploration. It is necessary to use gyrocoscopes because ordinary magnetic compasses are affected by changes in magnetism caused by metal deposits.

SEE ALSO: GYROCOMPASS • INERTIAL GUIDANCE • NAVIGATION • SURVEYING

Hair Treatment

The idea of putting waves and curls into straight hair dates back to ancient Egyptian and Roman times. Cleopatra is said to have set her hair in rollers made of baked mud. Early methods, which involved wetting the hair, winding it onto rollers and then drying it, achieved only a temporary set. It is the ability of hair to stretch when it is wet by as much as 20 to 50 percent of its original dry length that makes temporary setting possible.

Permanent waving was invented by Charles Nessler in 1905. Nessler's method involved winding the hair onto rods or rollers, applying an alkaline chemical (usually borax) to soften it, and then heating to fix the hair in its new shape. In the early days, permanent waving was a long, hazardous process because the action of the alkali was difficult to control; if it was too vigorous or was allowed to continue for too long, damage to the hair would result. Nevertheless, Nessler's invention was an important advance on previous processes; for the first time, the chemical structure, rather than just the physical shape, of the hair was altered during waving.

Hair structure

Hair is composed of three layers—a thin, outer layer of semitransparent, overlapping scales called the cuticle, an inner layer (the cortex) composed of thin threadlike fibers of the protein keratin, and a central marrow (the medulla). It is the cortex that is important in hair waving and straightening processes. The fibers of the cortex are held together by chemical linkages called disulfide linkages.

Permanent waving

The principle of permanent waving is to break these links so that the individual fibers in the cortex can move relative to each other as the hair is put into its new shape and then to reform the linkages to fix the fibers in their new positions. In modern permanent waving, the breaking and reforming of the disulfide linkages is achieved chemically and is usually carried out at room temperature, hence the term cold waving is sometimes applied to this process. A reducing agent, usually ammonium thioglycolate, is used to break the disulfide linkages while an oxidizing agent is used to reform them. Acid-balanced perms are better for delicate hair, a gentle curl, or just to add body. They require external heat and usually contain glyceryl monothioglycolate. Hydrogen peroxide used to be the most common oxidizing agent, but other more stable oxidizing agents are

preferred. Thus, permanent waving comprises three steps: applying a softening solution (containing the reducing agent), shaping the hair, and applying a neutralizing solution (containing the oxidizing agent) to fix the curl. The number of rollers used and their size depend on the result required and the type of hair—coarse or fine.

The softening and neutralizing solutions often contain additional chemicals, such as wetting or swelling agents, that improve penetration into the hair fibers. To avoid damaging the hair, the softening and neutralizing solutions are normally neither acid nor alkaline, although the action of the softening solution is sometimes enhanced by adding ammonia, which makes it slightly alkaline.

Straightening

Hair straightening is simply the reverse of permanent waving. As far as is known, it was first introduced in the United States to straighten the tightly curled hair of African Americans. The first hair straighteners were based on caustic soda, a vigorous alkali, but these were generally unsatis-

▲ Colorants can be applied all over the head or restricted to selected parts of the hairstyle, such as when highlights are added to give a more natural sun-lightened effect. Developments in colorants have made a wide range of colors available that will remain in the hair for just one wash or last several months.

factory because unless they were applied with great care, damage to the hair would result.

Modern methods of hair straightening employ chemicals similar to those used in permanent waving. The softening agent is normally applied in the form of a cream, which tends to hold the hair against the scalp while it is being straightened. The straightening is done by stretching the hair, preferably with the hands rather than a comb. After stretching, the hair is fixed using a conventional neutralizing solution. In recent years, hair straightening has become popular because, once hair has been straightened, it can be temporarily set into any desired style.

Hair colorants

Most modern hair color products no longer have the rotten-egg smell that used to accompany permanent waves or hair colors. Most can be applied easily to either wet or dry hair, almost like a shampoo, after which they are left to process, usually for around 30 minutes.

With a semipermanent color, the hair colorant contains tiny color molecules that enter the hair's cuticle and go into the cortex—they do not interact with the hair's natural pigment, and since the molecules are small, they migrate from the hair after between 6 and 12 shampoos.

Demipermanent color products last longer, between 24 and 26 shampoos. Here, precolor molecules penetrate the cuticle and enter the cortex, where they partner to create medium-sized color molecules. This larger size means they take longer to wash out. Such products do not contain ammonia, so the natural pigment cannot be lightened, but they do contain a small amount of peroxide, which can give a subtle color change.

In permanent-color products, both ammonia and peroxide are used. Tiny molecules enter into the hair cortex, where they react and expand to a size that cannot be washed out—the hair has to grow out to get rid of the color. These products lighten the hair's natural pigment to form a new base and then add a new permanent color. The end result is a combination of the natural hair pigment and the new shade.

Science is also searching for an answer to gray hair. Cancer researchers have discovered that liposomes, which are used to deliver drugs into the body, can be used to deposit melanin, the pigment that gives hair its color, inside follicles and color hair from the roots up. If further research proves successful, products could be available relatively soon. And one day, gray hair may be no more—after 30 years of research, L'Oreal's laboratories have developed a precursor molecule for melanin, dihydroxyl-5,6-indole,

which enables the natural process of hair pigmentation to take place biologically through a slow oxidization process.

Shampoos and conditioners

There are many different types of shampoos, but most are essentially perfumed detergents—soaps would leave a film on the hair, dulling it. These detergents, such as sodium laureth sulfate, simply loosen and strip dirt from the hair's outer cuticle. Many shampoos contain harmless additives, mainly vegetable based such as jojoba, that are claimed to bring additional benefits.

Many conditioners utilize silicone-based substances that form a film on the cuticle to give hair a slick, glossy feel. Research has highlighted the essential role played by lipids in the cuticle. These include ceramides, which ensure the cuticle remains cohesive and maintains its protective effect. Studies have shown that ceramides are destroyed during hairdressing and various forms of chemical treatment. L'Oréal's laboratories have synthesized ceramides with a view to incorporating them into haircare products to mend damaged hair cuticles. Ceramide R, whose structure is similar to that of the hair's natural ceramides, has been shown to accumulate in the cuticle, leaving the capillary fibers of the hair smooth and conditioned.

▼ Heat lamps are sometimes used to dry hair, instead of a hooded drier. This arrangement makes it more convenient for hairdressers who use different implements, such as these winding sticks, to achieve a particular style.

SEE ALSO: ACID AND ALKALI • PROTEIN

Halogen

The five elements fluorine, chlorine, bromine, iodine, and astatine form the seventh group in the periodic table of elements. They are called halogens, from the Greek words meaning salt producers, because they readily form salts, such as sodium chloride, by simple chemical combination with metals. The halogens each have seven electrons in the outer shell of their atoms and will readily accept a further electron (as in salt formation) to give the stable eight-electron configuration of the noble gases.

Fluorine

Fluorine (F) is a light, yellow gas at normal temperatures; it is the most chemically active element and reacts vigorously with most substances, including organic materials and many metals. It will even form compounds with the noble gases xenon and krypton. Traces of fluorine exist in seawater, bones, and teeth, and fluorine is widely distributed in such minerals as fluorspar and cryolite.

Fluorine is produced commercially by the electrolysis of hydrogen fluoride made electrically conductive by the addition of potassium fluoride. One of the chief uses of pure fluorine is in the manufacture of uranium hexafluoride (UF_6), which is used in the separation of the uranium isotope U-235 (used in nuclear reactors and in the atom bomb) from the more common isotope U-238. Most fluorine compounds, however, are manufactured from hydrogen fluoride and not fluorine itself. Hydrogen fluoride is made by heating finely powdered fluorspar with concentrated sulfuric acid. When dissolved in water, it forms a weakly acidic solution, which is used for etching and polishing glass.

Nearly three-quarters of the hydrogen fluoride produced is used in making organic fluorine compounds (containing both fluorine and carbon atoms). Examples of organic fluorine compounds include fluothane, a nontoxic and nonflammable anesthetic, polytetrafluoroethylene (PTFE), a plastic used as a nonstick coating for kitchen utensils, bromochlorodifluoromethane (BCF), a chemical used in firefighting, and Freons, low-boiling liquids used as refrigerants and aerosol propellants. These aerosol propellants, commonly known as CFCs, cause a depletion of the ozone layer—the layer of Earth's stratosphere that protects us from the harmful effects of ultraviolet radiation. Increased levels of ultraviolet radiation can lead to a greater incidence of skin cancer, and for this reason CFCs are banned in many countries.

It is known that tooth decay is less common in areas where fluoride salts are present in the drinking water supply. Fluoride is sometimes added to water supplies that are deficient in fluoride salts, and stannous fluoride (a fluoride of tin) is a constituent of some toothpastes.

Chlorine

Chlorine (Cl) is a greenish yellow poisonous gas that has a choking irritating smell and is corrosive to the respiratory tract. Chlorine is the twelfth most common element in Earth's crust, its chief sources being seawater and rock salt, in which it occurs as sodium chloride (common salt). The name of this halogen comes from the Greek word for green, *khloros*. Chlorine boils at –29°F (–34°C) and can be liquefied under pressure at room temperature. The gas has diatomic molecules (Cl_2), that is, they consist of two atoms. In this way, the atoms in the gas molecule achieve the stable eight electron configuration in their outer shells.

Chlorine gas was first prepared in 1774 by the Swedish chemist Carl Wilhelm Scheele, who reacted manganese dioxide with hydrochloric acid, but it was not until 1810, when the English chemist Sir Humphry Davy was unable to decompose the gas, that it was accepted as a new element.

Chlorine is a typical nonmetallic element, but it is too reactive to occur naturally and is therefore only found combined with other elements. Chlorine gas will combine directly with most elements to form chlorides. The main exceptions are carbon, nitrogen, oxygen, and the inert gases. The bonds formed in the chlorides may be ionic (electrovalent) as in sodium chloride, NaCl, which is a crystalline soluble salt, or covalent as in phosphorus trichloride, PCl_3, which is a volatile liquid.

Chlorine is prepared industrially by the electrolysis of brine in a diaphragm cell or a mercury cell. In the diaphragm cell, chlorine gas is released at the anode, and sodium hydroxide forms at the cathode. Because chlorine will react with sodium hydroxide, it is important to provide a barrier between the cathode and the anode that will prevent mixing of the two products but allow the electric current to pass between the cell electrodes. A porous diaphragm, usually made of asbestos paper, is used for this purpose. In the mercury cell, a stream of mercury is used as the cathode. Chlorine gas is liberated at the anode as in the diaphragm cell, but the sodium, which migrates to the cathode, dissolves in the mercury to form an amalgam. This amalgam is removed from the cell and passed through a water bath, where the sodium reacts to form sodium hydroxide and hydrogen. The purified mercury is then pumped back to the electrolytic cell.

Uses of chlorine

As in the case of fluorine, most of the chlorine produced is used in making organic chlorine compounds, such as vinyl chloride. This is an important compound because it can be polymer-ized to give the widely used plastic polyvinyl chloride (PVC). Chlorine is contained in certain weed killers and insecticides. The chemical perchloroethylene is a commonly used dry cleaning fluid. Chlorine compounds, such as hydrochloric acid, are also used for bleaching, especially in the paper and textile industries. Chlorine itself is a useful bactericide and, for this reason, is added in small quantities to swimming pools and drinking water. It is also used as a quenching gas in some Geiger–Müller tubes.

Chlorine combines with hydrogen to form hydrogen chloride, HCl, a pungent gas, which dissolves in water to form hydrochloric acid, a corrosive acid that has many industrial uses. It is also found in the stomach, where it aids digestion.

Compounds

When chlorine combines with a metal, a chloride is formed that usually contains the chloride ion, Cl^-. These compounds tend to be stable and unreactive. Sodium chloride, common salt, is found dissolved in the extracellular fluid of the body. It is essential to maintain a constant concentration of this salt in the body to keep the intra- and extracellular fluids in osmotic balance. (Osmosis

◀ Spreading out iodine-rich seaweed to dry in the sun in Hokkaido, Japan. Iodine salts are found in high concentrations in many sea plants and animals. When these plants are dry, the iodine is extracted by a simple chemical process. The iodine is used in medicine, radiography, and photography. Without iodine, the human body can develop a large swelling on the neck called a goiter.

is a process involving passage of small molecules through membranes.) Other metallic chlorides have industrial uses as catalysts and as intermediates in a large number of synthetic processes.

Organic molecules that contain chlorine have a wide range of uses. The dry cleaning industry uses trichloroethylene, $CHClCCl_2$, and perchlorethylene, CCl_2CCl_2, as solvents. A group of refrigerant gases, called Freons, are mixed organic chlorides and fluorides, such as difluorodichloromethane, CCl_2F_2. They are used in refrigerators and deep freezers. Chloroform, $CHCl_3$, was a compound used as an early anesthetic in 1847 by Sir James Simpson in Edinburgh, Scotland, but it has long since been superseded by safer anesthetics.

War gases

Chlorine gas is highly toxic and was the first poisonous gas to be used in World War I. Several other gases, like phosgene (carbonyl chloride, $COCl_2$) and mustard gas (dichlorodiethyl sulfide, $(CH_2ClCH_2)_2S$), were developed and used later on in the war. Milder gases are used by the police and army for controlling riots. An example is chloroacetophenone ($C_6H_5COCH_2Cl$), which is one of the tear gases often used by riot police.

Bromine

Bromine (Br) is a dense, volatile liquid at room temperature, giving off a highly poisonous brown vapor. Most of the world's bromine is extracted from seawater. The high concentration of salts in the Dead Sea makes it the world's richest source of bromine. Brine is taken from the sea, treated with dilute acid and chlorine, and passed down a tower into which air is blown. This releases bromine from the bromide salts in the seawater.

The chief use of bromine in industry now is as a flame retardant, but it was formerly used in large quantities in the manufacture of ethylene bromide, which was added to gasoline together with the antiknock agent tetraethyl lead. The ethylene bromide prevented lead deposits from building up in the engine by converting it to lead bromide, which is volatile at the operating temperatures of gasoline engines and thus passes out through the exhaust system. Lead-free gasoline has reduced demand considerably. Silver bromide is an active constituent of photographic film; crystals of this compound become activated when exposed to light. When treated with a photographic developer, the activated particles are reduced to black metallic silver while the unactivated particles remain unchanged. The color in a color photograph is produced by pigments coupled into the black-and-white image.

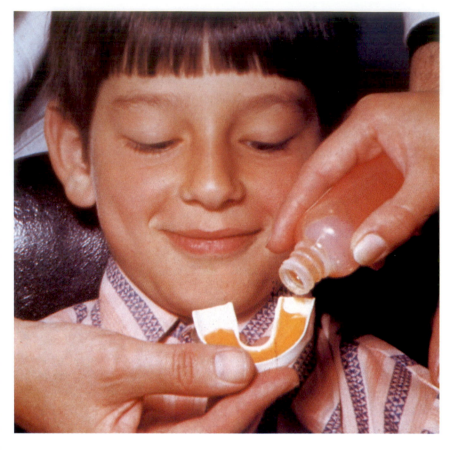

Iodine

Iodine (I) is not an abundant element but is widely distributed as salts in rocks, soils, seawater, and animal and plant tissue. Iodine salts are found in relatively high concentrations in certain sea organisms, such as corals, sponges, and seaweed and in cod-liver oil. Most of the world's supplies of iodine come from northern Chile, where it is found in association with the ore of Chile saltpeter. Iodine itself is a black solid at room temperature and vaporizes easily to give a violet vapor.

Iodine is used in medicine as an external antiseptic both as the free element and in the compound iodoform (CHI_3). It is essential in the human body, and deficiency of iodine leads to the disease known as goiter. Some iodine compounds are opaque to X rays and are used in radiography to distinguish various parts of the body. The radioactive isotope I-131 is used in nuclear medicine to study liver, kidney, and thyroid disorders.

Astatine

Astatine (At) is the least important of the halogens. Its most stable isotope, At-210, has a half life of only 8.3 hours. As far as is known, astatine resembles iodine in its chemical properties.

▲ Fluoride gel is applied to a child's teeth to prevent decay. A new coat must be applied every year or two. Fluoride encourages the enamel that covers developing teeth to be more resistant to the action of bacteria that can cause tooth decay. Fluoride can also be taken in tablet form. Dentists recommend fluoride treatment for children until all the permanent teeth (apart from the wisdom teeth) emerge, usually around the age of 12. After that age, fluoride toothpaste can protect permanent teeth.

SEE ALSO: Acid and alkali • Atomic structure • Chemical and biological warfare • Discharge tube • Element, chemical • Lightbulb • Noble gas • Periodic table • Salt, chemical

Hang Glider

Hang gliding, once the sport of a few daredevils prepared to leap from hills on short and dangerous flights, has progressed to a sophisticated form of sporting aviation. The modern hang glider is an elegant craft capable of flights covering distances of more than 200 miles (320 km). Hang gliders can ascend to heights in excess of 20,000 ft. (6,000 m) and continue to fly many hours.

Major advances in hang glider technology have produced improvements in performance, controllability and coordination. The result is that the efficiency and steerability of today's hang glider compare favorably with conventional fixed-wing aircraft. The most obvious difference in the means of achieving control is that the hang glider has flexible wings and is steered by the pilot shifting his or her weight from side to side.

To turn the machine to the left, the hang glider pilot shifts to the left; shifting to the right causes a turn to the right. For pitch control, the pilot either pulls forward, lowering the angle of attack to speed up the glider, or pushes rearward to increase the angle of attack, and so slow the glider.

By adopting a prone (horizontal) flying position, pilots have produced a reduction of pilot drag of around 50 to 60 percent. Harnesses have also undergone a series of design changes. The latest types are streamlined and cocoon the pilot from shoulder to feet. They are also padded and give protection from the freezing temperatures at the extreme altitudes commonly achieved.

Most glider designs are derivatives of the early Rogallo Delta shape (named after Dr. Francis Rogallo, a NASA scientist) and are tailless. Faster flight and greater efficiency have been achieved by making the wings longer and more slender.

Besides performance, an important advantage of the latest generation of hang gliders has to do

▼ When the control bar of a hang glider is in the central position (A), the glider is trimmed for normal flight. Pushing the bar forward (B) keeps the nose up through tight turns and enables the pilot to reduce air speed before landing. In position (C), the nose drops, and the glider can move through strong headwinds.

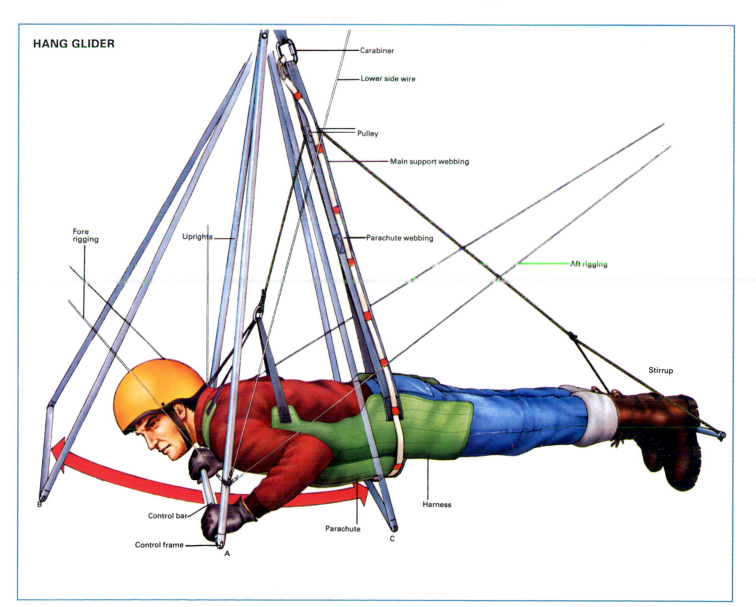

HANG GLIDER

Carabiner
Lower side wire
Pulley
Main support webbing
Fore rigging
Uprights
Parachute webbing
Aft rigging
Stirrup
Harness
Control bar
Parachute
Control frame
A
B
C

with safety. Modern hang gliders are immensely strong (they are designed to take a load of at least ten times the pilot's weight.) Their aerodynamic properties are such that they are extremely stable yet allow the pilot easy and confident handling. Gains in efficiency, however, are not made without some penalties. A wing of high aspect ratio can weigh twice as much as the early Rogallos.

Sixty years ago, hang gliding would hardly have been possible—because materials with the combination of strength and lightness had not been developed. In recent years, however, hang glider design has progressed dramatically, thanks to advanced materials originally produced for jet aircraft and yacht construction.

Powered glider

One of the limitations to hang gliding is its dependence on the need for a suitable hill site. It is therefore hardly surprising that enthusiasts have given a great deal of thought to motorizing their craft by adding a small engine. Motorizing was first done in the early 1980s and proved to be successful. As a result the design of powered hang gliders has rapidly changed these machines into a new type of light aircraft called ultralights or

▲ Hang gliding has become popular, yet the dangers for the unskilled are not to be underestimated. Hang gliding almost fulfills the human desire to fly.

microlights where the pilot is seated in a cockpit. Consequently, most governments have produced regulations covering this new type of flying.

Towing

Pilots of hang gliders living in flat lands are faced with the problem of not having hills from which to take off. Consequently, they have been developing other means of launching—including towing by a winch or automobile. Towing was first achieved by attaching the towline onto the glider's keel and control frame. The forces so produced, however, prevented the pilot from having control of the glider. Several accidents occurred that nearly put an end to towing. Luckily, and quite independently, pilots in Britain and Australia discovered that towing could be done safely by attaching the towline onto the pilot instead of the glider.

The risks

Early in the 1970s, when hang gliding was in its infancy, many accidents occurred. The public media were not slow to pick up these newsworthy stories, so many people believed hang gliding to be dangerous. Despite the controversy, the sport has survived and has matured into a popular pastime.

SEE ALSO: AERODYNAMICS • AIRCRAFT DESIGN • HELICOPTER • ULTRALIGHT AIRCRAFT

FACT FILE

■ The prototype model for Francis Rogallo's flexible-wing hang glider, from which the first modern hang gliders were developed, was flown in 1948; the wing fabric was made from a piece of flower-patterned chintz curtain, and a child's plastic toy was the pilot. The model was fan tested in the Rogallos' front room.

■ On April 29, 1905, Daniel Maloney cut loose from a hot-air balloon at an altitude of 4,000 ft. (1,220 m), attached to a tandem biplane hang glider with a horizontal tail. He took 20 minutes to reach the ground, always under control, and landed on his feet.

■ In 1969 the U.S. Air Force experimented with a Francis Rogallo wing attached to a jet pilot's ejection seat. The aim was to enable a pilot who had been shot down to leave the immediate area of the attack and, if possible, get back to his own lines, gliding on the Rogallo wing, with boost power coming from any fuel left in the ejection unit.

Head-Up Display

A head-up display (HUD) is a means of displaying information vital to the user, without the need to move the eyes from the normal line of sight. The largest developers of these systems are electronics and optical companies fulfilling contracts for the world's air forces, and to some extent civil airlines and the automobile industry.

Many modern single lens reflex (SLR) cameras have viewfinder displays that have some points of similarity with the more complex aircraft systems. The available displays might include information concerning focus, shutter speed, lens aperture setting, and the status of dedicated flash units. Some incorporate warning light-emitting diodes (LEDs) to indicate over- or underexposure.

Of course all these functions can be seen on the camera body, but if they are displayed against the backdrop of the scene to be photographed, the photographer has a great advantage. In the case of high-speed photography, it is particularly important that the eye need not leave the viewfinder merely to check settings. As both displayed information and the subject are viewed in the same optical plane, there is no need for the photographer to refocus his or her eyes to view either and thus cause fatigue and render the system useless.

Military application

In an air attack mission four factors are of great importance: the ability to fly fast, to be able to fly low (to avoid radar detection), to find the target, and to hit the target accurately. The pilot must be able to do all four things if necessary at night and in bad weather. These requirements demand the concentration of vision on the view of the outside world. Any time taken to check instruments that are not in the line of sight could impair the pilot's ability to fly the aircraft to the peak of its performance. The pilot must keep a constant check on height, speed, and heading, so this information must be supplied in a way that does not restrict the view. This is the purpose of the head-up display unit.

Information from the airplane's navigation computer, weapon-aiming computer, altimeter, air-speed sensors, and radar is fed into a central processor. The inputs are converted electronically to appear as green numbers, letters, and graphic symbols on a small cathode-ray tube. The light from the display then passes through lenses that project and magnify the image of the symbols. An angled mirror then reflects the images up to a combiner glass.

The combiner glass, housed directly in front of the pilot, must serve two functions. It must reflect the green display symbols into the pilot's eyes, and still allow a clear view. It may be useful to think of the combiner simply as a semi-reflecting mirror.

It is important that the display seen by the pilot should appear to be floating in front of the aircraft. Were it to be brought to focus on the surface of the combiner, the pilot would have to refocus each time it is viewed. As the pilot is using binocular vision, the result of looking at the display would mean that the view ahead would be a double image, and vice versa. This effect is easy to demonstrate. If a small circle of paper is placed on a window and the eyes focused on it from about 3 ft. (1 m) away, objects outside the window will appear double. If now the eyes are focused on something outside, two paper circles will be seen instead of one.

In the HUD unit, this problem is solved by placing collimating lenses between the angled mirror and the combiner. These lenses make the light rays stay in parallel lines. As such, the display will always appear to be in focus and a natural part of the pilot's forward view.

Below the combiner is a small control panel that the pilot uses to select the type of display required and to update the navigation system. The panel also has a control to vary the brightness of the display. Some systems do this automatically, with a manual override for unusual conditions.

▲ The advantage to pilots of a head-up display is that they can check instrument information without having to move their field of vision. This display is especially useful for fighter pilots who must be able to navigate across unfamiliar territory while flying fast and low.

The above description relates to a basic, refractive HUD unit, which, though quite efficient, has two main drawbacks. One is that the field of view is limited to about 20 degrees, which may not be sufficient for dogfight situations, for example, when the pilot needs as wide a view as possible. Small displays also make the information appear cluttered on the combiner. The other drawback is the loss of light coming through the combiner. Loss of light would be a particular concern in bad weather or at night.

HUDs using holographic techniques in the manufacture of the combiner improve this situation. Using laser light, a highly reflective hologram is produced. It is sandwiched between glass to form the combiner. The hologram is made so that it reflects only an extremely narrow section of the visible spectrum. The section chosen corresponds to the specific green color of the cathode-ray tube display. To all other colors of light, including other shades of green, it is virtually transparent. Thus, the pilot has excellent forward vision and a brighter display as well.

In practice, more than one hologram is used. They are made so that not only will they reflect a specific color, but they will reflect it at a precise angle. This leads to the elimination of the collimating lenses of the refractive system and also makes wider angles of view possible: 20 degrees by 30 degrees with little distortion.

Both systems, refractive or diffractive, can be fitted with a provision for recording the pilot's display, and both have stand-by sights in case the main display should fail or be damaged. The source of the stand-by sight would be either a quartz halogen bulb or, in some cases, LEDs.

Displays and use

The HUD may be considered as the pilot's contact with all the airplane's advanced technological systems. Before the airplane leaves the ground, the navigation computer is fed with data regarding its starting point, the position of the target (which may be hundreds of miles away), and the precise locations of a number of waypoints, or landmarks. Once airborne, the pilot switches the HUD to its cruise mode. The height, speed, and heading are all shown numerically or by a cursor on a vertical scale.

As the pilot approaches a planned heading, a small dot (the flight director spot) appears on the display. This is the navigation computer's way of informing the pilot that it knows how to fly to the next waypoint. The pilot then simply maneuvers the airplane until the circle of the airplane symbol surrounds the dot. By flying so that the dot is maintained in this position, the pilot is sure that the airplane is on course for the waypoint.

Civil aircraft HUDs

Civil airliners normally fly very predictable routes at high altitude using autopilot facilities and watched over by ground radar. They carry crew members to monitor instruments, navigate, and operate communications. The only time a HUD could be valuable to the pilot would be in a poor-visibility landing. Fold-down systems are in use to give the pilot a graphic display of the runway and position of the aircraft on it, but they have not been universally adopted. Some systems derive the positional information from the instrument landing system (ILS) radar fitted to most airliners.

Helmet HUD

As the name suggests, these devices make use of the pilot's helmet to mount the display. In some systems, the display is viewed through a collimating eyepiece, and in others, it is reflected off the visor. Although they can be used in fixed-wing aircraft, their main application is in helicopters, where all-round vision is most important. Flight information or warning cues can be displayed, as well as weapons-aiming guides, irrespective of where the pilot happens to be looking.

Automobile HUD

Another area of development for HUD is in automobiles. Instrument information, such as speed and fuel level, may be displayed directly onto the car windscreen, enabling drivers to maintain their view of the road.

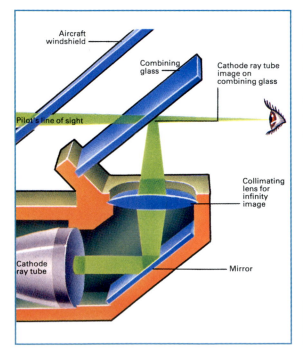

◀ The HUD optical system projects the computer-generated data into the pilot's line of sight, adjusting the light rays so that the display is focused at infinity and refocusing the eyes is not necessary.

 SEE ALSO: AIRCRAFT DESIGN • BOMB-AIMING DEVICE • CATHODE-RAY TUBE • COMPUTER • LIGHT AND OPTICS • MULTIMEDIA • NAVIGATION

Hearing

◀ Hearing tests are common tests for children growing up. The machine on the right is called an audiometer and produces sounds of varying pitch and loudness that are sent to one ear at a time through headphones. The sounds are decreased in volume until they become inaudible. The person being tested signals (here by raising a hand) each time they hear a sound. This type of hearing test, called pure-tone audiometry, is often used to assess the extent of a person's hearing loss and to investigate possible causes.

The ear is an extremely delicate and complex organ, giving us both our sense of hearing and our sense of balance. What is normally called the ear—the part we can see—is only part of the outer ear, itself the simplest of three sections. Behind it, stretching deep into the skull, lie the middle and inner ear, which in turn connect with the nose and throat.

The outer ear, called the pinna, has two important parts: the auricle, the fleshy part attached to the side of the head, and the opening called the external auditory canal. The auricle is shaped like a cup or radar bowl to collect sound waves and direct them into the external auditory canal. It is composed of fatty tissue and cartilage, a tissue softer than bone but harder than muscle, and although some individuals can move their ears, humans lack the ability to "prick" their ears as many animals do. The external auditory canal is the opening visible when looking directly at the ear. It is a passage about 1½ in. (3.8 cm) long, which guides sounds from the auricle to the middle ear. Its outer third is lined with fine hairs and wax-producing glands. The hairs and wax trap dirt and other foreign matter to stop them from entering and possibly damaging the ear. Sometimes this wax hardens and causes discomfort, earache, temporary loss of hearing, and ringing in the ears (tinnitus). In such cases, doctors can syringe the wax out.

The middle ear

The middle ear, or tympanic cavity, resembles a six-sided box. It is separated from the external auditory canal by the eardrum, or tympanic membrane, a thin sheet of tissue about ¼ in. (6 mm) across. Within the tympanic cavity, three small movable bones, called the auditory ossicles, link with each other to form a chain.

The outer bone, called the malleus or hammer, is attached to the eardrum. Next comes the middle bone, called the incus or anvil, which connects the malleus with the innermost bone, the stapes or stirrup. The outer and middle ears channel sound across these three bones to the inner ear, to which the innermost bone is attached.

Two parts of the head connect with the middle ear but are not part of it. The mastoid process is a series of small airfilled spaces, connecting with the tympanic cavity. Infection of these bone cells, mastoiditis, can cause severe earache. The Eustachian or auditory tube is about 1½ in. (3.8 cm) long and connects the nasal cavity at the back of the nose with the tympanic cavity. Its purpose is to equalize pressure on each side of the eardrum. Popping of the ears, as experienced in an airplane, is due to small movements of the eardrum caused by changes in the air pressure and can be rectified by nose blowing. This passage can also become infected, causing severe pain.

The inner ear and hearing

The inner ear, which lies partly within the temporal skull bone, contains so many intricate chambers and passages it is called a labyrinth. It consists of three connected parts—the vestibule, the semicircular canals, and the cochlea.

The vestibule is the central part of the inner ear, one side of which connects with the middle ear. Above and behind the vestibule are the three semicircular canals that give us our sense of balance. In front of the vestibule is the cochlea, which looks like a snail and contains the hearing organs, known as the Cortian fibers or the organs of Corti. For a person to hear, sound waves must reach these organs, and they do so in three ways.

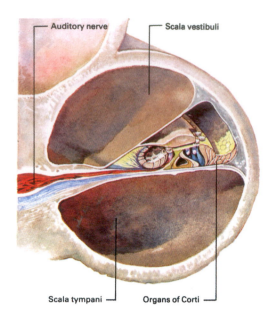

The first and most important way is by sound waves causing the eardrum to vibrate. These vibrations are carried across the middle ear by the auditory ossicles to the oval window, which is an opening between the middle and inner ear. Sound vibrations make the bone called the stapes move like a plunger in and out of the oval window, agitating the fluid in the cochlea and therefore the organs of Corti.

The second way is by sound waves traveling through air from the eardrum to the secondary eardrum, a membrane covering the round window, which is an opening in the middle ear located below the oval window. Sometimes, as a

◀ The organs of Corti, located in the cochlea, consist of some 30,000 highly sensitive hair cells. When sound waves distort the basilar membrane the tufts on top of the hair cells bend, stimulating the nerve endings at their base.

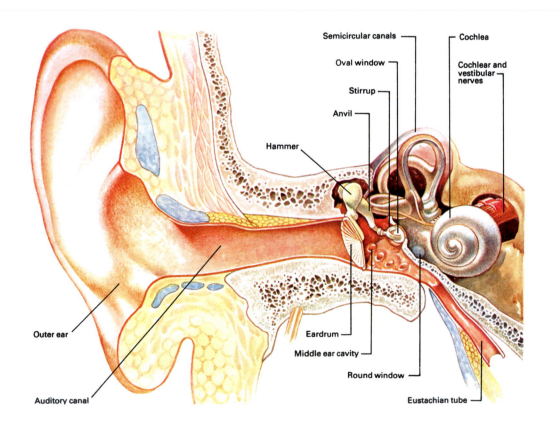

◀ When sound waves enter the ear, they travel along the external auditory canal until they strike the eardrum, making it vibrate. These vibrations are transmitted through the hammer and the anvil to the stirrup, the footplate of which rests upon the oval window. As it pushes in and out, the stirrup causes the fluid in the cochlea to move in waves, stimulating the tiny hairs that line the cochlea to bend.

result of injury or disease, a hole, or rupture, forms in the eardrum. A ruptured eardrum does not normally interfere with hearing. Sound vibrations pass through to the secondary eardrum where they are carried on to the perilymph, one of the fluids in the cochlea that resembles extracellular fluid.

The third way is by sound traveling directly through the bones of the skull and sending vibrations to the inner ear, where they are detected.

The inner ear transmits sounds to the brain. When sound waves move through the perilymph, they move the fibers of the basilar membrane within the cochlea. These fibers—there are 30,000 of them—stimulate the nerves that are attached to them, and these send messages through the auditory nerve to the temporal lobe, the center of hearing in the brain.

Scientists are divided as to the exact mechanism of hearing. The Resonance Theory says that the cochlea differentiates between sounds of different pitch—the normal person can hear sounds in the frequency range of 16 to 20,000 cycles a second—the fibers of the basilar membrane varying in length like piano strings. The shortest fibers respond to the high-pitched sounds, the lowest to low-pitched ones.

The Telephone Theory states that the ear acts very much like a telephone. Sound waves strike the eardrum, which corresponds to a telephone transmitter, to set up nervous impulses, somewhat like the electrical impulses in a telephone wire. These impulses, of identical frequency but coded for variations in pitch, go to the brain.

The Resonance Theory has been disproved, at least in part, by the German physiologist E. von Bekesy. He observed the basilar membrane with the aid of a stroboscope and discovered that it vibrates even for a pure single note.

Balance

The other vital function of the ear is aiding balance. If someone walking along a plank or riding a bicycle begins to wobble, the ear sends a message to the brain, which prompts the muscles necessary to adjust the body. The ear can detect this imbalance thanks to the three fluid-filled semicircular canals in the inner ear. They enable us to keep our balance when we sit, run, or walk and to recognize in what direction we are going even with our eyes closed. One of these canals is horizontal, the other two are vertical.

When the head or body is moved up, down, backward, or forward the fluid in the canals moves, affecting delicate hair cells at one end of each canal. These cells are equipped with fibers from the vestibular nerve, which carries impulses to the brain.

Dizziness or loss of balance occurs when the canals or receptor cells become diseased, as in Ménière's disease. If they are destroyed, the body loses its ability to maintain its balance or equilibrium, as the brain has lost an important source of information. Seasickness comes from excessive stimulation of the semicircular canals.

Hearing aids

The development of the electronic hearing aid was the biggest advance ever made in helping deaf people, and hearing aids are now used by millions of people all over the world. All hearing aids are fundamentally simple acoustic amplifying systems and consist of four basic parts: a microphone to pick up the sound and convert it to a very small electrical signal, an amplifier to increase the size of the electric signal, an earphone (often called a receiver in hearing aid circles) to turn the electric signal into an acoustic one that is then fed into the ear through an ear mold, and a source of power for the amplifier, usually a small battery. The ear mold is not part of the hearing aid but is essential for fitting the aid to the user. It is made of plastic and molded from an impression taken of the user's ear.

Hearing aids can be divided into three groups: body-worn aids, head-worn aids, and educational aids such as group hearing aids and auditory training units. Because of their larger size, body-worn aids are capable of the widest possible performance and can be used for all types and degrees of deafness. They are, however, large and

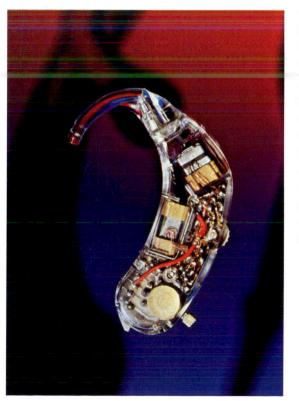

◀ This picture shows the inside workings of Bosch's behind-the-ear Star 6 hearing aid. Modern electronics make possible the manufacture of high-performance hearing aids of such small size (the picture is enlarged to about twice the actual size). The selector switches along the outside rim control the functions, such as tone and volume.

many people do not like to be seen wearing them, preferring the smaller head-worn aids. These can be divided into three main groups: those worn behind the ear, in eyeglass frames, and completely in the outer ear itself. A head-worn aid is not capable of producing the high output of a body-worn aid, but otherwise it has similar characteristics. The smaller the aid the more restricted is its performance. Group hearing aid equipment is used in schools for the deaf and partially hearing units where size is unimportant. The large, high-quality microphones and earphones used ensure the best possible performance.

Performance

The performance of a hearing aid is largely controlled by the transducers, that is, the microphone and earphone. The performance of the transducers can be indicated by means of a frequency-response curve, which shows graphically how the microphone or earphone responds over a range of frequencies from 100 to 10,000 Hz. The graph shows that at low frequencies the limitation is largely due to the microphone, while at high frequencies it is the earphone that restricts the performance of the hearing aid.

The amplifier consists of three or more transistors, depending upon the amount of amplification required. The frequency response and power output from the amplifier are such that they place almost no limitation on the performance of the aid. The amount of noise generated by the first transistor stage is important, however, because if this is too high, the listener will hear a continuous background rushing noise. The maximum amount of sound available from the aid, called the maximum acoustic output, will depend upon the power-handling capability of the output transistor and earphone. In addition, the power available will be limited by the amount of current that can be drawn from the battery.

The smaller the battery, the smaller the current that can be drawn while still giving a reasonable battery life and the lower the maximum amount of sound available from the aid. The amount of acoustic amplification required depends upon the degree of deafness that the aid is required to help and may vary from 40 dB, that is, 100 times amplification, to 80 dB, that is, 10,000 times amplification. Because the transducers have less than 100 percent efficiency, the electrical amplification necessary is considerably greater than the acoustic amplification. Amplification varies with frequency, and most hearing aids amplify high frequencies more than low ones. It has been found that this method gives more intelligible speech.

A laryngograph enables a deaf person to modify his or her own voice patterns. Two tiny electrodes are placed on the front of the person's neck. They record every movement of the vocal cords and show the result on an oscilloscope.

The earphone will alter the performance of the aid in terms of frequency response, gain, and maximum acoustic output, and on a body-worn aid, this is used as a means of altering the performance and then fitting the hearing aid to suit individual requirements. The main limitation on earphones is at high frequencies.

Frequency-response curves

The performance of hearing aids can be roughly divided into three main groups in terms of the maximum acoustic output or power: low, medium, and high power. A low-power aid will have maximum output of around 110 dB sound pressure level (SPL), a medium-power aid 120 dB SPL, and a high-power aid 130 dB SPL or more. This output level can be compared with the noise from a jet engine close by, which is only about 130 dB SPL. Some deaf people are not able to hear at this level, but can hear at 135 dB SPL or more.

On many hearing aids, there is a switch that disconnects the microphone (marked M) and switches on an inductive pick-up coil (marked T, because it was originally designed for telephone use). This coil enables the user to pick up alternating magnetic signals produced by an electric current flowing through a loop of wire around the room, enabling him or her to move anywhere in the loop and hear the signal without direct connection to the amplifier. Such a system can be used in schools and in the home, where it is used for listening to the radio or television, for example.

The future

A recent advance for those suffering from total sensorineural deafness is the possibility of cochlear implants. These devices convert sound into electric impulses that are channeled, via the auditory nerve, to the brain and interpreted as sound, giving limited sound information to the otherwise totally deaf.

SEE ALSO: ACOUSTICS • AMPLIFIER • BIOENGINEERING • CELL BIOLOGY • MICROPHONE • RESONANCE • SOUND • TRANSDUCER AND SENSOR • TRANSISTOR • VOICE RECOGNITION AND SYNTHESIS

Heart

The heart is an impressive example of natural engineering. A typical healthy human heart will function for more than 70 years without requiring attention and will pump at least one million gallons (4.6 million l) of blood in this time. In contrast, the mechanical pumps that circulate water in a central-heating system and deliver fuel to a car engine have a working life of around 5 years and require maintenance every 12 months or so.

How a healthy heart functions

The human heart is in fact a double pump, divided into a left and right side by a central wall. The right side, defined from the viewpoint of the heart's "owner," pumps blood to the lungs where it gives up carbon dioxide and absorbs oxygen; the left side pumps oxygenated blood that returns from the lungs around the rest of the body.

The right and left sides are further divided into two chambers each: an upper chamber, called an atrium (plural atria), or auricle, and a lower chamber, called a ventricle. The role of the atria is to receive incoming blood from veins. The ventricles periodically accept blood through nonreturn valves that connect them to their respective atria; the contraction of the ventricle walls then causes pressure to rise in the ventricle.

The increase in ventricular pressure during contraction causes the valves between the ventricles and the atria to slam shut. The ventricular pressure also opens a second set of nonreturn valves, through which blood flows from the heart into arteries. At the end of the contraction, the pressure in the arteries causes these valves to close and the cycle starts again.

Both sides of the heart contract and relax at the same time: the contraction phase is called the systole; the relaxation phase, the diastole. The valve closures between these two phases are responsible for the two audible pulses of the heartbeat that can be heard through a stethoscope.

Components of the heart

Although the two sides of the heart contract at the same time and in the same manner, the structures and names of the components of the two sides of the heart differ somewhat. The vessels that lead oxygenated blood from the lungs to the left atrium form the pulmonary vein. The veins that lead blood to the right ventricle after its journey around the body include the inferior vena cava and the superior vena cava. A smaller blood vessel, called the coronary sinus, returns blood that has passed through the muscles of the heart.

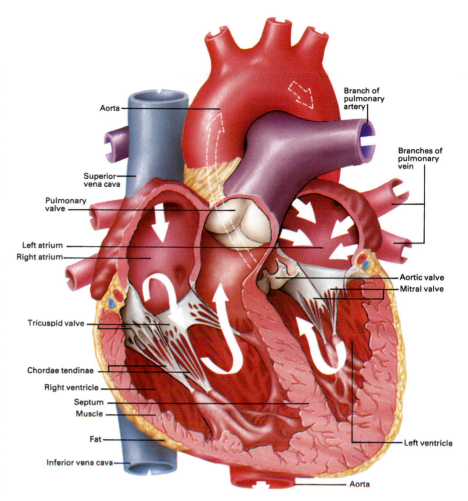

The atrioventricular valves—those that separate the atria from the ventricles—have similar structures: they both consist of flaps of tissue secured to a ridge in the heart wall and tethered by fibers called *chordae tendinae* to prevent them from inverting. The difference between the two is that the tricuspid valve (right side) has three flaps, whereas the mitral valve (left side) has only two.

Each of the exit valves of the heart consists of three sail-like sacs that inflate under the back pressure from the arteries, thereby closing the exit holes. The aortic valve prevents blood from flowing back from the aorta to the left ventricle during diastole, while the pulmonary valve seals the pulmonary artery from the right ventricle.

Muscles and nerves

The heart is able to contract because its walls consist mainly of muscular tissues. Like other forms of muscle, these tissues contract as a response to electrical stimuli from the nervous system. These stimuli originate in the sinoatrial node, which is located in the wall of the right ventricle near the point where the superior vena cava enters. A system of nerve fibers radiates from the sinoatrial node through the walls of the two atria. These are the "wires" that carry the stimuli that cause the atria to contract early in systole.

▲ This cross section shows the human heart as seen through the rib cage. In this mirror image, the right ventricle appears at left, and vice versa.

The stimuli from the sinoatrial node also pass to the atrioventricular node, located between the right atrium and the pulmonary valve. This node introduces a delay before issuing the stimuli that trigger the contractions of the ventricles. The delay allows time for blood to pass from the contracting atria to the relaxed ventricles. The stimuli pass through the atrioventricular bundle, a system of nerves that passes through the septum between the two ventricles and spreads through the walls of the ventricles, making them contract.

The heart muscles have their own circulatory system, called the coronary circulation. Two coronary arteries tap blood from the aorta and divert it to a system of tiny blood vessels, called capillaries, that suffuse the heart muscles with blood. The spent blood from the muscles collects into veins and ultimately passes into the right atrium through the coronary sinus.

Heartbeat and activity

During physical activity, the muscles of the body take chemical "fuel" and oxygen from the bloodstream and convert them into carbon dioxide and other waste products. The more intensive the activity, the greater the demand for fuel and oxygen, so the heart beats faster to increase the supply of blood to the muscles. Blood also starts to circulate more rapidly through the lungs, which remove carbon dioxide from the bloodstream and replenish it with oxygen.

During sleep, when physical activity is low, the heart can slow to around 60 beats per minute. During physical exertion, the rate accelerates to around twice this rate. Short bursts of extreme physical exertion can provoke heart rates of 200 beats per minute or even more.

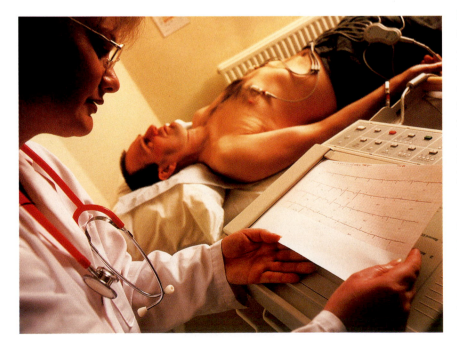

▼ The minute electrical impulses that trigger the contractions of the heart can be detected by sensors attached to the skin. A printer produces a trace of electrical activity plotted against time that can help in the diagnosis of heart complaints. Such an examination is often called an EKG, an abbreviation of the German name for the chart that results from the test—*Elektrokardiogram*.

Congenital heart defects

A fetus acquires its blood oxygen and disposes of carbon dioxide through its umbilical cord, so the circulation of blood through the lungs is unnecessary. Until birth, the function of the heart is to pump blood from the inferior vena cava, which carries oxygenated blood from the umbilical cord, to the aorta, which distributes that blood through the body. Accordingly, the lungs are switched out of the circuit of blood by a valve that directs incoming blood from the right atrium to the left atrium. At birth, this "short circuit" normally ceases to function and the interatrial valve heals up as the lungs assume their role in oxygenating blood and eliminating carbon dioxide.

In some cases, however, the interatrial valve fails to heal completely, so that a proportion of the blood that arrives at the right atrium passes to the other side of the heart rather than following the normal course through the right ventricle and thence to the lungs. This is one of several abnormal heart conditions that arise because the connections in the fetus fail to rearrange completely for the normal function of the heart outside the womb. Collectively, these conditions are described as "congenital," meaning "with birth," and they have various degrees of impact on the ability to lead a healthy active life.

In another congenital defect, a passage that connects the pulmonary artery to the aorta fails to close at birth. The proportion of blood that reaches the lungs is so small that the baby becomes fully deoxygenated. This condition is called blue-baby syndrome, because of the abnormal coloration caused by dark-blue deoxygenated blood. The condition is life-threatening but can often be remedied by emergency surgery.

Coronary heart disease

One of the conditions associated with the aging process is atherosclerosis, whereby fat and cholesterol form a deposit of plaque on the inner walls of arteries. As the deposit thickens, the space available for the circulation of blood diminishes, reducing the supply of oxygenated blood to the parts of the body fed by the affected arteries. The rate at which plaque forms varies from person to person and is determined by factors such as the amount of fat in the diet and genetic heritage.

Atherosclerosis of the coronary arteries is the starting point of coronary heart disease. As the plaque thickens, the supply of oxygen to the heart muscles becomes restricted. Sometimes, a lump of plaque dislodges from the wall of the coronary artery and blocks a narrower artery in the heart. This event, called coronary thrombosis, deprives the heart muscles of their blood supply. Starved of oxygen, the heart muscles cease to function properly. The result is a myocardial infarction, commonly called a heart attack. Unless normal heart function can be restored, death ensues within four minutes, as the brain and body are deprived of oxygenated blood.

Detached plaque is not the only cause of the arterial occlusion, or blocking, that leads to a heart attack. Clots of blood platelets are capable of obstructing arteries narrowed by atherosclerosis, and spontaneous spasms of the coronary arteries can pinch off the blood supply whether arterial plaque is present or not.

Resuscitation and recovery

One of the principal causes of death in a heart attack is ventricular fibrillation, which is when the ventricles lose their normal rhythm and assume a fluttering motion that pumps little or no blood. In many cases, normal ventricular action can be restored by passing a pulse of heavy current between two metal paddles of a defibrillator applied to the victim's chest. If a defibrillator is unavailable or ineffective, some blood can be pumped around the body by pressing firmly and

◀ This calf has been fitted with an artificial heart as part of a research program at the University of Utah. Sensors monitor its performance as the calf exercises on a treadmill.

repeatedly on the left side of the victim's chest. In combination with artificial respiration, which introduces oxygen to the lungs, this technique is called cardiopulmonary resuscitation, or CPR.

If the patient survives the attack, chances of prolonged survival can be improved by intravenous injection of so-called clotbusters as soon as possible after the attack. This class of compounds includes streptokinase, an enzyme that stimulates the production of thrombin, which decomposes blood clots that could cause further attacks. Small daily doses of aspirin can also help prevent heart attacks by reducing the clotting ability of blood. More radical treatments include surgery to broaden or bypass congested arteries.

Other heart disorders

Congestive heart failure is a progressive weakening of the ventricles caused by the effort of forcing blood through congested or constricted blood vessels. It can be avoided or halted by drugs that inhibit the formation of substances that cause blood vessels to contract.

Heart block is the dysfunction of the nervous system that controls the contraction of heart muscles. It can be overcome by the use of an artificial pacemaker to provide electrical stimuli.

Myocarditis is an inflammation and destruction of heart tissues caused by bacterial or fungal infections. In most cases, its progress can be halted by a course of powerful antibiotics.

FACT FILE

■ *The risk of heart attacks can by reduced by diets low in saturated fat and cholesterol, thereby reducing the availability of raw materials for the formation of arterial plaque. Regular exercise increases the rate of blood flow through the arteries and so can help remove arterial plaque before it accumulates in dangerous amounts.*

■ *Research shows that good nutrition during pregnancy and the first years of infancy does more to prevent heart disease than any change of diet in later life.*

■ *Seattle, Washington, is one of the safest places to have a heart attack. An estimated 50 percent of heart attack victims survive heart attacks as a result of prompt action by passersby trained in resuscitation.*

■ *Many shopping malls, conference centers, and other public venues are equipped with portable defibrillators. In the hands of trained personnel, these devices save lives that would otherwise be lost while waiting for the arrival of medical teams.*

SEE ALSO: AMBULANCE • BLOOD • ELECTRONICS IN MEDICINE • FAT • HEART PACEMAKER • HEART SURGERY • NUTRITION AND FOOD SCIENCE

Heart Pacemaker

A heart pacemaker—also called a cardiac pacemaker—is a device that produces electrical impulses to stimulate and coordinate the contraction of cells in the atria, which are a pair of chambers in the heart. In a healthy individual, this function is performed by a lump of fibrous tissue, called the sinoatrial node, located at the top of the heart. The condition in which the sinoatrial node ceases to function normally is called heart block; it may be a permanent state or a temporary condition caused by the trauma of heart surgery.

Timing circuitry

The key element of any artificial pacemaker is a signal generator, which produces the stimulant impulses that act on the atrial cells via electrodes. The precise nature of this circuitry varies between different types of pacemakers.

Early devices, called asynchronous pacemakers, produced regular impulses at a rate of 70 to 75 beats per minute. They overrode any natural impulses from the sinoatrial node to produce a regular heartbeat at a rate sufficient for a patient lying in bed. (The normal rate ranges from about 55 beats per minute during sleep to more than 200 beats per minute for heavy exercise.)

Asynchronous devices have now been superseded by synchronous pacemakers. These devices rely on sensors to detect any impulses from the sinoatrial node and remain passive as long as such impulses are detected, thus allowing the heartrate to rise and fall according to the body's oxygen requirements for various levels of activity. If the circuitry detects that the heart rate has fallen below a critical value—70 beats per minute, for example—the pacemaker takes over the regulation of the heartbeat so as to avoid loss of consciousness and possibly death.

External versus implanted

Two configurations of cardiac pacemaker exist: external and implanted. The most appropriate choice for an individual depends on the precise nature of his or her condition.

A patient recovering from heart surgery and showing symptoms of heart block would be a typical candidate for the application of an external pacemaker. In this case, a fine tube, called a catheter, is introduced into a vein, usually in the patient's arm. A surgeon then delicately maneuvers a fine wire through the catheter and vein until an electrode at its tip reaches the entrance of the heart. The wire is then secured in place and its free end connected to a signal generator.

◄ This implant pacemaker of 1972 used radioactive plutonium as a power supply. The smooth surface and composition of its silicone casing helped reduce the risk of rejection by minimizing the immune response when implanted.

The signal generator occupies a box taped to the patient's chest. If recovery from surgery brings an end to the episodes of heart block, a simple procedure withdraws the electrode and catheter, and the entry wounds heal rapidly.

An external pacemaker has the advantages that its power cells are easily replaced, and the procedures for its application and withdrawal are relatively noninvasive—they do not require major surgery. The disadvantages are the encumbrance of the signal generator and power pack and the risk of infection through the entry wound.

For chronic sufferers of heart block, the convenience of an implanted pacemaker may outweigh the hazards of invasive surgery. If so, a surgeon creates a cavity in the chest, just below the collarbone, and inserts a combined power pack and signal generator. The surgeon then implants electrodes in the wall of the heart or feeds them through a vein before testing the pacemaker and, if it works, closes the wound.

An implanted pacemaker is intended to last at least ten years before replacement. Accordingly, its power supply must be extremely durable. Lithium cells are the preferred power supply, although devices that produce power from radioactive plutonium have also been used.

The external surface of the device must be smooth and consist of a biocompatible substance, such as a silicone polymer. Otherwise, the pacemaker could trigger an immune response that would necessitate its removal.

SEE ALSO: Battery • Bioengineering • Electronics in medicine • Heart • Heart surgery • Muscle • Transplant

Heart Surgery

Heart surgery, also called cardiovascular surgery, encompasses surgical techniques that correct or alleviate congenital heart defects and acquired conditions such as coronary heart disease and that mend wounds caused by the penetration of the heart by bullets, knife blades, or other objects.

The scope for treatment of complaints by cardiovascular surgery increased vastly with the introduction and development of open-heart surgery in the early 1950s. More recent advances, including minimally invasive surgery, have improved success rates and reduced recovery times.

Stopping the heart

For many cardiovascular procedures, the heart must be temporarily stopped so that its rhythmic contractions do not impede the surgeon's work. The connections between the heart and the circulatory system must also be clamped to prevent massive blood loss through the surgical opening. When these measures are taken, the body's supply of oxygenated blood from the lungs is disrupted—an occurrence that would normally cause the degeneration of the brain and other organs and would eventually kill the patient.

In most cases, the patient is kept alive by cardiopulmonary bypass, whereby blood that arrives at the heart through the inferior and superior venae cavae is diverted to a heart-lung machine. Such devices have oxygenators that imbue blood with oxygen and remove carbon dioxide before pumps inject the blood through catheters that feed into the patient's aorta. The blood then follows its usual path through the body.

In the first stage of a cardiopulmonary bypass, tubes called catheters are inserted into the appropriate veins and arteries to make the connections with the heart-lung machine. The machine is primed with a sufficient volume of donor blood to fill its working parts. The pumps are then switched on so that the heart-lung machine works in parallel with the patient's heart.

Once the heart-lung machine is working satisfactorily, the surgeon seals the entrances and exits of the heart with clamps and injects the heart muscles with a solution of potassium salts, which halts their contractions. Temporarily isolated and paralyzed, the heart is in a suitable condition for surgery to commence. At the end of surgery on the heart, the clamps are removed and blood flows into the heart. As soon as the paralysis owing to the potassium salts ends, the heart-lung machine is disconnected and the catheters withdrawn before the patient is stitched up.

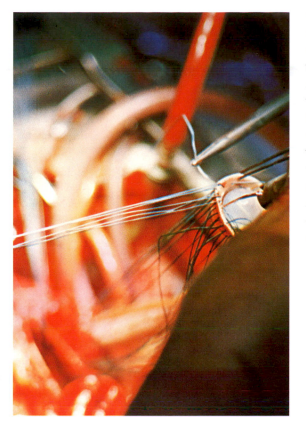

◄ This picture shows a surgical procedure to replace a defective heart valve with an artificial substitute. A surgeon first threads loose sutures between the polyester rim of the artificial valve and the edge of the opening where the valve will be positioned. Tightening the sutures by pulling on the ends of the thread then draws the valve into place.

Hypothermic techniques

Before the invention of the heart-lung machine in 1953, hypothermia was the only means of sustaining life while the heart was temporarily stopped for surgery. Hypothermia—abnormally low body temperature—reduces the rate of the metabolic processes that drain oxygen from blood. In this way, the body's demand for oxygen would be diminished to such an extent that the oxygen content of static blood would be sufficient to maintain basic organ functions while the heart was stopped for up to five minutes of surgery.

The limited stoppage times allowed by early hypothermic techniques imposed severe restrictions on the amount of surgery that could be done without running an unacceptable risk of brain or other organ damage or even death. For this reason, hypothermic techniques fell into disuse soon after the invention of the heart-lung machine.

The use of heart-lung machines is not entirely free of problems, however. Blood that has been in contact with the metal, glass, and plastic inner surfaces of heart-lung machines can form clots and cause inflammation when it returns to a patient's body. These effects put the patient at risk of side effects and prolong recovery times. For these reasons, a group of surgeons from the Novosibirsk Institute of Circulatory Pathology, Russia, generated worldwide interest when they announced their success in using refined hypothermic techniques to allow heart stoppages for up to 90 minutes of open-heart surgery.

HEART-LUNG MACHINE

Heart-lung machines oxygenate blood and pump it around the body while the heart is stopped. Such machines are used if the heart is stopped for surgery or if the heart or lungs fail to function adequately as a result of disease or a congenital defect.

The patient's blood enters the machine from catheters inserted into the major veins that normally feed the heart. An addition of the drug heparin at this stage discourages the formation of clots during the subsequent oxygenation process.

There is a choice of three apparatuses for introducing oxygen into the blood: bubble, film, and membrane oxygenators. As its name suggests, a bubble oxygenator passes a stream of oxygen through blood to encourage uptake of the gas. A film oxygenator promotes oxygenation by spreading a thin film of blood on metal plates or rotating disks in an atmosphere of oxygen. These two types of devices cause gradual hemolysis—degradation of the blood—as a result of direct contact

between blood and oxygen gas. Membrane oxygenators introduce oxygen to blood via permeable membrane. This process causes less hemolysis than occurs with bubble or film oxygenators, so a membrane device is preferable to those devices when a patient must remain connected to a heart-lung machine for a prolonged period.

A second cause of hemolysis is the mechanical stress imposed by the pumps that cause the blood to circulate through the heart-lung machine and through the body of the patient. In most cases, the pumps used for this purpose are roller or peristaltic pumps, in which a flexible tube that carries the blood is squeezed against a U-shaped wall by rollers mounted on axles around the periphery of a rotating disk. Successive pairs of rollers pinch the tube to form pockets, then move those pockets through the tube in the required direction of blood flow. Such pumps have the advantage that their moving parts never come into contact with the blood.

Before oxygenated blood returns to the patient's main arteries near the heart, it passes through a filter that removes solid debris and a defoamer that eliminates gas bubbles. Compatible donor blood from a reservoir compensates for the volume of blood in the machine. A heat exchanger adjusts blood temperature to slightly lower than the normal body temperature so as to slow the metabolic processes that damage organs during surgery.

▼ This diagram shows the main components of a heart-lung machine. Blood enters the machine from catheters inserted into major veins near their entry to the heart. The flow of blood is partly assisted by a peristaltic pump. After passing through an oxygenator, the blood passes through a heat exchanger, which adjusts its temperature for reinjection. The blood then passes through a filter, which removes particulate matter and clots, before it returns to the body through catheters that feed major arteries where they exit the heart.

▼ Detail of a membrane oxygenator. Blood flows through a manifold across the top of the folded assembly of membrane, filmers, spacer, and tape. Oxygen flows through a similar manifold below the assembly.

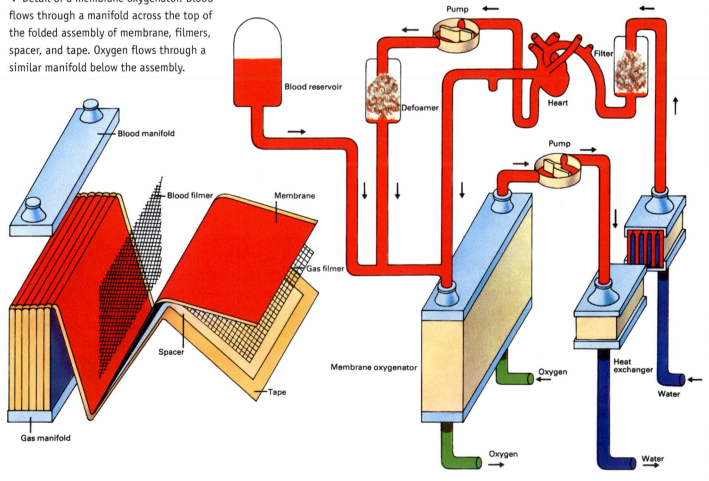

Blood manifold

Blood filmer

Membrane

Gas filmer

Spacer

Tape

Gas manifold

Membrane oxygenator

Blood reservoir

Pump

Defoamer

Heart

Filter

Pump

Heat exchanger

Oxygen

Water

Oxygen

Water

◄ The three peristaltic pumps of this heart-lung machine are visible in the foreground of this picture. A rotating-disk film oxygenator occupies the cylindrical glass casing behind the pumps.

► This heart-lung machine has a disposable plastic bubble oxygenator and is mounted on a cart so that it can be moved around an operating room with ease.

In the Russian approach, the anesthetized patient is first wrapped with ice in insulating plastic, reducing the body temperature from its normal value of around 98.6°F (37°C) to around 75°F (24°C). An ice-filled helmet cools the brain even further to around 60°F (16°C). The additional cooling of the brain is important, since the brain is more prone to damage through oxygen deprivation than are other organs.

Once the required temperature has been reached, the surgeon clears ice away from the operation site and starts surgery. On completion of surgery, the patient is warmed to normal body temperature and revived from anesthesia. Recovery rates are rapid and free of the potential side effects caused by heart-lung machines.

Congenital defects

One of the principal applications of open-heart surgery is in the correction of structural defects of the heart and nearby arteries and veins that are present at birth. Such defects occur when the fetal configuration of valves and openings does not change to the mature configuration at birth or when either the aortic or the pulmonary valve is malformed such that it obstructs the flow of blood from the heart to the respective artery.

Relics of fetal valves and openings are treated by performing cardiopulmonary bypass before opening the heart and stitching the valve or opening closed. Malformed valves can often be made to perform more adequately by making small incisions to increase the size of their openings. In either type of condition, the severity of the condition varies greatly from case to case, as does the urgency with which it must be treated. Congenital defects that are life threatening require treatment within the first days of life, while others cause only mild weariness and can wait to be treated later in life if necessary.

Valve surgery

Open-heart surgery can be used to treat valve conditions that develop during life as opposed to being present from birth. If the flaps of a valve have fused together, a simple incision can separate them so that the valve functions normally. If calcium deposits have caused the flaps to lose flexibility, a surgeon may remove those deposits. If the flaps of a valve have become too loose and floppy to function correctly, the surgeon can reshape the flaps and tighten the tendons that prevent them from inverting.

If a valve opening has become too slack, it may be supported by the addition of a ring of synthetic material or of tissue grafted from elsewhere in the body. Torn or perforated flaps may be patched together to some extent to improve their function, but sometimes the best treatment for a slack valve opening or delapidated flaps is valve replacement using an artificial valve of carbon-fiber flaps seated in a polyester ring or a valve that is made from animal tissues. Such valves function for many years before they have to be replaced, but they have the disadvantage of requiring lifelong treatment with blood-thinning warfarin.

Bypass surgery

Coronary-artery bypass graft (CABG) surgery is sometimes necessary as a treatment for atherosclerosis of the coronary arteries. This condition is the accumulation of a plaque of cholesterol and fat that restricts the blood flow through the coronary arteries and therefore the supply of oxygen to the heart muscles. Apart from causing chronic fatigue and chest pains (angina pectoris), this condition is a precursor of life-threatening myocardial infarctions (heart attacks).

In bypass surgery, a surgeon inserts blood vessels taken from other parts of the patient's body to bridge one or more obstructed arteries. The choice of blood vessel taken depends on the diameter of the artery that needs to be inserted. Certain arteries from the arms, legs, and chest are the most popular candidates for use in this procedure, since these parts of the body have abundant blood supplies and do not become deprived of blood if one artery is removed.

In a related procedure, the downstream end of a chest artery (a thoracic or mammary artery) is cut from its normal location and sewn into place at the point where the blood supply from the coronary artery has become restricted. In this way, oxygen-rich blood that would normally have contributed to the supply to the chest tissues becomes diverted to the heart muscles.

Minimally invasive surgery

The traditional forms of valve and bypass surgery require a 6 to 8 in. (15–20 cm) surgical wound through which the rib cage is opened and retracted to allow access to the heart and to make room for connections to a heart-lung machine. At the end of surgery, the ribs are wired together and the chest is sewn up. The severity of this type of surgery places an enormous strain on the body and requires almost a week of postoperative monitoring and recovery.

Less invasive techniques use a smaller surgical wound—typically 3 in. (7.5 cm)—through which the surgeon operates on the heart between the ribs without opening the rib cage. In minor bypass surgeries, the operation may be performed on a beating heart (albeit with a slower heart rate induced by drugs) so that the use of a heart-lung machine is unnecessary. In other cases, the connections to the heart-lung machine are made through blood vessels in the groin so that those connections do not interfere with the surgery through the smaller wound. The advantages of minimally invasive surgery include reduced bleeding, trauma, and postoperative pain, recovery times of around three days compared with the traditional week, and smaller scars.

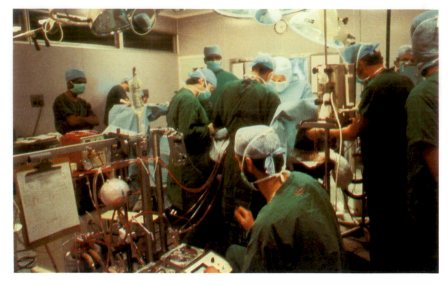

Cardiac catheterization

Balloon angioplasty is an example of a form of heart surgery that requires no incision in the chest area. The technique takes advantage of a procedure called cardiac catheterization, in which a fine tube is inserted into a blood vessel in the groin and fed through blood vessels to the heart.

The catheter contains an amount of contrast material, such as a barium salt, that reveals the path of the catheter on an X-ray fluoroscopy screen similar to that used in airport security checks. Using the display for guidance, the surgeon maneuvers the tip of the catheter until it reaches the appropriate position for surgery.

In balloon angioplasty, a balloon at the tip of the catheter is repeatedly inflated and deflated so as to flatten the arterial plaque against the walls of the artery and to widen the artery so as to allow an increased flow of blood. In some cases, a cylindrical metal cage, called a stent, is then inserted into the widened area to prevent reclosure. For insertion, the stent is extended along its cylindrical axis so that it lies flat against the catheter. Once in place, the stent is released so that it becomes shorter and wider, thereby holding the artery open. The stent may be made of stainless steel or nickel alloys that make it spring back to its original form when released from the catheter.

In one related technique, arterial plaque is cut away by a rotating diamond-coated tool at the tip of the catheter; in another, a balloon inflates on one side of the catheter to push it against the artery wall. A rotating blade then cuts the plaque through a side window in the catheter. The recovery time for such procedures is a few hours.

▲ This picture shows cardiovascular surgery in progress. While the surgeon's team operates (background), a heart-lung machine (foreground) provides oxygenated blood to keep the patient alive.

SEE ALSO: BIOENGINEERING • CARBON FIBER • ENDOSCOPE • HEART • HEART PACEMAKER • LUNG • MICROSURGERY • MUSCLE • TRANSPLANT

Heat Engine

The term heat engine is used by engineers in two entirely different ways. First, it is used loosely and generally to include any engine that produces work or power continuously from the combustion of a fuel in air. In this sense, the following are heat engines: gasoline and diesel engines, gas turbines, jet engines, and steam turbine power plants.

The second sense is the precise one used in the science of thermodynamics. In thermodynamics, a heat engine is a device that operates in a cycle and produces a net quantity of work from a supply of heat. Note that a heat engine run backward becomes a refrigerator. By this definition, a gasoline engine is not a heat engine because it does not take in heat but a mixture of gasoline and air. A distinction like this may appear to be splitting hairs, but it is more satisfactory for both engineers and scientists if engines that burn fuel internally are given their correct name—internal combustion engines. In contrast, certain kinds of heat engines that burn their fuel externally, such as Stirling engines, are known as external combustion engines.

There are few practical types of heat engines, and the most important example is the steam turbine power plant used in electricity-generating stations. This heat engine consists of a boiler in which water is evaporated into steam using heat transfer from hot gases, a turbine that produces power as the steam flows through it, a condenser in which steam is converted back into water again, and a feed pump to pump the water back into the boiler. The working fluid (in this case, steam or water) flows continuously around in a closed circuit.

The efficiency of heat engines

The thermodynamic theory of heat engines is important because it tells us about a key limitation in the conversion of heat into work. Heat energy is available from the combustion of fuels such as coal and oil, but not all the heat generated by a source can be converted into mechanical power. By examining the behavior of a perfect heat engine running on an ideal cycle called the Carnot cycle, the greatest possible conversion of heat to power can be determined. All heat engines involve two important temperatures, that at which heat is produced and that of the environment into which the heat not converted to mechanical power must be released. In

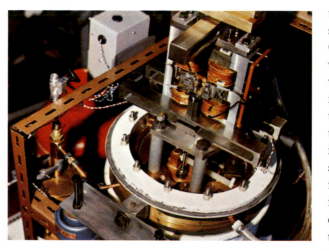

▲ The Harwell Thermomechanical Generator. The alternator windings can be seen near the top.

the Carnot cycle these are represented by two heat reservoirs. The Carnot cycle consists of four reversible stages: in the first, the working fluid takes heat from a reservoir at a constant temperature and expands doing work. In the second stage, the heat source is removed and the fluid expands adiabatically (with no heat transfer) doing further work. Then the fluid is subjected to an isothermal compression with heat being transferred to a cold reservoir and work done on the fluid by external forces. Finally, the fluid is compressed adiabatically until it is at the temperature of the hot reservoir again. Now if the hot reservoir is at temperature T_1 and the cold reservoir at T_2 and the amount of heat taken from the hot reservoir is Q while the net work produced by the cycle is W, it is possible to determine the highest value of W that can be obtained.

Using the Second Law of Thermodynamics, it can be shown that the efficiency of even a perfect heat engine must be less than 100 percent and that the efficiency is related to the temperatures of the heat reservoirs that the engine works between. The efficiency is given by $(T_1 - T_2)/T_1$ with the temperatures T_1 and T_2 being measured on the absolute temperature scale in degrees Kelvin: 0 K is $-459°F$ ($-273°C$).

When the efficiency of a power plant as a heat engine is measured, it is found to be fairly low, a typical figure being around 40 percent. So 60 percent or more of the heat in the fuel is lost to the cold reservoir. It might seem that the designers are not doing a very good job, but this is a false impression, as can be shown by considering the maximum possible efficiency.

Although the fuel burns at a temperature of around 2700°F (1500°C), restrictions on the materials used in the boilers mean that the maximum steam temperature is around 923 K, this being T_1. Allowing for a temperature difference between the coolant and the condensed steam, T_2 is around 300 K. Putting these figures into the efficiency equation shows that the maximum efficiency of a heat engine between these temperatures is 67 percent.

SEE ALSO: Stirling engine • Thermodynamics

Heat Exchanger

A heat exchanger is a device in which heat is transferred from a hot fluid to a cold fluid without the two streams mixing. A common example of a heat exchanger is an automobile radiator. Here the engine is kept at the proper working temperature by water cooling and the waste heat in the cooling water is disposed of in the radiator by the passage of air through the radiator.

The main applications of heat exchangers are to cool working fluids—as in the above example—or to make use of heat that would otherwise be wasted. For example, many chemical processes are carried out at high temperature in a reaction vessel, and considerable energy savings can be made by passing the hot products through a heat exchanger to heat up the raw ingredients on their way into the reaction vessel. A special application of heat exchangers lies in some nuclear reactors, where intermediate heat exchangers are used to transfer heat from the radioactive working fluid within the reactor core to a secondary working fluid, such as steam, which is then used to generate electric power.

Engineering principles

Heat is a form of energy now measured in joules (the international unit of energy) and represents an amount of energy taken from a hot body to a cooler one. Energy transfer (or heat transfer) results only where there is a temperature difference and always from the higher temperature to the lower temperature in the process; the temperature of the hotter body drops because energy has been removed from it, and conversely the temperature of the cooler body increases. This process continues until there is no temperature difference left to cause any heat transfer.

Any engineer wishing to maximize the heat transferred from a hot fluid to a cooler fluid will use a heat exchanger. The features that affect the design of such a device to obtain maximum heat transfer are the temperature difference between the fluids and the area of surface interaction. The designer may not have much control over the temperature difference, which is fixed by the nature of the job to be done, so a high area of surface contact must be incorporated to achieve the best heat transfer.

Double-tube heat exchanger

A double-tube heat exchanger consists of one tube placed inside a second larger tube. To transfer heat from a hot fluid, such as the lubricating oil from an engine, to a cold fluid, for example, the cooling water, one fluid is passed through the inner tube and the other through the annular space between the two tubes. Because of the temperature difference between the two fluids, there will be an exchange of heat through the wall of the inner tube separating them.

Such designs are also called concentric tube, or tube-and-annulus, heat exchangers. In the above

OCEAN ENERGY

The Ocean Thermal Energy Conversion (OTEC) was first proposed in the early 1880s by the French engineer Jacques-Arsìne d'Arsonval. Surface water in oceans and seas may be as much as 122°F (50°C) warmer than water found at depths of only 300 ft. (90 m) below the surface. OTEC uses this temperature difference to produce electricity. In the closed system depicted here, surface water is used to warm a refrigerant, such as ammonia, which evaporates at room temperature. The expansion drives a generator turbine—the refrigerant is then cooled using water pumped from the ocean depths, and the cycle is repeated.

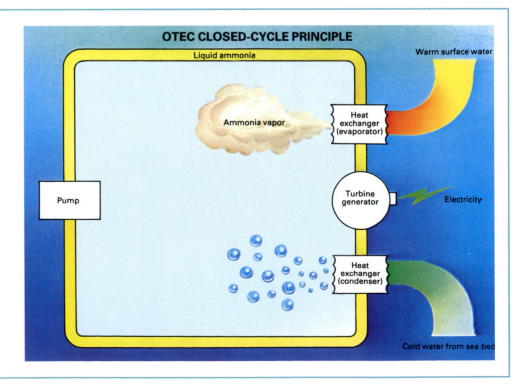

OTEC CLOSED-CYCLE PRINCIPLE

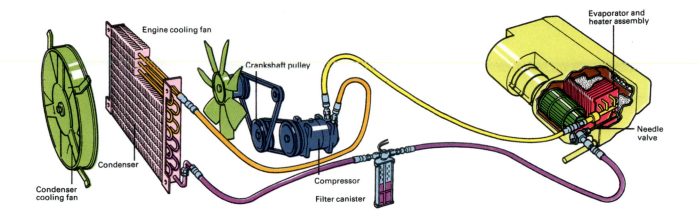

example of an oil cooler, the oil would most probably be passed through the inner tube, which would be more capable of withstanding the high oil pressure than the outer tube, but in general, the hotter fluid could be passed through either tube.

Flow arrangements

When the two fluids flow in the same direction through a double-tube heat exchanger, it is known as a parallel-flow type. In the counter-flow type the fluids flow in opposite directions. Counter-flow heat exchangers are intrinsically more efficient and must be used in applications where maximum heat transfer is required.

To explain counter-flow exchangers, consider a hot fluid, such as oil, at a temperature of 200°F (90°C) and a cold fluid, say water, at a temperature of 50°F (10°C). The greatest possible heat transfer occurs when either the temperature of the oil drops to 50°F or the water rises to 200°F. The relative magnitudes of the two flow rates determine which of the two occurs. If the water flow rate is considerably higher than that of the oil, the temperature rise of the water will be less than the drop in temperature of the oil.

In a parallel-flow heat exchanger, the two fluids leave at the same end. Given any amount of heat transfer, the hotter fluid will get colder and the colder fluid will get hotter, as in the counter-flow type, but the best that can be achieved from the exchanger is when the fluids leave at the same temperature. This temperature will be somewhere between the two extremes, depending on the two flow rates.

Other designs

The double-tube heat exchanger is an extremely simple design but does not leave much room for improvement to the interacting surface area, which is determined solely by the surface area of the inner tube. For larger surface areas, more elaborate designs are necessary.

▲ An automobile's cooling system. The compressor pumps the refrigerant around, and waste heat is disposed of through the radiator.

One of these is the shell-and-tube heat exchanger, which consists of a bundle of parallel tubes passing between the flat ends of a cylindrical casing, or shell. One fluid flows through the tubes while the other flows through the shell. This type of heat exchanger is widely used in the chemical-process industry.

The plate heat exchanger is another important type, consisting of a multilayer sandwich with hot and cold fluids flowing through alternate layers. Some air heaters for cars are made in this way; they use hot water from the car's cooling system.

Regenerative exchangers

In the regenerative heat exchanger, the hot fluid is first passed through the heat exchanger elements to heat them up. Then the cold fluid is passed through the hot elements and picks up the heat from them. The elements are normally formed into some type of matrix to give a large area for heat transfer and may be made of a range of materials, such as metals or ceramics, depending on the precise application.

The flow of fluid through the heat exchanger can be controlled by valves, or the exchanger elements can take the form of a heat wheel. In this design, the exchanger core is slowly rotated through parallel streams of hot and cold fluids with any given element being first heated by the hot fluid and then moving into the cold fluid stream to give up its heat before returning to the hot fluid for reheating. A typical application of this design is in gas turbines where ceramic elements capable of working at high temperatures are used to extract heat from the hot exhaust gases and preheat the air feed, giving a substantial increase in turbine efficiency.

SEE ALSO: ENGINE COOLING SYSTEMS • HEAT ENGINE • HEAT PUMP • INTERNAL COMBUSTION ENGINE • NUCLEAR REACTOR • TEMPERATURE • THERMODYNAMICS

Heating and Ventilation Systems

Heating and ventilation systems enable humans to live comfortably in conditions of varying ambient temperature. Humans need to maintain a body temperature of about 98°F (37°C) and begin to feel uncomfortable when exposed to temperatures that fall below 70°F (21°C). Warm clothing can be worn to insulate the body, but this solution tends to be heavy and cumbersome. The body may also experience discomfort when exposed to excessive heat. Therefore, various methods have been developed to heat, cool, and ventilate interiors.

Heating systems

Heating systems can be divided into those that heat the area in the immediate vicinity of the heat source, or direct heating, and those where the heat source is remote from the rooms heated, or central heating. The earliest methods of heating were direct, consisting simply of burning a fuel, such as wood or turf, usually in the middle of a room, the smoke produced escaping through a hole in the roof. This method inevitably resulted in very smoky interiors, so chimneys were developed to carry the smoke away from the living space to the exterior of the building. In Europe, the first chimneys appeared during the 12th century.

One problem with chimneys is that the heat tends to escape up the flue as combustion gases, making open fires an inefficient use of fuel. Fires also need a supply of air to burn, and in the case of open fires, this air is drawn from the room, resulting in drafts. An improvement on the open fire was the enclosed stove, first used in China around 600 B.C.E. In this system, the heat of the fire is absorbed by the stove walls, which then emit this heat to the surrounding room.

Central heating

The first central heating system was invented by the Romans and consisted of an elaborate form of underfloor heating called hypocausts. Two systems were devised that worked in similar ways. In the channeled hypocaust, a network of tunnels ran under the rooms to be heated, while in the pillared hypocaust the floors of the rooms were raised on a series of pillars, creating a hollow area underneath. In both cases, however, hot gases from a furnace ran through the spaces under the floor, warming the rooms above. As the Roman Empire declined, the system of hypocausts ceased to be used, and central heating was not reintroduced until 1,500 years later.

▲ The archaeological remains of a Roman hypocaust. The system of supporting brick columns indicates that this was a pillared hypocaust. Hot gases from a furnace would have passed below this floor, warming the room above.

Modern developments

Modern techniques of central heating were developed in the 19th century in North America and Europe where they were used to heat industrial buildings. These systems used piped steam to circulate heat supplied by a coal- or oil-fired furnace. The pipes connected to standing radiators that provided a large surface area for the efficient emission of heat. Eventually, central-heating systems were introduced in houses and offices, and different methods of transferring heat were developed. By about 1830, engineers realized the advantages of using hot water, which can operate using lower temperatures than steam. This is the method still favored in Europe, whereas in the United States, the most popular method of central heating is through forced air. In both of these cases, the central-heating boiler or furnace may also be used to heat water for the domestic hot-water supply.

Hot-water systems

An advantage of using hot water for circulating heat is that it carries more heat per unit volume than air. Therefore, the pipes that carry the water can be relatively small. The water is heated in a boiler and pumped through the network of pipes to radiators that emit the heat in a combination of convection and radiation. The water, having lost its heat, then returns to the boiler where it is reheated in a continual circulating process. Another system that uses hot water is radiant heating. In this case, the water pipes pass under the floors where they release their heat, eliminating the need for radiators. Radiant heating creates convection currents that produce a more uniform and therefore more comfortable ambient temperature.

Forced-air heating

In forced-air heating, the air is heated in a furnace and then circulated around the building in ducts. Because warm air rises, it is possible to rely on gravity to circulate the hot air around the building. Friction, however, slows the movement of air, so the ducts have to be large. In addition, gravity is an inefficient way of ensuring that warm air is distributed evenly throughout a building,

▶ Top: hot-water heating systems use a boiler to heat the water, which is then pumped through the system to radiators. Center: radiant heating systems also heat water using a boiler, but the water is then pumped to underfloor pipes. Bottom: steam-heating systems work in a way similar to hot-water systems, but the steam condenses when it gives up its heat nd circulates by gravity, instead of a pump.

CENTRAL-HEATING SYSTEMS

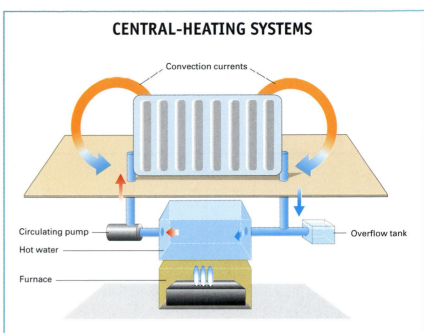

In hot-water heating systems, water is heated by a furnace and then pumped through radiators. As the radiators heat the air, convection currents develop.

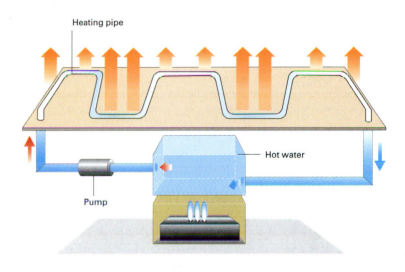

In radiant heating systems, hot water is pumped through pipes embedded in the floor. This creates a more even distribution of convection currents.

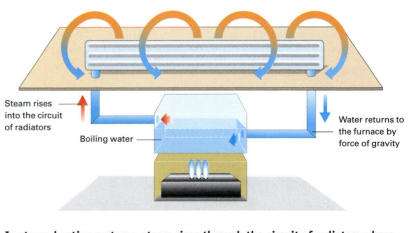

In steam-heating systems, steam rises through the circuit of radiators where it releases its heat. The water then returns to the furnace under gravity.

the rooms farthest from the heat source tending to be cooler than those close to the source. In the 1930s, motor-driven fans were introduced that enabled warm air to circulate more rapidly and evenly through the system of ducts without the aid of gravity. Forced-air heating is often combined with air-conditioning by the addition of a cooling unit and filters. In summer, the air is merely cooled rather than heated, the rest of the process being much the same. In recent years, hot-water heating systems have developed in popularity in the United States.

Thermostats and timers

Central-heating systems employ thermostats to regulate the temperature in a room. In some systems, a single thermostat may be used, whereas in others, each room or radiator may have its own thermostat. In the first instance, the thermostat regulates the flow of fuel to the boiler or furnace; the fuel is cut off when a certain predetermined temperature is reached and is then allowed to flow again when the temperature falls. In the second case, the flow of a heated gas or liquid to a radiator or convector is controlled by individual thermostats.

Automatic timers allow for an efficient use of fuel, the heating system being turned on only when the building is in use. A manual override switch provides flexibility, enabling the heating system to be turned on at times when the building is not normally used.

Alternative energy sources

Most modern heating systems are powered by either oil or natural gas. These systems require very little cleaning and can be fully automatic. In recent years, however, concerns about the use of fossil fuels have created an interest in more environmentally friendly sources of energy for heating, such as solar energy. Passive systems of solar heating use the heat of the sun to warm the building directly. Large areas of glass facing the direction of the sun and buildings shaped in such a way that they trap the sun are both passive methods of heating. Active methods involve the use of solar collectors, blackened panels that convert sunlight to heat and then transfer this heat to a liquid (usually water) that is carried in pipes. The hot water is then pumped to an insulated storage tank to be used later or is pumped directly to the rooms to heat radiators.

Ventilation

The creation of enclosures in which to live and work has separated people from access to unlimited fresh air, and the deficiency has to be compensated for by incorporating devices in

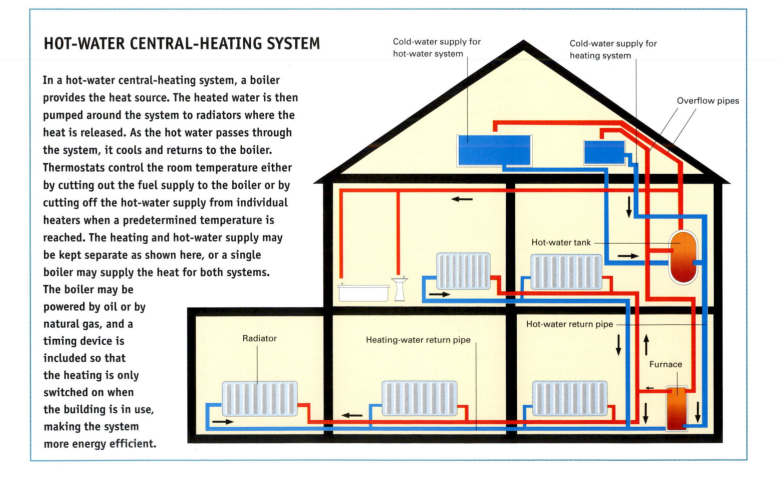

HOT-WATER CENTRAL-HEATING SYSTEM

In a hot-water central-heating system, a boiler provides the heat source. The heated water is then pumped around the system to radiators where the heat is released. As the hot water passes through the system, it cools and returns to the boiler. Thermostats control the room temperature either by cutting out the fuel supply to the boiler or by cutting off the hot-water supply from individual heaters when a predetermined temperature is reached. The heating and hot-water supply may be kept separate as shown here, or a single boiler may supply the heat for both systems. The boiler may be powered by oil or by natural gas, and a timing device is included so that the heating is only switched on when the building is in use, making the system more energy efficient.

Cold-water supply for hot-water system

Cold-water supply for heating system

Overflow pipes

Hot-water tank

Hot-water return pipe

Radiator

Heating-water return pipe

Furnace

buildings, tunnels, mines, ships, and aircraft to ensure that humans are neither deprived of essential oxygen nor subject to impurities released in the enclosure. A constant supply of fresh air is also essential to humans because air is the major heat-exchange medium in nature's system for keeping blood temperature constant regardless of the body's rate of exertion and of the degree of external heat or cold.

In simple enclosures, differences in air pressure set up by the wind or heat cause air to flow in or out of windows, doors, and ventilators. This seemingly haphazard method takes care of the ventilation of nearly all homes and the majority of small commercial buildings in parts of the world that have a temperate climate.

Because air expands with increasing temperature, it tends to rise and float in cooler, denser air. Hence, air warmed by human occupancy (as in assembly halls) or by radiators in offices and dwellings or by machinery and processes in industrial buildings rises to the top of the enclosure to exit through static exhaust ventilators in the roof or high in the walls, while cooler, heavier air flows in through all openings at lower levels. This thermal current ventilation operates on well-defined laws of physics and forms the basis of mathematically designed large-scale industrial ventilation schemes.

Powered methods

Wherever natural ventilation is unsuitable, as for example, in large office buildings, multistory industrial buildings, railway tunnels, and subway systems, and where toxic fumes or harmful dusts are released, mechanical ventilation is essential. The fans employed, usually driven by electric motors, are broadly classified as axial or centrifugal, according to their action on the air.

Axial fans cause air to move substantially parallel to the axis of the fan. Blades are mounted radially on a hub, which in turn is secured on the shaft of a motor. Each blade is inclined at an angle from the plane of the imaginary disk formed by its rotation. These fans have many design variants, ranging all the way from the simple propeller fan with pressed steel metal blades attached to a hub spider to ones with high-precision airfoil sections, variable pitch, and cast aluminum blades, running in a tubular fan housing.

Their main characteristic is that for a given power output from a driving motor, they will handle large volumes of air when flow is relatively unobstructed. When, however, resistance to flow is set up by filters, heaters, and long or tortuous runs of ducting, recirculation, or backward flow, may occur through the fan itself. It is caused by

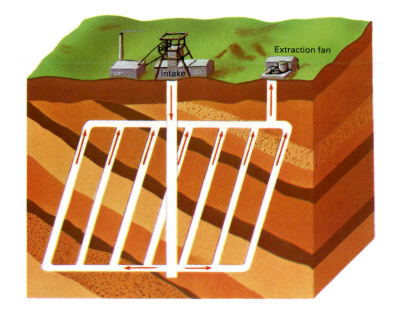

▲ A deep underground mine requires powerful fans to maintain air flow.

the inability of slower-moving parts of the blades close to the hub to equal the pressure caused nearer the blade tips, where circumferential speed is greatest. Propeller fans are therefore used mainly in simple housing, for example, in stale-air exhausts in manufacturing plant roofs or as fresh-air supply units in short duct systems. Window fans, free-standing stirrers, and cooling fans used not to change the air but simply to create a breeze within an enclosure are also usually of this simple propeller type.

Centrifugal fans have their blades mounted parallel to the rotating shaft and equidistant from it. Their action is to sling air radially by centrifugal force. Blades may be many or few, deep or shallow sectioned, forward or backward curved, or even flat, according to the pressure, volume, and noise characteristics required of them. Such fans are used in the majority of large ducted systems wherever substantial pressure differences must be maintained to force or draw air through filters, humidifiers, heaters, or coolers.

Dangerous environments

The ventilation of buildings containing toxic, flammable, or explosive substances is subject to stringently enforced regulations. These lay down the maximum allowable concentrations of toxic products, and the ventilation systems must be designed and operated well below the permissible limits. Where possible, the contaminant is drawn away from the breathing zone by an exhaust opening close to the harmful source and arranged to cause air drawn into it to pass the contaminants release area at a speed above the capture velocity, that is, the velocity at which the toxic particles are certain of being pulled into the flow of the air stream.

◀ Installing a reverse-cycle sliding-chassis heat pump unit like this requires only basic skills and is suitable for small commercial and private users.

Where explosive atmospheres or flammable vapors are liable to occur, all powered ventilation equipment must be fitted with flameproof motors.

In mines, subways, and long road and railway tunnels, air must flow through all parts continuously at a speed of not less than 100 ft. per minute (30 m/min.), to prevent the collecting of gases (either natural or added by vehicles) into light and heavy strata. Full technical data, including likely composition, density, and rate of emission of gases, heat, and moisture, must form the basis of each scheme design. There is no uniformity of treatment, but because of the fire danger when unidirectional flow is used, the practice of laying supply and exhaust shafts alongside road tunnels, with inlet or exhaust slots opening into the tunnels at frequent intervals, is now favored. In this system there is little or no longitudinal flow, yet exhaust gases are removed and fresh air supplied throughout the tunnel.

The railway tunnel beneath the Severn River in Britain is kept under negative pressure by a 40 ft. (12 m) diameter exhaust fan handling nearly half a million cubic feet of air per minute. The exhaust duct runs parallel with the tunnel and breaks into the tunnel roof midway along its length, causing fresh air to be drawn into the tunnel at both ends.

Since World War II, production methods have favored large undivided areas in single-story manufacturing plants. This setup gives fires such large reservoirs of air and oxygen that they can no longer be stifled by lack of ventilation. Because in plants and warehouses the danger of fire spreading is great inside the roof spaces (where hot combustion products are forced to spread horizontally), it is now usual to distribute fire ventilators in the roofs of such buildings. When

▶ The impeller of a large variable-pitch ventilation fan being assembled in a plant.

triggered by smoke detectors or by fusible links, they automatically fly open to release heat and smoke to the sky. A single ventilator can remove heat at a rate sufficient to convert ten tons of water per hour into steam, an indication of a fire's destructive power if allowed to spread inside the building. Research carried out at the Fire Research Station in Borehamwood, Britain, has established the design laws upon which many fire ventilation schemes are based.

Air-conditioning

Air-conditioning is the creation of an artificial climate, making it possible to maintain constant, pleasant conditions inside buildings and provide a steady flow of purified air.

Air-conditioning is essential in underground spaces, movie theaters, dance halls, crowded stores, hospitals, tall office buildings, and many industrial processes that are sensitive to atmospheric conditions.

Methods used

Air is purified, cooled or heated, humidified or dried, according to the need, by the air conditioning plant and circulated through the building by means of ducts, which may be of metal or may be formed out of the structure itself.

There are various stages in a large air-conditioning plant: not all plants include every component, and in the smallest air-conditioning unit,

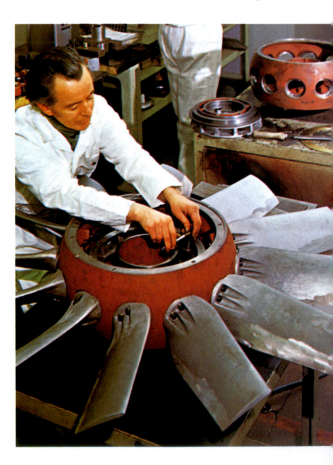

the components are combined in one casing not much larger than a television set.

Air first enters the section where it mixes with recycled air from the building—only a certain proportion of fresh air is needed. Next, the mixed air passes through a filtering section, which may be in two stages. The first stage takes out coarse dust using a fibrous medium, rather like cotton, either in the form of a screen of individual filter cells that can be replaced when they become dirty or an electrically driven roller screen. Following this step is the second-stage filter—generally an electrostatic type—that removes the finer particles, such as cigarette smoke. In this filter, a high voltage is used to charge incoming dust particles, which are then attracted to a grid of oppositely charged plates.

The air temperature is controlled by passing the air through two tube banks. One is supplied with hot water or steam and the other with chilled water or refrigerant fluid. Inside the room to be ventilated is a temperature sensor—usually an electric resistance thermometer—that is set to the desired value. The difference between the required and the actual temperature automatically determines whether the heating or cooling tubes are used.

The next stage is the odor filter, made of activated carbon, a substance that is capable of directly absorbing odor molecules from the air. This filter needs to be reactivated by heating from time to time to drive off the absorbed material.

Finally, moisture is added to produce the desired humidity, either by injecting steam into the air or by spraying a mist of very fine water droplets. This step too is controlled from a sensor inside the room, the electric resistance of which varies with the humidity. If moisture has to be removed from the air, the usual method is to arrange for it to be both cooled and then reheated if necessary at the temperature-control stage. The moisture will condense on the cooling tubes.

The air is normally moved through the system by a centrifugal fan, the rotor of which resembles a paddle wheel. Air enters at the center and leaves around the edge of the wheel. This type of fan can move large volumes of air despite the appreciable drag of the plant and ducting.

Silencers are always placed after the fan to prevent the noise of the plant from reaching the room. They usually consist of a labyrinth of sound-absorbing material.

Air is finally delivered through metal ducts to the room diffusers, which take various forms, such as long slots or grilles in the walls close to the ceiling, vaned outlets flush with the ceiling, or perforated sections of the ceiling itself.

▶ When hot currents rise from the electric arc furnaces in this steel manufacturing plant, ventilators in the roof open to release the heat.

Air-conditioning systems

The same principles are used from the smallest to the largest air-conditioning system. Small room units contain a simple washable filter, refrigerating compressor, and electric air heater.

More powerful units are made to supply larger rooms, and frequently the relatively noisy refrigerating section (compressor and condenser) is placed outside the building.

For large buildings, there are three main systems: all air, air-water, and all water. In the first, the plant supplies all the air that is needed at a fixed temperature. Local duct heaters are needed in different rooms or zones of a building to give final temperature control. An alternative is to have two ducts, one carrying cool air, the other warm air. The two air streams are blended, as in a mixer faucet, to give the required temperature. In the variable-volume system, the temperature is regulated by controlling the amount of air supplied instead of its temperature.

In the air-water system, the central plant only delivers the minimum fresh air needed for ventilation. Each room then has a separate heating and cooling unit using heated or chilled water. In the all-water system, only the heating or cooling water is supplied from the central plant, and fresh air is brought in through room ventilators.

AIR-CONDITIONING SYSTEM

During hot summer months, air-conditioning units are used to keep buildings cool. Air exits the room through an exhaust duct and is mixed with fresh air from outside the building. It then passed through a series of filters that clean the air of pollution and impurities. A cooling unit reduces the temperature of the air to the level required, and it is then filtered once more, this time to remove odors. To maintain comfort, it is necessary that the air in a room has certain levels of humidity. This level is achieved by passing the air through humidifying sprays of water. Finally, after the air has passed through these various conditioning stages, it passes through a silencer and into the ducts that carry it throughout the building. Many air-conditioning systems can also be used to heat air in winter; the cleaned air passes through a heating unit rather than a cooling unit.

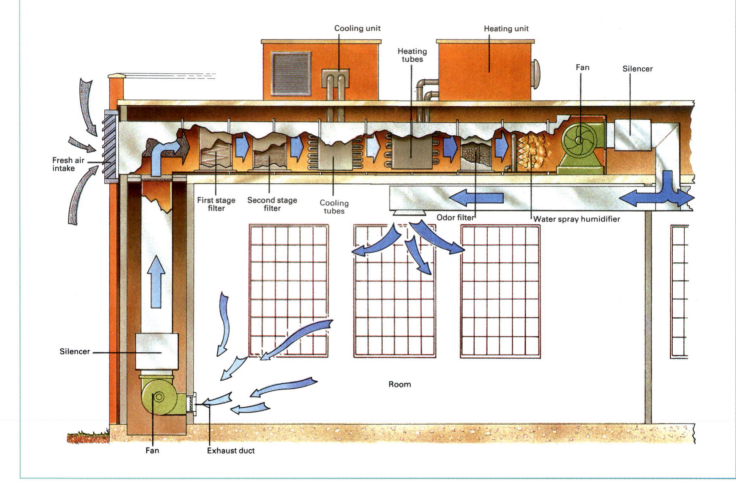

Cooling unit • Heating unit • Heating tubes • Fan • Silencer • Fresh air intake • First stage filter • Second stage filter • Cooling tubes • Odor filter • Water spray humidifier • Silencer • Room • Fan • Exhaust duct

Air-conditioning today

Air-conditioning is used widely in office buildings, shops, supermarkets, restaurants, and entertainment centers, where the main problem is to keep the building cool in summer. Temperatures in modern buildings can become uncomfortably high through heat from lights, crowds of people, and sunshine through increasingly large windows.

The heat from artificial lighting is sometimes sufficient to keep a building warm in winter, and some buildings have been specifically designed to do just that: the hot air generated by the lights is picked up and returned to the plant.

In medicine, air-conditioning is essential for the operating room. In this case, the air must be sterile and must keep the area around the operating table free from contamination. In industry, air-conditioning is needed to control the environment for a process or product. In so-called white rooms, for example, in the manufacture of transistors, the atmosphere is cleaner than ever occurs naturally.

The largest single air-conditioned space is the vehicle assembly building at Cape Canaveral: 525 ft. (160 m) high and nearly 371,000 sq. ft. (35,000 m²). The cooling power is sufficient to turn 10,000 tons (9,000 tonnes) of water into ice in a day.

Chlorofluorocarbons (CFCs), such as Freons have been used as refrigerants in air-conditioning cooling systems. Freons, however, cause a depletion of the ozone layer, which protects us from harmful ultraviolet radiation. For this reason CFCs have been gradually phased out and replaced with other less harmful refrigerants.

SEE ALSO: BUILDING TECHNIQUES • HEAT EXCHANGER • POLLUTION MONITORING AND CONTROL • REFRIGERATION • THERMOMETRY • THERMOSTAT • WATER

Heat Pump

It is a basic law of nature that heat will flow from a hot body to a colder body, but not the reverse. With a heat pump, however, this reverse operation becomes possible: that is, heat is taken from the colder body and pumped to the hotter body. In the process, the hot body becomes hotter and the cold body becomes colder.

A heat pump does not violate any laws of nature however; to achieve this end, power must be supplied to the pump to make it work. It therefore operates like a heat engine in reverse.

A heat engine operates between a hot body and a cold body (these are usually called reservoirs), and part of the heat, as it flows from the hot reservoir to the cold reservoir, is converted into mechanical work. To conceive the reverse of this process, imagine work being put into the engine and heat flowing in the opposite direction. This is the basic principle of the heat pump.

A heat pump is therefore identical in operation to a refrigerator—differing only in purpose. A refrigerator is used specifically to cool something down still further by removing heat from it, whereas the heat pump places the emphasis on where the heat is going to—namely, increasing the temperature of the already warm body.

Working principles

The term heat pump is somewhat misleading since heat is not a fluid like air or water and cannot in fact be pumped—except in a metaphorical sense. Some medium is required to make it possible for this transfer of heat to take place.

A heat pump functions rather like a steam power plant (which is a heat engine) working backward, except that steam is unlikely to be the working fluid. A vapor or refrigerant, such as ammonia, carbon dioxide, or a halocarbon, is more likely. The fluid flows around a closed circuit driven by a compressor or pump. The fluid enters the pump as vapor and experiences a rise in pressure and temperature. The vapor then enters the condenser (which is a heat exchanger), and heat is transferred to the warm reservoir, which is cooler than the vapor entering the condenser. Here, the vapor condenses and leaves as a liquid, still at a high pressure.

The liquid then flows through an expansion valve—a restricted passage through which the liquid spurts into a low-pressure area. This reduction in pressure causes the liquid to vaporize partially and is accompanied by a reduction in temperature. The liquid–vapor mixture now flows through the evaporator, which is situated in

A type of heat pump used in air-conditioning plants. In warm weather, it provides a cooling draft. In the winter, it can be converted to extract heat from the outside air to add to the heating system.

the cold reservoir (this is the second heat exchanger in the system). Because the liquid–vapor mixture is now colder than the cold reservoir, it takes heat from the reservoir and moves on to the compressor at a higher temperature than when it went in. This is the complete cycle.

Coefficient of performance

A typical application of a heat pump might be to take heat from a cold reservoir, such as a river, and transfer it to a building that requires heating (this is the warm reservoir). In the process, work or power must be supplied to the pump to drive it. The heat pump might, for example, receive 1,000 kJ from the river, absorb 400 kJ in power from an external source to drive it, and deliver 1,400 kJ in heating to the building.

The performance of the heat pump is measured by the ratio of heat delivered to the warm reservoir to the work absorbed by the pump to drive it. For the above example this ratio is 1400/400, which works out to 3.5; this figure is called the coefficient of performance.

The ideal coefficient of performance for a heat pump is that of a reverse Carnot cycle working over the same temperature range. If the hot reservoir is at temperature T_1 (degrees absolute) and the cold reservoir at temperature T_2, then the maximum coefficient of performance is given by $T_1/(T_1 - T_2)$. Thus, for a hot reservoir temperature of 77°F (25°C, 298 K) and a cold reservoir temperature of 36°F (2°C, 275 K), the ideal coefficient of performance is given by 298/(298 – 275)

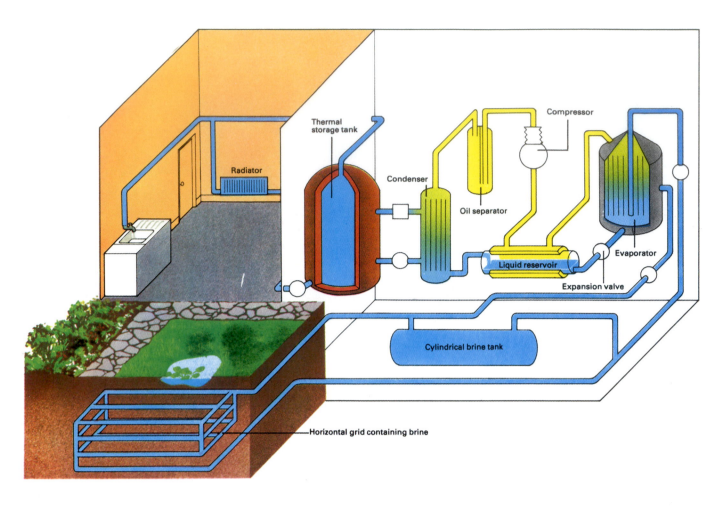

Thermal
storage tank

Compressor

Condenser

Oil separator

Radiator

Liquid reservoir

Evaporator

Expansion valve

Cylindrical brine tank

Horizontal grid containing brine

= 12.96. In practice, of course the actual coefficient of performance will be considerably smaller.

The heat pump is at first sight a most attractive proposition—we seem to get something for nothing. If the coefficient of performance is 3.5, it means that we get 3.5 kW of heat by supplying 1 kW of electric power to the heat pump—a considerable improvement over the electric space heater. The remaining heat is obtained from the river, where it was not wanted. But as always, there is a snag. From the above temperature expression for maximum coefficient of performance, it can be shown that as the hot reservoir heats up through the action of the heat pump, the maximum coefficient of performance will automatically fall. A more serious problem in real applications is that the need for heating is normally greatest when the outside temperature, and so the temperature of the cold reservoir, is at its lowest. Therefore, heat pump systems designed for use in cold climates often have a conventional heating system to top up the heat supplied.

Applications

For many applications such as space heating, air-to-air heat exchangers can be used, extracting heat from the outside air to release it inside. Typical designs can work with outside air temperatures as low as –4°F (–20°C). In many cases, such units are designed so that they can be reversed to become an air conditioner during hot weather, thus transferring heat from the inside of a building to the air outside. A problem with this system is that in winter, when the system needs to transfer heat from outside to the inside of a building, there is a tendency for the pipes outside to collect ice. The pump deals with this problem by temporarily reversing its function to that of air-conditioning, which has the effect of heating the pipes outside. The air-conditioning function would also cause the system to pump cold air into the building—an undesirable effect in winter. The system may then heat the cold incoming air with electric strip heaters or gas burners.

Other designs transfer the heat to a water circuit that can be connected to a conventional central heating system. Often heat pumps are used as add-on systems to work in conjunction with conventional heating systems, so reducing fuel usage. However, it is worth noting that the overall fuel efficiency of a heat pump system is questionable when the total energy balance includes the thermal inefficiencies in the power plant that generates the electricity used to drive the heat pump.

▲ An arrangement of a heat pump to heat a building. Heat from the soil is absorbed into brine in a grid and transmitted inside the building.

SEE ALSO: ENERGY STORAGE • HEAT ENGINE • HEATING AND VENTILATION SYSTEMS • REFRIGERATION • THERMODYNAMICS

Helicopter

Helicopters belong to a class of aircraft known as rotorcraft, the other members of which are autogiros (or gyroplanes) and convertiplanes. Helicopters and autogiros are superficially similar to one another in that both are wholly sustained in flight by the lift generated as a result of the rotation of long thin wings, or rotor blades, in a horizontal plane.

The blades of an autogiro, however, are rotated by the action of air blowing through them, in the manner of a windmill, while those of a helicopter are driven directly by an engine. Autogiros cannot therefore land or takeoff vertically in calm air. Helicopters, on the other hand, can takeoff or land vertically, hover, and fly forward, backward, or sideways irrespective of the wind.

The principles of helicopter flight have been known for centuries. Leonardo da Vinci designed one, and many helicopter models were made by early flight pioneers, such as Sir George Cayley in 1927. The first helicopter capable of carrying a person, built by Paul Cornu in France in 1907, was powered by a 24-horsepower engine, but stability and engineering problems held back further development for decades.

It was not until January 1942 that the world's first practical helicopter, the VS-316A, was built by a Russian-born U.S. engineer Igor Sikorsky. This machine had the simplest possible configuration, the design of which is still used most widely today.

Construction

The main structural element of a helicopter is the fuselage, housing the crew, payload, fuel, and power plant, which until the mid 1950s was a piston engine but is now usually a gas turbine. The output shaft from the engine, turning at several thousand revolutions per minute, is connected to a transmission, which steps down the speed to between 300 and 400 rpm to drive the rotor (the assembly carrying the hub and the attached blades) since the rotor tips must be restricted to subsonic speeds to ensure efficient operation.

The reaction of the rotor spinning in one direction would cause the rest of the helicopter to rotate uncontrollably in the opposite direction. In order to prevent this problem, a secondary rotor, of smaller diameter, is mounted on the rear end of the fuselage and driven by a second shaft from the gear box at such a speed that it exactly neutralizes the turning action of the main rotor.

Each of the blades of the main rotor (modern helicopters have any number from two to seven)

is inclined (with its leading edge upward) so that it meets the air at a small angle to the horizontal. This is the pitch angle, analogous to the pitch of a propeller or a screw thread.

Pitch control

When hovering, the combination of rotor speed and the pitch of the blades provides a lift force that is exactly in balance with the weight of the

▲ A British Royal Air Force search-and-rescue helicopter display, airlifting a man from a dinghy. The ability of helicopters to hover and to land in small spaces makes them useful for rescue purposes such as these.

▶ These illustrations show how a helicopter is prevented from twisting with the force of its rotor. Top and bottom right: the twist can be prevented by the two main rotors turning in opposite directions. Center: the rotors can also be placed one above the other. Below: a small tail rotor is the most common way to keep the body from twisting.

helicopter. In order to climb, the rotor has to generate more lift, and this is achieved not by increasing the speed of the rotor (the rotor speed of a particular helicopter at all times remains virtually constant, irrespective of what the aircraft is doing), but by increasing the pitch of the blades. More lift, however, also means more drag and so extra power is needed from the engine to maintain rotor speed.

The pitch of the blades is controlled from the cockpit by means of the collective pitch lever, so called because it changes the pitch of all the main rotor blades by the same amount. This lever is mounted on the floor and is one of the very few differences between the cockpit of a helicopter and that of a conventional fixed-wing aircraft. Operated by hand, it is moved up to gain height and down to descend.

Since most maneuvers, including climbing and descending, necessitate changes of power, the collective pitch lever has a twist-grip throttle control at the top so that engine power and blade pitch can be controlled and coordinated with one hand.

Flight control

Helicopters have no wings or tailplane, and so the main rotors are required to generate between them not only the forces needed to provide lift but also those needed to control it. In order to make the helicopter travel forward or in any other horizontal direction, the rotor has to be tilted in that direction. Its reaction, or total lifting force, is then inclined away from the vertical and can be considered as being made up of two components: one acting vertically to balance the weight and the other, much smaller force, acting along the direction in which the pilot wishes to travel.

To make the helicopter travel faster, the rotor blade has to be tilted further so that more of the reaction of the rotors acts in the desired direction. At the same time, the vertical component of lift must always be maintained, so even more engine power has to be applied.

The rotor is made to tilt by arranging that one half of the disk traced out by the rotating blades generates more lift than the other half, and this tilt is achieved by increasing the blade angle

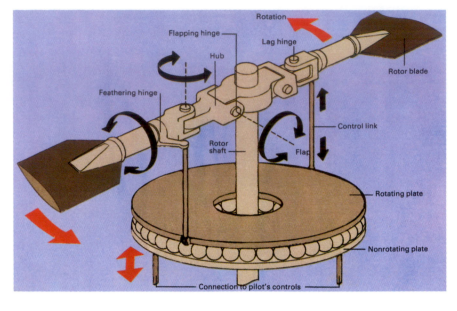

▲ A helicopter's control incorporates two swash plates that tilt up and down together under the pilot's control. The bottom plate is fixed, the top one rotates. They are linked to the blades, which twist in different directions and at different speeds from each other. As the pilot tilts the swash plates up or down, the control link translates the movement into a rotating movement for the blades, generating lift for the helicopter.

on one side and decreasing it on the other. Thus the pitch of a helicopter blade goes through a complete cycle, from maximum to minimum and back again, during one full revolution.

The cyclic pitch control, which determines where on the rotor disk variations of lift shall occur to perform the desired maneuvers or change the speed, is commanded by a conventional control column in the cockpit. Changes in heading are made by collectively altering the pitch of the tail rotor blades by means of conventional rudder pedals. Thus, four controls need to be adjusted in order to perform one basic maneuver.

Maximum speed

As the forward speed of the helicopter increases, the velocity of the forward-moving blade is increased by an amount equal to the speed of the aircraft, while that of the rearward-moving blade is decreased by the same amount. Eventually a situation is reached when the forward-moving blade approaches the speed of sound over a considerable portion of its travel. Undesirable aerodynamic effects then cause the drag of the blade to increase rapidly and its lift to decrease. At the same time the relative velocity of the retreating blade, traveling momentarily in the opposite direction to that of the helicopter itself, is too low to provide useful lift and it may become stalled. These effects limit the speed of a conventional helicopter to about 250 mph (400 km/h), fast enough to be useful in many situations.

Autorotation

If engine power is suddenly removed, the rotor slows very rapidly, lift is lost, and the helicopter begins to drop. To prevent loss of rotor speed the collective pitch lever has to be rapidly lowered, so as to set the blades at a negative pitch angle. This means that the leading edges of the blades are inclined slightly downward from the horizontal, but as the air is moving upward through the rotor, the blades still meet the airflow at a small upward angle.

As the helicopter begins to descend, usually in a forward glide, the air blowing up through the rotor disk generates forces on the blades that keep them spinning, thus providing some lift. This situation is known as autorotation and is the basis of the operation of the autogiro.

As the helicopter nears the ground, the collective pitch lever is raised slightly so as to reduce the rate of descent, using the kinetic energy stored in the rotor to provide, for a short time, the extra lift necessary to decelerate the machine for touchdown.

Rotors

The use of two smaller main rotors in place of a single large one can be an advantage, particularly with bigger helicopters. The rotors are arranged to spin in opposite directions so that the reaction torque of one cancels that of the other. There is thus no tendency for the fuselage to rotate, so the tail rotor can be dispensed with, thus reducing the weight somewhat and enabling all the power developed by the engines to be put to useful work in lifting and moving the aircraft.

The rotors may be mounted transversely across the fuselage or they can be located at either end of the fuselage, as on the Boeing Vertol CH-47 Chinook. They may be set one above the other and driven by concentric shafts, as on the Kamov Ka-26, or they may be carried on separate shafts mounted at a slight angle to one another; in this case, the rotors intermesh with each other and the drives to the blades have to be synchronized so the blades do not collide with one another.

Power plant

The general adoption of gas turbine propulsion for helicopters in place of piston engines in the mid 1950s resulted in a tremendous improvement in performance. Today, piston engines are to be found only on the older or very smallest helicopters. Instead of generating a high-velocity stream of hot gases to thrust the aircraft through the air, as in the jet engine, the power of the engine is extracted mechanically by fitting it with extra turbines and connecting these to the shaft that drives the rotor. This type of power plant is known as a turboshaft engine, and only a small proportion of the gas energy emerges as thrust.

Uses

Helicopters have developed into useful and in many cases indispensable machines. As air taxis they can cover 100-mile (160 km) journeys inside an hour, taking up and setting down passengers in confined spaces close to their destinations.

Helicopters have many applications in rescue work, particularly at sea, and every year, hundreds of swimmers and seafarers are saved around the world's coastlines. Helicopters have greatly

assisted the operation of offshore oil and gas rigs, as crews may be changed and spare drills and essential supplies may be ferried out irrespective of sea conditions.

In inaccessible areas of the world they have many uses, such as the supply of outposts and the maintenance of telephone and power lines. Large hospitals often depend on specially equipped helicopters to transport patients quickly and safely.

In firefighting, helicopters are frequently used for dealing with forest and bush fires and, in large cities, for rescuing people from high buildings. Large helicopters are often used in difficult construction situations, for example, for lifting church steeples into position.

In wartime, they confer tactical mobility, transporting troops, guns, and materials rapidly into the battle zone and ferrying out casualties

▲ Traffic supervision from a helicopter over the highways in Stuttgart, Germany.

▼ The Bell AH-1Q TOW American Cobra helicopter carries eight TOW (Tube launched, Optically tracked, Wire-guided) missiles. The Cobra has a slim but tall fuselage seating just two crew in a tandem fighterlike cockpit, with the gunner in the nose and the pilot seated above and behind.

and equipment that might otherwise have to be left behind. They may be equipped with cannon and rocket launchers and used as gunships.

Dangers

Helicopters are often required to hover close to vertical surfaces, such as cliffs. Because such vertical surfaces tend to restrict the airflow through the rotor blades on the side closest to them, that side of the rotor will generate less lift than the opposite side, causing the rotor disk to tilt and the helicopter to move toward the vertical surface. As the helicopter approaches the vertical surface, this effect becomes more acute and will result in a collision unless the pilot takes quick corrective action.

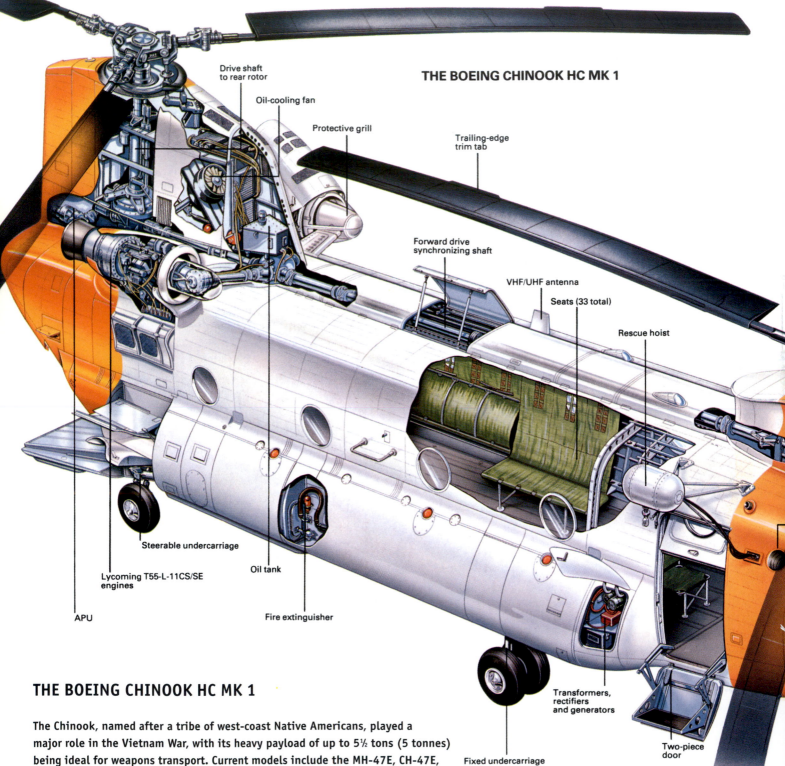

THE BOEING CHINOOK HC MK 1

Drive shaft to rear rotor
Oil-cooling fan
Protective grill
Trailing-edge trim tab
Forward drive synchronizing shaft
VHF/UHF antenna
Seats (33 total)
Rescue hoist
Steerable undercarriage
Oil tank
Lycoming T55-L-11CS/SE engines
APU
Fire extinguisher
Transformers, rectifiers and generators
Fixed undercarriage
Two-piece door

THE BOEING CHINOOK HC MK 1

The Chinook, named after a tribe of west-coast Native Americans, played a major role in the Vietnam War, with its heavy payload of up to 5½ tons (5 tonnes) being ideal for weapons transport. Current models include the MH-47E, CH-47E, and the CH-47D—all capable of carrying a payload of 12½ tons (11 tonnes). Apart from military use, Chinooks have been used for search and rescue, firefighting, disaster relief, and heavy construction.

Convertiplanes

The convertiplane is basically an aircraft with an engine and rotor mounted at the end of each wing, with the plane of the rotor disks at 90 degrees to the plane of the wings. For takeoff and landing, the wings are rotated so that the rotors are horizontal, as in a helicopter, to provide the necessary lift. When the aircraft is airborne, the wings are rotated back to the conventional position so that the lift is provided by the wings and forward propulsion by the rotors, which are then operating as ordinary propellers.

Autogiro

An autogiro is an aircraft that derives its lift from an unpowered rotor system mounted above the machine, with blades rotating horizontally.

Autogiros differ from helicopters in that their rotor blades are driven by the air flowing upwards past them—the principle known as autorotation. Helicopters, meanwhile, have mechanically driven blades set at a greater pitch angle, so as to screw upwards through the air.

To take off, maintain height, or climb, an autogiro needs an engine and a propeller to drive it forward. By tilting the lift rotor system slightly backwards, the rotor blades will lift the aircraft, even though the air flows up and through the rotor. An autogiro needs some forward speed to maintain height, so, unlike the helicopter, it cannot hover or takeoff vertically—its greatest limitation.

The motion of the rotor and the resulting upward thrust, or lift, depend entirely upon autorotation resulting from the air flowing up and through the slightly tilted rotor blades as the machine moves forward through the air.

Nature has applied the principle of autorotation for millions of years, seen in the whirling flight of a sycamore seed as it falls to the ground. Autorotation slows its descent and the wind has greater opportunity to disperse the seeds over a wider area.

In the case of an autogiro, the rotor blades are set at a angle of about three degrees to the horizontal plane in which they rotate. The shape is that of an airfoil, which enables the blades to turn into the airflow rather than be pushed around by it. These factors are what allow an autogiro to fly.

When turning fast, these rotor blades offer considerable resistance to the upward airflow, and it is this resistance that can be used to provide lift. The amount of lift created depends upon a compromise between the airspeed of the rotors and the resistance the rotating blades offer to the airflow past them. The advancing blade bends upwards in the airstream to store energy, which it releases by springing back downwards as it retreats.

Takeoff

For takeoff, the rotor must produce adequate lift, and it is necessary, therefore, to bring the rotor up to the required speed. This goal can be achieved in two ways.

The first and simplest way is to propel the machine forward and, by tilting back the rotor system, use the airflow through the blades to build up the rotor speed, all of which requires a suitably long runway. The second method involves more complex machinery but makes possible very short takeoff distances. Here the rotor is brought up to speed by a linkage to the engine used to provide the forward motion. When the rotor has the correct speed, the linkage is disengaged. The machine is then allowed to move forward, and takeoff is achieved by tilting back the rotor system. Some autogiros can jump-start by overspeeding the rotor using the engine. The drive is then disengaged, and the rotor pitch increased. The aircraft jumps, using the stored energy, and continues then in autorotation.

Landing

When the engine and propeller speed are reduced, the forward speed decreases and the autogiro goes into a steady descent path. The autorotation principle still applies, as the air flowing up and through the rotor maintains the rotor speed. A lifting force is therefore produced that, although insufficient to maintain the machine's altitude, prevents it from falling like a stone. Even when the propeller is stopped, the autogiro will descend safely, gliding with forward speed to a normal landing.

In this respect, the autogiro is at some advantage over the helicopter, since in the case of helicopter engine failure, the climbing pitch angle of the rotors (about 11 degrees) would quickly stop them, with disastrous results. To keep the rotors turning, the blade pitch angle must be quickly reduced to an angle that provides autorotation for a safe forced landing.

rotor hub and oil tank

Air inlet

IFF antenna

Cyclic-stick grip

Cover for vibration absorbers

Heated pitot tubes to measure speed

Yaw sensors

Overcoming instability

The first successful autogiro was designed by the Spanish aeronautical engineer Juan de la Cierva and was flown on 9 January 1923, at Getafe Airdrome near Madrid. This was his fourth design; the other three had suffered from an alarming tendency to roll over when moving forward.

The instability was due to the use of rigid rotor blades. With the machine moving forward and the rotor turning, the blade turning into the airstream undergoes a greater lifting force than the opposite blade, which is moving downstream. With rigid rotor blades, this imbalance is transmitted to the whole machine, producing, a rolling motion. To overcome this instability, Cierva designed a rotor system with blades suitably hinged at the root so that, rather than transmit the imbalance to the whole machine, it was taken up by the individual blades, which could move accordingly.

At the root of each blade, he fitted two hinges. One, the flapping hinge, allowed the blade to flap

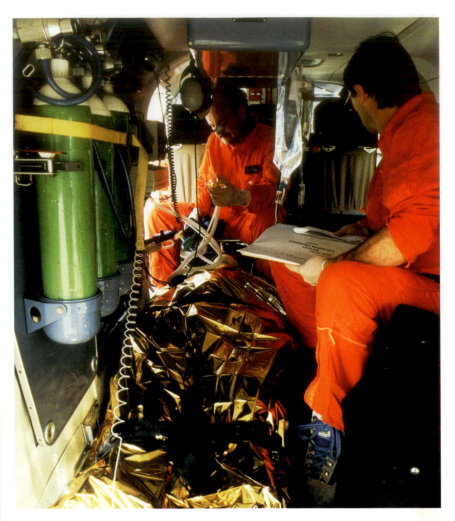

▲ Paramedics with a patient inside a helicopter ambulance. Air ambulances are equipped with life-support systems and medical staff to handle emergencies. Helicopters can provide a rapid response to emergencies in otherwise inaccessible locations.

up and down; the other, the drag hinge, permitted the necessary sideways movement.

The autogiro rotor blade (or that of the helicopter) is not, by itself, stiff enough to carry the weight of the machine. It is the enormous centrifugal force of rotation that keeps the rotors moving in an almost flat path, and even though they have flapping hinges at their roots, the weight of the machine is carried here.

Modifications

The autogiro was the forerunner of the helicopter and did much to help its development. The late 1920s and the following decade saw the autogiro's heyday, with many improvements and modifications that were to become permanent features of the then-new vertical takeoff and landing machines called helicopters. After a period of stagnation, however, there are signs of a revival of the autogiro. Its relative simplicity of construction and maintenance, combined with stable and efficient operation, are useful for surveying and reconnaissance.

FACT FILE

■ *The Westland Sea King helicopter is a self-contained submarine hunter. It uses dipping sonar, which it can immerse repeatedly in the sea at the end of a cable and at various depths, and can also drop a number of sonobuoys, the signals from which can be used to pinpoint a submarine by means of the Sea King's inboard computer. It also carries up to four torpedoes or depth charges.*

■ *The X-wing project worked on by Sikorsky and NASA involved a new concept. The aircraft was designed with an X-shaped, wide-bladed rotor for takeoff and hovering, that could be locked in position for fixed-wing flight. Unfortunately, the technical complexity of this design prevented it from developing beyond the prototype stage.*

■ *Nicknamed the Water Wagtail (Bachstelze), the Fokke Fa330 had rotors that kept it aloft when towed behind a surfaced U-boat in World War II. Produced in large numbers as a reconnaissance unit, it could be folded up for stowing and reassembled in ten minutes. Several pilots were drowned when their parent boat crash dived under air attack.*

SEE ALSO: AERODYNAMICS • AIRCRAFT DESIGN • AVIATION, HISTORY OF • GAS TURBINE • V/STOL AIRCRAFT

Hi-fi Systems

The term *hi-fi* is an abbreviation of high fidelity. Hi-fi systems are so called because they are designed to reproduce recorded or broadcast sounds with as much fidelity, or faithfulness, to the original sounds as possible within the limits of technology and acceptable cost. Since the term *high fidelity* was coined in the 1950s, its usage has become increasingly loose. As such, midprice music systems that provide reasonably faithful sound reproduction are often described as hi-fi systems, whereas true high-fidelity systems are now classed as reference equipment.

At the core of any hi-fi system are one or more amplifiers. An amplifier's primary function is to boost signals from input devices to such an extent that they are capable of driving loudspeakers or headphones. Potentiometers, or variable resistance devices, modify the output signal to suit the environment and mood of the listener. One such device, the volume control, varies the overall output strength for all speakers. Another, the balance control, adjusts the relative strengths of the signals fed to different speaker channels—left and right or front and rear, for example.

Input devices

The principal input devices that provide audio signals for amplifiers include compact disc (CD) players, digital audio tape (DAT) players, and digital radio tuners. Analog input devices such as record players, audio cassette players, and analog tuners continue to form part of many hi-fi systems, but the inherently poor reproduction of analog devices compared with digital input devices is eroding their popularity. In contrast, MP3 and minidisc players, which record sound as digital computer files, are growing in popularity.

Some hi-fi systems can be used in home-entertainment systems. The audio output signal of a video cassette or digital versatile disc (DVD) player provides the input signal for the soundtrack that accompanies the on-screen images.

Output devices

The principal output devices of hi-fi systems are speakers, in which the output signal passes through a coil in the back of a flexibly mounted rigid cone. Variations in the signal cause corresponding changes in the magnetic field of the

▲ At the mixing desk of a sound-recording studio, a mixing engineer (center) "designs" the sound that will be recorded. The mixing-desk controls modify the strengths and frequency profiles of input signals and determine their places in the stereophonic or polyphonic sound field. The function of a hi-fi system is to reproduce faithfully the sound that a mixing engineer creates.

coil. The varying field causes a permanent magnet to alternately attract and repel the coil so as to cause the cone to vibrate and produce sound.

The earliest hi-fi systems were monophonic: they had a single output channel. Such systems are now all but extinct, and modern systems use multiple output signals and speakers to create an impression of a three-dimensional soundscape. Stereophonic hi-fi systems reproduce the left and right fields of a sound recording through a pair of speakers placed to the left and right of the listening position. This arrangement is sufficient to create a reasonable impression of watching a performance on stage. Quadrophonic systems create the impression of being in an auditorium by means of an additional pair of channels for loudspeakers at left and right behind the listener. Quadrophonic recordings are rare, however.

Surround-sound hi-fi systems, for use with video devices, have up to six speakers. In addition to pairs of left and right speakers at front and rear, surround-sound systems have a central-front main speaker for principal dialogue and a central subwoofer that boosts low-frequency ambient sounds, such as the rumble of an earthquake.

Frequency response

A typical human ear can detect frequencies in a range from 20 Hz (hertz) to 20 kHz, so an ideal hi-fi system would reproduce each frequency in that range without emphasizing or diminishing any give frequency relative to the others. This ideal behavior is called a flat frequency response, since a plot of amplification against frequency would be a horizontal straight line.

Real hi-fi equipment varies from the ideally flat frequency response, emphasizing certain frequency ranges relative to others. For this reason, the term *frequency response* is sometimes used to describe the frequency range over which a given

piece of equipment responds within a stated deviation from the flat response. Good hi-fi equipment is characterized by a wide frequency range and narrow limits of deviation.

The unit of frequency response is the decibel (dB). The dB is an expression of the ratio of input and output voltages, currents, or power levels and is a multiple of the base-10 logarithm (log) of the input value divided by the output value. When comparing voltages or currents, the log of the ratio is multiplied by 20; for power ratios, the log of the ratio is multiplied by 10.

If a hi-fi device produces an output signal of 50 W at one frequency and 100 W at a second, provided the input powers are the same, the response at the second frequency is 10 x log ($^{100}/_{50}$) dB = 10 x log 2 dB = 3.01 dB relative to the first. A negative number indicates a reduction in signal strength, so –3.01 dB represents a drop from an output of 100 W to an output of 50 W for a given strength of input signal. Note that the same value would be consistent with a reduction from 80 W to 40 W, since it refers to the ratio of values.

One method of measuring the frequency response of an amplifier is to feed it with a sine-wave signal at 1,000 Hz and adjust the input and volume controls such that the output has a power of 1 W. This output level is taken as the 0 dB standard. The frequency of the input signal is then varied without changing its power, and the output power is measured at corresponding frequencies. The power output figures obtained are then related to the 0 dB standard to give an indication of the linearity of the amplifier's frequency response and its effective upper and lower frequency limits. The frequency response can then be quoted, for example, as 25 Hz to 20 kHz ± 1.5 dB. Variations as great as 2 dB are hardly detected by the human ear, so such a frequency response would indicate high-quality equipment.

▲ This compact hi-fi system combines minidisc and CD players—both digital sources—with a high-performance amplifier to give faithful sound reproduction. The speakers' protective covers can be removed (right) to reduce interference with their performance, and a remote control allows tracks and amplifier settings to be selected without moving from the listening position.

Tone controls and equalizers

While a flat frequency response is the mark of good high-fidelity equipment, it is not a guarantee that the listener will hear a faithful reproduction of the original performance. Inadequacies of the recording process or of the acoustics of the listening environment can boost certain frequency ranges while diminishing others, as can weaknesses of analog recording media such as audio cassettes and vinyl discs. As such, it is sometimes desirable to modify the frequency response of an amplifier to compensate for such factors.

In some cases, the strengths of the high- and low-frequency components of the output signals are controlled by treble and bass tone controls, respectively, while a loudness control can diminish the midfrequency signal to compensate for the limited ability of the human ear to hear low and high frequencies at low volumes.

Some amplifiers replace tone controls with equalizers, whose three or more variable resistors control the output strengths of specific frequency ranges. An equalizer may be an integral part of the amplifier unit, or it may be a separate device that takes the diverted input signals of an amplifier and modifies their frequency profile before returning the signal to the amplifier circuitry.

Equalizers can be used to compensate for the acoustics of a listening environment. Some equalizers include white-noise generators that produce a sound in which all frequencies are present at equal signal intensities. A microphone placed at the listening position detects the white noise as modified by the amplifier, speakers, and acoustics. The controls of the equalizer are adjusted so as to produce a flat frequency response. In some cases, this process is automatic; in others, the equalizer produces a display of the frequency response, and the equalizer is adjusted manually.

Some equalizers include programmed settings that mimic listening environments, such as concert halls, jazz clubs, and discotheque dance floors, by introducing the characteristic frequency responses and reverberations of such environments. While such features are popular selling points for some systems, they contribute nothing to the faithfulness of sound reproduction.

Forms of distortion

The frequency distortion characterized by deviation from a flat frequency response is one of many forms of distortion that can hamper faithful sound reproduction. In general, distortion is any process that causes undue changes or additions to a signal. A typical effect of distortion is an increased harshness of sound quality.

An effect called amplitude distortion is the source of two common forms of sound distortion: harmonic distortion and intermodulation (IM). Amplitude distortion is due to the nonlinear transfer of the signal from one section of the equipment to another, such as from one stage of the amplifier to the next. This occurs when the amplitude of the output signal from the section at a given instant is not exactly proportional to the amplitude of the input signal.

Harmonic distortion is caused by the unwanted generation of harmonic frequencies within the equipment. A harmonic frequency is a multiple of the fundamental frequency, that is, the frequency of the signal passing through the equipment. If the fundamental is 1,000 Hz, the second harmonic will be 2,000 Hz, the third harmonic will be 3,000 Hz, and so on.

Intermodulation can occur when equipment handles two or more signal frequencies. In IM, the equipment generates frequencies that are the sums or differences of input frequencies.

▼ Component-based hi-fi systems enable people to put together a sound system that meets their own requirements. This hi-fi has DVD and minidisc players rather than the more usual CD and audio cassette components.

Harmonic and intermodulation distortion are often quoted as percentages of the output signal; for instance, if the total harmonic distortion (THD) is stated as 0.1 percent, then that percentage of the output signal will be the harmonic distortion content. Of these two types of distortions, intermodulation usually has a greater impact on sound quality than does harmonic distortion.

Clipping is a form of overload distortion that occurs when an input signal is too strong for the equipment that it feeds. The peaks of the waveforms then become stunted, changing the quality of sound. Manufacturers sometimes quote overload distortion as the percentage of signal strength present as distortion at a given level of overload, so 0.1 percent distortion for 20 dB overload indicates that 0.1 percent distortion will result if the input signal level rises 20 dB above the maximum recommended input.

Noise and hum

Noise is a random signal introduced mainly by the so-called quiescent current that flows through the circuits of an amplifier even when it is not carrying a signal. Another source is interference from electrical equipment such as switches.

One form of noise is called white noise, since it includes all frequencies in the audible range, just as white light includes all frequencies in the visible range. Hum is an extraneous signal that arises from the frequency of the alternating current mains supply—typically 50 or 60 Hz—and its harmonic frequencies.

For the purposes of evaluating equipment, hum is included with other forms of noise in a signal-to-noise (S/N) ratio, which is the ratio between the level of wanted signal and that of the hum and noise content. Signal-to-noise ratios are

◀ Loudspeakers have undergone many changes since the days of the flared horn attached to wind-up phonographs. Most speakers now use a thin diaphragm mounted close to a fixed plate that vibrates when a signal causes a variation in the electrostatic force between the two. The lightness and tightness of the diaphragm enables it to move accurately, reproducing the sound with near perfect fidelity.

measured in decibels, so –66 dB at 50 watts indicates a noise power less than 50 μW at 50 W output power. Such figures are quoted for perfect signal and ground connections. Poor-quality signal cables can introduce noise, and bad grounding connections can generate hum.

Power output

As a consequence of the complexity of electrical audio signals, the power-handling capacity of hi-fi equipment can be expressed in a variety of ways. The most meaningful value is the RMS (root-mean-square) value, which is calculated from the square root of the mean of the signal amplitude squared. The RMS power output of a system is the maximum continuous power output under which the equipment conforms to the stated values of total harmonic distortion.

Instead of RMS values, many manufacturers quote PMPO (peak music power output) values for equipment. Such values indicate the capacity of equipment to handle transient signal peaks, such as drumbeats. PMPO values are difficult to measure accurately and may be as much as double the RMS value for a given system. PMPOs can give the impression that equipment is more powerful than it really is. For this reason, it is advisable to compare RMS values rather than PMPO values when choosing hi-fi equipment.

Although high power output levels are not needed for normal domestic purposes, it is better to have an amplifier capable of delivering more power than is usually required. The amplifier will then be running at less than its maximum output under most circumstances, with a reserve of power to cope with loud musical peaks and less risk of clipping distortion or of overheating the output transistors during prolonged use.

Impedance and sensitivity

Impedance is the alternating current equivalent of resistance. The impedance of a component consists of its direct current resistance and additional resistive effects caused by inductance and capacitance as a result of the oscillating nature of signals. Since these effects are frequency dependent, manufacturers quote impedance for a given frequency—generally 1 kHz.

For the most efficient transfer of power from one component of a system to the next with minimum distortion, the respective output and input impedances of the two components should be as closely matched as possible. In general, a satisfactory match occurs when the input impedance is up to five or six times the source impedance.

The sensitivity of an amplifier is the input voltage necessary for it to be able to develop its rated maximum output power—the lower this input voltage, the greater the sensitivity of the amplifier. A typical amplifier can handle up to four or five times its stated sensitivity without overloading.

Components versus midi systems

A midi system is an integrated collection of an amplifier and source components, usually in a single housing and often with matching speakers. Midi systems are an alternative to systems in which individual components are bought separately and connected by cables.

Both types of hi-fi systems have advantages and disadvantages. Midi systems have the advantages that their components are likely to be well matched in terms of impedance and sensitivity, and their soldered connections avoid the risk of noise owing to inadequate cable connections. They have the disadvantage that certain compo-

▼ Digital technology has done much to improve the quality of hi-fi sound reproduction systems, though some enthusiasts say it lacks the warmth of analog vinyl disc recordings.

nents of the system might not be the best available, and the failure of one component might necessitate the replacement of the whole system.

The main advantage of component systems is their flexibility. The best available models of each type of component can be combined, and the system need include only components that its owner is likely to use, thereby saving unnecessary expense. If one component fails, it can be replaced without having to replace the whole system. The disadvantage of component systems is their potential for the mismatch of components and for inadequate connections.

Digital versus analog

Since the widespread acceptance of compact disc players in the 1980s, digital sources such as CDs, DATs, and minidiscs have become the dominant source components for hi-fi systems. The dominance of such components stems mainly from their quality of reproduction and their relative resistance to damage from dirt and scratches. The media for such devices carry sounds as digital signals, and error-correction software can eliminate the effects of physical damage and electrical interference to a large extent. In connection with an adequate amplifier and speakers, the result is a crystal-clear reproduction of the recorded sound.

Some music enthusiasts claim that the clarity of digital reproduction is inappropriate for certain types of music and express a preference for the "warmer" sound of analog reproduction from vinyl discs and audio cassettes. The disadvantages of analog recordings are many, however. Vinyl discs are prone to noise from scratches and dirt, and audio cassettes can lose their magnetization through aging or exposure to magnetic fields. Both media are prone to wow and flutter, which are periodic speed variations at rates of less than or greater than 10 Hz, respectively. In the case of record players, constant speed can be maintained by the use of a phase-locked loop—a type of tuning circuit that automatically corrects deviations from the nominal rotation speed. Record players are also prone to rumble, which occurs when the pickup transmits the noise of the turntable drive to the amplifier. A similar effect can cause feedback if the turntable is too close to a speaker.

In addition to the problems of noise and speed variations encountered with some record players, tracking and tracing errors arise because the pickup does not match the movements of the needle that cut the original disk. Tracking errors occur because of the deviation of the pickup arm from an exact tangent to the groove and because of the lateral force necessary to move the pickup arm as the record turns. Tracing errors occur because the elliptical profile of a pickup stylus causes it to follow the groove in a manner slightly different from that of the pointed cutting stylus.

▲ The sound-control booth of Glyndebourne Opera House, England. The inputs from several microphones on stage are mixed in the same way as for a sound recording. The output from the mixing desk and associated amplifiers feeds speakers in the auditorium to ensure a hi-fi quality sound for the audience.

SEE ALSO: AMPLIFIER • COMPACT DISC, AUDIO • LOUDSPEAKER • PHONOGRAPHY • SOUND MIXING • SOUND REPRODUCTION

High-Speed Photography

High-speed photography is used to study events that last for a very short period of time or to freeze very rapid motion. For example, the technique can be used to study the behavior of a bullet as it penetrates a target or capture the rapid development of an explosion.

In high-speed photography, light from the subject being photographed will fall on the film for only a very short period of time and must therefore be of high intensity to achieve a proper exposure. For this reason, the subject is normally illuminated with flash apparatus unless it is self-luminous, such as a flame or spark. The equipment used will depend on the results required; if only a single picture is needed the equipment must be capable of producing a single high-intensity flash of short duration and must include a triggering arrangement so that the picture is taken at precisely the right moment. If the result required is a study of motion, then a series of pictures must be taken in very rapid succession. Each picture will require a separate high-intensity flash, and each successive image must fall on a different section of the film.

Flash equipment

The flashguns employed in normal photography use flashbulbs that produce a flash lasting from about $\frac{1}{80}$ to $\frac{1}{1000}$ of a second or an electronic discharge tube, which produces a flash lasting for $\frac{1}{750}$ to $\frac{1}{1000}$ of a second. While these flash times are suitable for most normal applications, they are too long if the event itself lasts for only a few microseconds or if the motion to be photographed is very fast. For example, a bullet traveling at three times the speed of sound will travel approximately 3 ft. (0.9 m) in $\frac{1}{1000}$ of a second.

The most common flashlamp for high-speed photography is the xenon-filled discharge tube. The flashes from such tubes are similar to daylight in their color content except that they emit rather more light at the blue and ultraviolet end of the spectrum. This feature is useful because photographic emulsions are more sensitive to light at that end of the spectrum. The discharge tube is connected to a specially designed control circuit that ensures the duration of the flash is very short, typically 0.5 microseconds. For studying rapid motion, the flash tube must deliver a

▲ A very-high-speed flash was used for this studio shot, which was triggered automatically when the tongue flicked out toward its prey.

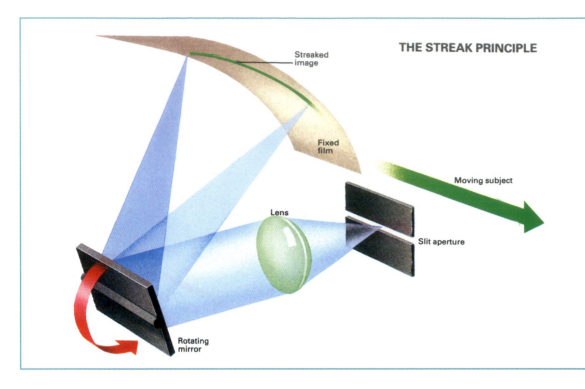

THE STREAK PRINCIPLE

Streaked image

Fixed film

Moving subject

Lens

Slit aperture

Rotating mirror

◀ In a rotating mirror camera, the mirror is operated by a gas-driven turbine that, in effect, wipes the image of the moving subject across a short, stationary strip of film.

large number of flashes per second. A flash rate of 4,000 flashes per second is quite common. Thyristors are used in the control circuit to ensure that each flash is distinct from the next. A multiple-flash apparatus of this sort is called a stroboscope.

Cameras

If a series of pictures is to be taken, the camera must arrange for each successive picture to fall on a fresh part of the film. Such pictures can be taken with a normal still-picture camera by moving the camera or deflecting the light entering the camera from the subject by using a rotating mirror. With this method, a series of pictures can be taken using the same roll of film, but of course, only a small number of pictures can be taken before the film is used up. Often it will be necessary to take a large number of pictures, for example, if a movie film is to be made. Conventional movie cameras cannot be used in high-speed photography because the

◀ A photograph showing the passage of a bullet through a card—an event measured in microseconds. Because of the extremely short exposure, the image of the bullet is only slightly blurred.

number of pictures they can take per second is limited by the mechanical film-advancing mechanism, which momentarily stops the film while each frame is exposed. In high-speed cameras, the film passes continuously through the camera and its motion relative to the image is compensated for optically, using rotating mirrors or prisms. In this way the film and the image can effectively be made stationary relative to each other, although the film may be moving through the camera at speeds of up to 200 mph (322 km/h). High-speed rotating-prism cameras of this type can operate at picture frequencies of up to about 10,000 per second when using a full 16 mm picture size, or up to some 40,000 per second when using 16 mm film with a picture height of 2 mm.

In high-speed cameras, the speed of the film is never absolutely constant, and it is therefore important to record a time base on the film if the time intervals between the various events recorded are to be determined. This end can be achieved by recording flashes, whose precise frequency is known, onto the edge of the film.

When recording animate subjects, such as insects in flight, it is important to ensure that the flash occurs at exactly the correct moment. Infrared trip beams are often used to perform this function, the camera being prefocused on the beam and activated when the beam is broken by the subject.

Digital high-speed photography

Electronic cameras are being developed that do not need to use film and so do not suffer from the mechanical limitations of conventional cameras. These cameras use arrays of charge-coupled devices (CCDs) to record images that can be read electronically and stored for future use. At present, the resolution of CCDs is far worse than that of conventional film-based recording.

More recent developments, however, use CMOS (complementary metal-oxide-silicon) technology instead of CCDs. CMOS technology has extremely low power requirements, allowing the development of cooler running systems and resulting in more compact cameras. In addition, CMOS has enabled manufacturers to create digital video cameras that can operate at high speed with better levels of resolution than cameras using CCDs.

The newest commercially available models, such as the Phantom v5 produced by Vision Research, stretch the bounds of photographic clarity for high-speed digital video technology. Cameras such as these are capable of offering 1,000 pictures per second with 1024 x 1024 pixel resolution, and by reducing image sizes, speeds of

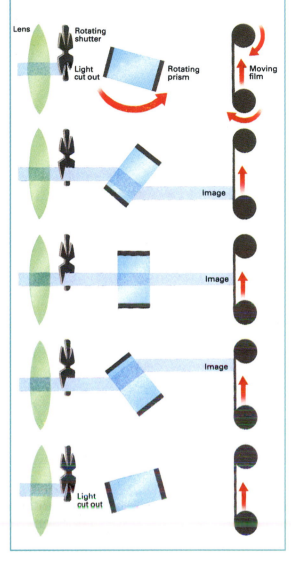

ROTATING PRISM PRINCIPLE

Some high-speed cameras use a rapidly rotating shutter that alternately blocks the light and allows it to pass through to the film. A rotating prism causes the image to follow the moving film and so prevent blurring.

Lens · Rotating shutter · Light cut out · Rotating prism · Moving film · Image · Image · Image · Light cut out

up to 60,000 pictures per second are also possible. These cameras also offer synchronous shuttering like conventional cameras, enabling very rapid shutter speeds as fast as 5 microseconds. To extend picture quality in harsh lighting conditions, a system called extreme dynamic range (EDR) has been developed. These kinds of digital cameras find applications in aviation, military, industrial, and automotive research. The fact that the images are instantly available to be viewed on desktop computer is an obvious advantage over conventional photography.

SEE ALSO: CAMERA • CAMERA, DIGITAL • CHARGE-COUPLED DEVICE • INTEGRATED CIRCUIT • MOVIE CAMERA

Holography

Holography is a technique for recording three-dimensional images in two dimensions. The word *hologram* is a combination of two Greek words: *holos*, meaning "whole," and *gram*, meaning "message." Holograms are recorded on film or glass plate coated with a light-sensitive photographic emulsion that records the image.

Whereas conventional photography yields two-dimensional images in which all scenic depth has collapsed into the plane of the print, holography captures scenes in three-dimensions. The perceived image depends on viewing angle, so an observer's eyes see two slightly different images, just as they would if viewing a three-dimensional object. The brain then reconstructs a three-dimensional image from the two different views.

Apparent three-dimensional images can also be obtained by stereoscopy, whereby slightly different images are viewed by each eye. Stereoscopy, however, presents only one viewpoint of an object, whereas a hologram can be viewed from a range of angles, so an observer can see parallax effects—the relative movement of two objects in the scene—as the observer moves.

Holography and laser light

Holography was considered and predicted in 1947 by the British scientist, Dennis Gabor, but the practical demonstration had to await the invention of a suitable light source—the laser—in the early 1960s. The critical feature of laser light is that it is coherent: all its photons have the same frequency and are in step with one another. Furthermore, when a laser beam splits in two at a half-silvered mirror, for example, the two beams remain coherent and will have the same phase at the same distance from where the beams split.

When the path length of the two beams is slightly different, the two beams will be out of step where they recombine. If the difference in path lengths is an exact multiple of wavelengths, the photons in the two beams will be in phase: their points of maximum positive amplitude will coincide. The two beams reinforce each other, causing a bright spot on a screen or plate.

When the path length is an exact multiple of wavelengths plus one half wavelength, the two beams will be in opposite phase when they combine. The positive peak of one beam coincides with the negative peak of the other, resulting in a dark spot on a screen or plate. In this way, an interference pattern holds information about differences in path length that can be recorded in the photographic emulsion of a hologram.

Recording a hologram of the clear acrylic object at left. A beam of laser light from a source at right is first split into two beams. The reference beam bounces off a mirror and spreads over the recording plate behind the object. A second beam reflects off the object and interferes with the reference beam to record an image where the two beams meet on the recording plate.

Recording a hologram

Holograms are recorded using a reference beam and recording beam split from a single laser source. A lens spreads and directs the reference beam to cover the whole of a photographic plate. A second lens spreads the recording beam over the object of the hologram. The relative positions of the laser beams, object, and plate ensure that light reflected from the object falls on the plate.

When light reflected from the object interacts with the reference beam at the surface of the holographic plate, the difference between the path lengths of the two beams at the holographic plate depends on how far the recording beam has traveled to reach the object and then the plate. The phase difference between the recording beam and the reference beam at each therefore varies with the distance between that point on the plate and the point on the object's surface at which the recording beam reflects.

Variations in the phase relationship between the two beams at different points on the plate produce variations in light intensity that are recorded by the light-sensitive emulsion. The recorded information on the plate therefore contains both intensity and phase information about light from the object. By contrast, a photograph captures only intensity variations.

Reconstructing the original scene

When a beam similar to the reference beam illuminates a developed hologram, a complete three-dimensional image of the object can be seen, because variations in the refractive index of the developed emulsion generate changes in the phase of light transmitted by each point of the hologram. These variations reconstruct the variations in the original recording-beam intensity, which an observer perceives as an image.

The simplest holograms are transparent, and they are intended to be viewed from "behind" the hologram with respect to the original recording setup. In this way, an observer sees a virtual image of the object as if it were in its original position. A focused image also forms on the observer's side, and it can be viewed by placing a screen behind the hologram. In practice, however, most holograms are modified to suppress the real image and enhance the desired virtual image.

Types of holograms

Laser-transmission holograms were the first and most basic type of holographic images. They produce the sharpest images with the best spatial reproduction, but they have the drawback that they can be viewed only in laser light.

White-light-reflection holograms can be viewed in white (normal) light. The image is reconstructed by light reflected from the surface of the film plate because the interference pattern in the emulsion is designed to reflect. A white spotlamp is used to reconstruct the image for this type, giving a single-color image, because the interference pattern reflects only one color efficiently.

In rainbow-transmission holograms, white light from a normal spotlamp passes through the film to create the image. Such holograms diffract different frequencies of light through different angles, so the same image is seen in varying colors as the observer's viewing angle changes.

Dispersion-compensated transmission holograms are backed with a diffraction grating that corrects the dispersion—frequency-related diffraction differences—caused by the hologram. This correction prevents the laser-transmission hologram's virtual image from breaking up into a blur of color under white-light illumination and results in a relatively sharp image.

Full-color holograms

The color of an object viewed in white light depends on the amount of each frequency of light that is reflected by the surface of the object. A red ball has its color because it reflects red light more strongly than other colors, for example.

When a single-frequency laser beam is used to record a hologram, parts of an object that have different colors will reflect that frequency of light with different intensities, but these variations will appear as variations in brightness rather than color, since no other frequencies of light are present to construct the true colors. In theory, a full-color hologram could be recorded using at least three laser frequencies in combination with emulsions sensitive to those frequencies.

▼ To record a hologram (top), a light-sensitive emulsion is simultaneously exposed to a reference beam and a recording beam that reflects off the object to be recorded. Both beams derive from the same laser source. To view the hologram (bottom), a laser beam similar to the reference beam illuminates the developed plate. A virtual image is then visible from behind the plate.

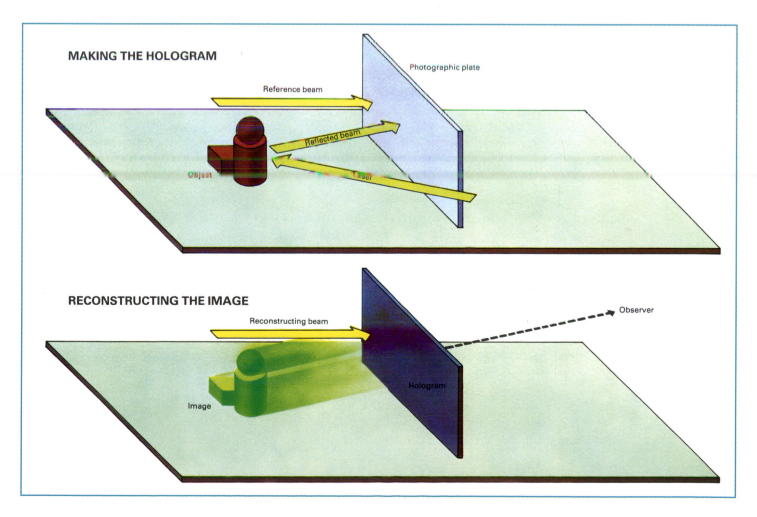

MAKING THE HOLOGRAM

Photographic plate

Reference beam

Reflected beam

Laser

Object

RECONSTRUCTING THE IMAGE

Reconstructing beam

Observer

Hologram

Image

▶ Recording a hologram of a nuclear fuel cell as part of an examination for surface defects. The dots on the plate in the background are the diffraction pattern. When developed and viewed from behind using a laser light, that pattern will create a virtual image of the fuel cell. The image is magnified, so it reveals more detail than is visible to the unaided eye. It also has the advantage that, unlike the object, it can be handled without risk of exposure to radiation.

Embossed-foil holograms

In a relatively low-cost mass-production process, white-light rainbow-transmission holograms are first recorded as microscopic ripples on a metal plate. This plate is then used to emboss the pattern on a foil-backed plastic film. Simple embossed holograms are frequently used to decorate book, magazine, CD, and DVD covers. More complicated designs, which are difficult to forge, are used to authenticate credit cards, bank notes, event tickets, and administrative seals.

Holographic optics

The complex optical properties of holograms are put to use in specialist light filters. Instead of using a silver-halide–gelatin emulsion, in which exposure to light forms grains of silver, such holograms use a dichromate–gelatin (DCG) system, in which exposure to light causes the chromate ions to cause modifications in the gelatin itself. Bright, high-precision holograms are the result.

One of the most fascinating aspects of DCG holograms is that they can be made to act as lenses or mirrors that are specific to the frequency of the laser that generated the hologram. Other frequencies of light simply pass through the hologram. Optical components made in this way are particularly useful for manipulating laser light itself, since they can be made for a fraction of the cost of high-precision optical glass components.

One application for DCG holograms is in the head-up display (HUD) screens used to view instrument data in some aircraft. The holograms act as narrow-bandwidth reflection filters, selectively reflecting light from instrument displays into the pilot's field of view, while allowing a clear view through the hologram to the outside world. Standard information in such a display might include air speed, bearing, and attitude relative to the horizon. Specialist HUD equipment is of particular use to fighter pilots, since the head-up display can project the path of weapon fire for the current aim at any time without the pilot having to look away. At night, an HUD can project computer-generated outlines of the ground below.

Another application of DCG holograms is in telecommunications, where they allow several signals of slightly different wavelengths to be transmitted down the same optical fiber. At the receiving end, DCG holograms act as highly wavelength-selective filters, separating narrow frequency channels for individual processing.

Holographic bar-code scanners

Holographic optics are even applied in supermarkets, where they help in the automatic reading of the bar codes that identify goods. A holographic bar-code scanner shoots out an exploring pattern of harmless laser beams to find the code, wherever it is on the package. The laser beam passes through a spinning disk about 8 in. (20 cm) in diameter and divided into sectors.

Each sector is a holographic lens that sweeps the beam on a different path through the space around the package, so the bar code can be sought and read from any direction. The returning beams travel back through the disc to a detector that is placed to pick up light that returns along exactly the same path. In this way, stray light from the surroundings is disregarded.

Holographic interferometry

If an object is recorded in two holographic images on a single plate, interference between the two images reveals any deformation in the object between the two exposures. Pulsed lasers are the typical illumination source, providing precisely timed exposures, and displacements of as little as 0.3 µm are easily distinguished.

Holographic interferometry is used as a tool for stress analysis in engineering applications, giving insights into the weak points of new designs by monitoring their deformations under applied stress. The technique is also used as a quality-control tool in the manufacture of high-precision components, such as turbine blades and pressure vessels, when comparison with a standard component reveals deviations in structure.

Multiplexed holograms

A multiplexed hologram consists of several holograms in a single unit. The two types of multiplexed holograms are volumetric and lateral.

A volumetric multiplexed hologram consists of several standard-transmission holograms stacked together. Each hologram carries an image of a slice through an object taken at a specific distance from the plate. When superimposed, the holograms form a transparent three-dimensional image of the object in question.

Lateral multiplexed holograms consist of several holographic images placed side by side on a single plate. The separate images are generally intended to be viewed sequentially. One application of lateral multiplexing is in holographic movies, where 200 to 300 vertical strips contain sequential images of an object as it moves or changes shape with passing time.

Real-time holograms

Temporary and variable holograms can be created by playing two lasers on a sheet of a material whose optical properties respond to light. Interference between the two beams creates the hologram, which can be changed or switched off at will. The hologram so created can be used to modulate or process a signal light beam passing through it. Such techniques open the way to real-time optical-signal processing and, in the future, the potential of an all-optical computer, many times faster than any current device.

Holographic archiving

Holograms have enormous potential for use in the storage of information. There are two main reasons for this. First, a single holographic plate can contain many separate images, each corresponding to a particular angle of reference beam

◀ A hologram of an apple generated and read by use of green lasers. Since lasers are monochromatic, the holographic image has no color definition.

and transparent at all other angles. The pages are then read by selecting the appropriate reading angle. Second, a hologram is a parallel storage mechanism: each part of the image contains information about the whole of the image. Therefore, although destroying one part of the hologram reduces the clarity of the image, the overall image is maintained.

Holographic records can also replace archives of solid objects, often making huge savings in space. This approach has been used to replace plaster molds as dental records. The holographic records, which are each the size of a playing card, may be used to take measurements in three dimensions as part of the forensic identification process for bodies that have been damaged beyond recognition by fire, for example.

Tumor visualization

One of the main difficulties facing surgeons who have to remove dangerous tumors from the human body is visualizing the extent of the growth and, consequently, how to plan the procedure. Whereas a video display can show the tomographic image produced by an X ray or other type of body scanner slice by slice, a composite hologram of the same results produces a transparent three-dimensional image of the tumor.

◀ Hologram lenses form part of the optics that guide laser beams around this package to read its identifying bar code.

SEE ALSO: CAMERA • HEAD-UP DISPLAY • LASER AND MASER • PHOTOGRAPHIC FILM AND PROCESSING

Hormone

Hormones are the body's regulators. They coordinate the functions of the body's cells so that they respond correctly to the environmental demands placed upon them. For example, cells involved with the digestive tract may be called upon to secrete saliva and enzymes; other cells may need to contract so that a limb may be moved.

The term *hormone* was first used in 1904 by the British physiologists Sir William Bayliss and Ernest Starling when they described the action of secretin, a substance that increases the flow of pancreatic juices. Many bodily functions are under the direct control of the brain via the nervous system. Hormone action is something apart from this system. Some cellular activity is regulated by hormones, which are manufactured in endocrine glands, and the study of hormones is called endocrinology.

Hormone production

Endocrine glands have a large number of blood vessels passing through them, so hormones can be secreted directly into the bloodstream. The endocrine gland normally produces a prohormone, which is a physiologically inactive molecule. When the hormone is needed, the cell changes the prohormone into the hormone.

Prohormones are stored in the cells that produce them until they are needed. The cell packages them in membrane-bound granules, which are formed by the large numbers of Golgi complexes—systems of smooth-surfaced, double-membraned vesicles.

When the hormone is needed, it is secreted into the bloodstream. Secretion is also often mediated by other hormones. Once in the bloodstream, hormones are protected from being broken down by being linked to plasma proteins until the site of action is reached. These hormone-protein complexes are in equilibrium with free hormone, so as the free hormone is used up, more hormone dissociates from the protein carrier to maintain that equilibrium.

Exerting control

The effects of hormones and the effects of the nervous system are different. The nervous system's direct control leads to a particular, specific, and limited action, which may be a single muscle contraction, an eye changing focus, and so on. On the other hand, hormonal signals mediate the action of cells by slightly modifying their action, so modulating their normal behavior over a longer time frame. Since each hormone has a

▲ Hormones released in male impala during the mating season cause aggressive and competitive behavior. These two males are fighting for the opportunity to mate with the best females.

specific target, it has a specific action, and a deficiency in one hormone will normally have a noticeable effect.

Types of hormone

The human body has upward of 50 hormones, which have many different chemical structures, varying greatly in molecular size. The smallest hormones are derived from amino acids, and examples are epinephrine (adrenaline) and thyroxine. Other hormones are polypeptides and proteins—these include oxytocin, insulin, and thyroid-stimulating hormone. Finally, there are the steroids, which are derived from cholesterol. Sometimes the first two categories are put together and described as peptide hormones.

The simplest way that hormones can be classified is according to the gland that secretes them. Thus thyroxine is the hormone that is secreted by the thyroid gland, parathormone is secreted by the parathyroids, and the adrenal gland secretes adrenaline, which is also called epinephrine. Steroid hormones, such as aldosterone and corticosterone, are secreted by the cortex of the adrenal glands.

The pituitary

The most important structure of the human endocrine system is the pituitary, which is a small pea-sized gland positioned near the bottom of the brain. This small gland produces some 25 different hormones, which, in turn, regulate the whole endocrine system. Among these are the adrenocorticotrophic hormone, which controls the production of steroids in the adrenal glands, the antidiuretic hormone (ADH), which controls the volume of blood plasma, and growth hormone, which stimulates and controls growth.

Hormone action

Epinephrine is one of the body's most important hormones. It governs the so-called flight or fight mechanism. Under conditions of extreme fear or stress, a surge of epinephrine makes the body ready for peak physical response. At such times, the concentration of epinephrine in the blood increases by up to 300 times its normal level.

Epinephrine interacts with receptors in many organs, causing elevation of the heart rate, increase in blood pressure, and the release of extra glucose from the liver to fuel the anticipated extra muscular demands.

Thyroxine is produced by the thyroid gland. Thyroxine is responsible for controlling metabolism—the rate of energy production in the cells. If the thyroid gland is producing insufficient thyroxine, the result is a medical condition known as hypothyroidism, in which the sufferer is slow, soporific, and apparently lazy, with a tendency to put on weight. If the condition occurs during infancy, the child becomes dwarflike and mentally retarded. If the thyroid becomes overactive and overproduces thyroxine, the condition is called hyperthyroidism. The symptoms of an overactive thyroid are weight loss, wasting of the muscles, and night sweats. Hyperthyroidism may be treated using iodine or radioactive iodine. Sometimes a partial thyroidectomy, in which part of the thyroid is removed, is the only effective treatment. Both conditions are measured in terms of Basic Metabolic Rate (BMR). The standard BMR is 100, but hypothyroidism lowers it to 50 or below, and hyperthyroidism raises it to 150 or above.

The body's carbohydrate metabolism is regulated by a number of hormones mostly produced by the pancreas and the adrenals. These hormones have two main functions: to increase carbohydrate reserves by increasing glycogen synthesis and to break down glycogen.

Insulin is one of the pancreatic hormones, and its role is to regulate the uptake of glucose into tissues. Persons suffering from insulin deficiency are called diabetics: the cause of the condition is the inability of cells to take in plentiful supplies of glucose from the bloodstream. The body then has to use fats and proteins to obtain its energy requirements. Excessive insulin is equally serious—glucose flows into the liver and muscles

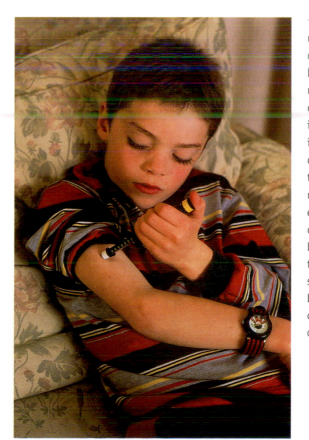

◀ This young boy has a medical condition called diabetes, in which his body is unable to manufacture sufficient quantities of the hormone insulin. Diabetics have to inject themselves with doses of insulin two or three times a day before meals so that there is enough hormone circulating in the bloodstream to cope with the rapid increase in blood sugar that results from the breakdown of complex carbohydrates in foods during digestion.

so that other organs, and the brain in particular, become starved of glucose. Starving the brain of glucose produces a coma and can lead to death in extreme cases.

The cortex of the adrenal gland also secretes a group of hormones, called glucocorticoids. This family of substances includes cortisone and cortisol, and their effects include increasing glycogen uptake by the liver and increasing the breakdown of proteins and amino acids. It has been suggested that the glucocorticoids are in a tug of war with insulin to control carbohydrate metabolism.

Vasopressin is a hormone produced by the pituitary. Its role is to control the amount of water released by the body as urine. The substances released as urine are known as mineralocorticoids and include such hormones as aldosterone. Aldosterone helps to reduce the loss of sodium, chloride, and bicarbonate ions, while at the same time increasing the excretion of potassium and phosphate ions. Another hormone connected with regulating ion release is calcitonin, which, as its name suggests, is involved with calcium ions. Its exact role is to inhibit the release of calcium from the bones.

Growth hormone is released by the pituitary four times per day. Its presence seems essential for normal growth—absence of growth hormone leads to a condition called pituitary dwarfism. Overproduction of growth hormone leads to giantism—a person may grow seven or eight feet tall.

The glucocorticoids and the mineralocorticoids are two main types of steroid hormones. The third class are the sex hormones. These are primarily estrogen in the female and testosterone in the male. Other sex hormones are folliclestimulating hormone (FSH) and luteinizing hormone (LH), which regulate some of the stages of pregnancy.

Estrogen is itself divided into three major hormones—estriol, estrone, and estradiol. Together these influence the development and functioning of the female reproductive tract, the mammary glands, and the development of female body shape. These hormones are mostly created in the ovaries, but they are also produced in the placenta of pregnant women, and small amounts are produced by the adrenal glands in both men and women. The function of estrogen in men is not entirely understood.

▼ The pituitary gland and some of its hormone activities. Four of the pituitary hormones activate an organ to produce another, related, hormone. Some of this hormone in the blood feeds back into the pituitary, thus regulating its production. Some of the hormone passes through the hypothalamus, stimulating neurosecretions. These secretions travel to the portal blood vessels and are carried in nerve fibers back into the pituitary, where they control the release of various hormones.

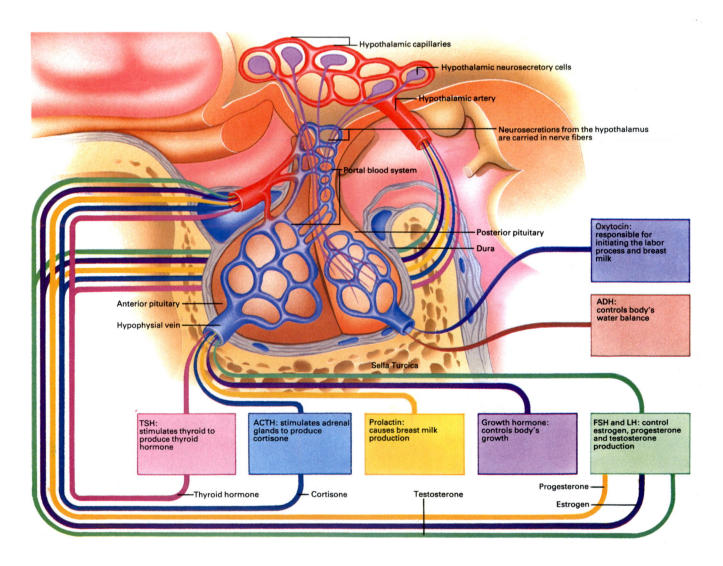

Testosterone is made in the male testes and some is also made in the adrenal glands. This hormone is responsible for the development of the male genitals and for other male characteristics, such as the deepening of the voice that occurs during puberty and the growth of body and facial hair.

Hormone regulation

The effects of over- or underproduction of hormones can be disastrous to the body, leading to a range of medical conditions, or even death. The body therefore needs to regulate the amounts of hormones in the bloodstream. The way it does this is to make sets of hormones whose target organs are the endocrine glands. The trophic hormones are made in the pituitary and include thyrotrophic, adrenocorticotrophic and gonadotrophic hormones. With some hormones—if their concentration becomes too high—their action automatically stimulates the release of other inhibiting hormones.

Hormone receptors and messengers

Hormones affect cell function by forming complexes with special molecules already in place in the cell, thus triggering a sequence of events. Hormone receptors are special molecules that are capable of binding strongly to specific hormone molecules. These receptors occur in very small numbers within the target cells. The positioning of the receptors within the cell varies. In the water-soluble hormones—epinephrine, glucagon, and insulin, for example—the receptors are placed on the cell's surface because these kinds of

◄ Deficiency of iodine causes the thyroid to malfunction and swell, leading to endemic goiter—the condition from which this woman is suffering.

hormones cannot pass through the cell membrane. Sex hormones and adrenal cortex hormones are lipid-soluble and can pass through the cell wall, so the receptors are located within the cell, in the cytosol.

After the hormone binds to its receptor, an intracellular messenger molecule is formed, which interacts with some biochemical activity within the target organ. Water-soluble hormones, such as epinephrine, form the intracellular messenger by stimulating a second messenger called 3,5-cyclic adenylic acid, or cyclic AMP. For steroids, the hormone-receptor complex becomes the intracellular messenger, and no second messenger is needed.

An important aspect of the second messenger model is that the hormone need not enter the cell. Once the hormone has bonded with the receptor, cyclic AMP inside the cell is stimulated. It is the concentration of cyclic AMP that regulates the cell's response, not the concentration of the hormone.

FACT FILE

■ *Certain insect abilities appear to be beyond the capabilities of their normal neural structure and may be accounted for by hormonal effects. Examples include the ability of a foraging worker honeybee to learn the layout of certain mazes faster than laboratory rats. Another example could be the ability of Monarch butterflies to navigate an annual migratory trip from Canada to Mexico and back again.*

■ *Seabirds, such as some ducks and seagulls, are able to drink seawater because of hormonal regulation of special organs. The hormone prolactin stimulates orbital salt glands, which eliminate excess sodium chloride ingested by the birds.*

■ *Pigeon's milk consists of the cells that line the food crops of adult pigeons. They use it to help feed newly hatched young. Hormonal action causes the cells to be sloughed off into the crop, from where they are regurgitated, along with partly digested food, to feed the young.*

SEE ALSO: BRAIN • CARBOHYDRATE • CELL BIOLOGY • ENDOCRINOLOGY • ENZYME • METABOLISM • PHEROMONE

Horticulture

Traditionally, horticulture refers to the growing of fruits and vegetables as food and flowers, flowering shrubs, and trees grown for their beauty.

Commercial horticulture has grown from a hobby or small business to a major industry now very much on a par with many sectors of arable agriculture. Although the land area involved is much smaller than for traditional agricultural crops such as potatoes, wheat, and corn, horticulture demands a higher technological input and an appreciably higher financial investment in the production of each crop.

Because the value of many of these crops is high and their weight slight, a worldwide air-freight industry has been established to meet year-round demands, making obsolete the phrase "in season." The cut flowers sold in New York City may come from Colombia; the trees and shrubs offered in Oregon may have been grown in Florida. To meet competition from foreign countries, American growers have expanded the use of greenhouses to extend their growing seasons.

High-tech greenhouses

Far from simply providing protection from frost, snow, and other unfavorable weather conditions, greenhouses can be warmed and, more recently, have been equipped with powerful lighting, both to allow tropical plants to be grown in a temperate climate and to permit year-round production of temperate zone horticultural crops.

Greenhouses equipped with artificial lighting not only extend growing seasons but also increase the yield of crops in all seasons. Under 24-hour lighting, for example, the yield of roses can be doubled. However, such lighting is expensive to buy, install, and operate. Research now in progress aims to find the right balance between the costs of lighting and the expected profit and determine when, in the life cycle of the plant, additional lighting offers the most benefit.

While hobbyists often use fluorescent lighting on indoor plants, commercial growers prefer high-intensity discharge lighting—the kind used in street lamps—which is up to 33 percent more

▼ Modern commercial greenhouses are high-tech ventures where conditions can be carefully controlled to provide the optimum environment for raising crops. The crops themselves are often bred to exhibit specific characteristics, such as hardiness, flower color, resistance to pests, increased yield, and out-of-season cropping times.

efficient. They are also working with utility companies to try to schedule artificial lighting during off-peak hours, when electricity rates are lower. Eventually, greenhouse lighting may be controlled by computers that take into account utility rates, the brightness of natural light, and the plants' stage of growth.

Yields of many crops have been greatly increased by boosting the level of carbon dioxide (CO_2; the atmospheric gas that plants convert into sugars and starch through photosynthesis) inside greenhouses. By boosting the CO_2 concentration to provide as much of the gas as the plants can absorb, growers have almost doubled yields of greenhouse-grown tomatoes and cucumbers in the last decade.

Ongoing research programs continue to seek a balance between product quality and concerns about pollution and water conservation. It is important to know how much water a crop needs and when it should be applied through irrigation. Similarly, the excessive application of nitrate fertilizers has led to water pollution problems. Researchers are seeking to determine plants' nitrogen needs and ensure that sufficient nitrogen is applied with no wastage and timed correctly so that it is fully used by the plant.

▲ The identification and isolation of the gene responsible has allowed plant breeders to develop this strain of branchless columnar apple called *Maypole*, ideal for even the most restricted garden.

Benefits of breeding

Since plants were first cultivated, growers have sought to improve yields, size, and quality. Initially this goal was achieved by selecting only the best specimens from a crop and sowing their seeds. Then came the crossing of top quality plants in an attempt to combine the best features of each.

Until the end of the 20th century, breeding was hit-and-miss, with thousands of progeny being raised to see if the desirable characteristics had been incorporated. Now researchers are mapping chromosomes, establishing the location of gene sequences for desirable characteristics. Genetic engineering technology dramatically expands the possibilities; it allows, for example, the transfer of potent genetic resistance to insect attack from one plant family to another completely unrelated one.

Particularly in flowering plants and shrubs, the efforts of plant breeders are visible when comparing the wild originals with the range of glamorous cultivars now available. Today's plant breeders concentrate not only on quality and productivity but also on building in natural pest and disease resistance so pesticide usage may be minimized.

FACT FILE

- Cut flowers and ornamental plants and shrubs, once sold only in specialty stores, now appear in supermarkets and mass-merchandising department stores everywhere. To provide the increased volume and low cost these markets demand, growers and distributors have been forced to mechanize.

- Seeding in flats is speeded up by devices that range from simple boxes with rows of holes in them to elaborate machines that use vacuum nozzles to pick up individual seeds, compressed air to deposit them in the soil, and electric eyes to count them. Such machines can place up to 60,000 seeds per hour.

- Some growers seed in "plug flats" made of thin plastic sheets into which hundreds of small cylindrical compartments have been formed. The compartments are filled with soil, and seeding machines place one or more seeds in each compartment. When seedlings are large enough for their roots to hold the soil together the plugs are pulled out and transplanted to pots that have been filled with soil by other machines. Automated transplanting machines are now in development.

- Just as mechanization has brought the end of the family farm, it and other changes may put small growers out of business. "Mom and Pop" operations may not be able to afford to invest in seeding and potting machines, artificial lighting, and other innovations.

Hosiery and Knitwear Manufacture

◄ The knitting head of a circular-knitting machine producing single stockings from which pairs are gathered, although most hosiery today is the one-piece panty hose style. At this stage of manufacture, the garments are undyed.

Hosiery, meaning a protective foot covering to fit inside a shoe, is first mentioned in 8 B.C.E. by the Greek poet Hesiod, who wrote of *piloi*, which were probably made from animal hairs matted together. Knitted socks first appeared between 3 and 6 C.E., although similar garments have also been found in Egyptian tombs—the earliest examples of knitting were found on the site of the town of Antinoë in Egypt. The world's first knitting machine was designed and built in Britain by the Reverend William Lee of Calverton, in 1589 during the reign of Queen Elizabeth I. Although the original produced fairly coarse cloth, it was soon adapted by his brother to produce fine silk stockings.

The Reverend Lee's discovery led to the foundation of the cottage knitting industry, which prevailed until the start of the 20th century. After the industrial revolution, power was applied to knitting machines, and circular machines were built that knitted tubular fabric with a constant rotating motion at high speeds of operation. By the early 18th century, hosiery manufacture was a well-established trade.

The advent of nylon

Circular-stocking manufacture began during the 19th century but only reached its present production levels in the 1960s, following the development of stretch nylon yarn—previously stockings had been made from cotton, wool, silk, or rayon (artificial silk). When nylon yarn was introduced in the 1940s, its thermoplastic properties meant that the knitted tube could be molded into the desired shape. Early stockings were seamed up the back, but with further improvements to the

process, by the 1950s, seamless stockings had become extremely popular. In the 1960s a new, easy garment combined single-leg stockings, which required a suspender belt to keep them in place, into a single garment, known as panty hose in the United States and tights in Britain. With the legs extended and joined at the top to form an elasticated, waist-height body element, these garments were easier to wear than stockings, although they have never completely ousted them in terms of popularity.

Yarn

So widespread is the use of nylon fiber that in some countries the term *nylons* has come to be synonymous with stockings and panty hose. Although other types of fiber are used occasionally, such as silk, wool, or cotton, the bulk of the industry uses nylon yarn that has been specially processed by heat setting and twisting to give good stretch and recovery properties, enabling the manufacture of stockings and panty hose that can stretch to fit and follow the contours of the leg.

Nylon is ideal for the manufacture of hosiery because it is resistant to chemicals, it does not fade in sunlight, and it has a natural luster. When the yarn is delivered to the hosiery manufacturer, it is stored in temperature- and humidity-controlled warehouses to ensure that it remains in good condition. Batch sampling of the yarn is carried out by the laboratory to ensure that correct standards are maintained.

Denier

At this stage the yarn is white and is wound onto plastic-coated tubes called pirns. The weight or thickness of the yarn is measured in deniers—a denier is equivalent to the weight in grams of 6 miles (9,000 m) of yarn, and hosiery is made in 15, 20, 30, and 60 denier nylon, 15 being the sheerest—the smaller the denier number, the finer the yarn. Stocking weight depends on yarn size and the machine's needle spacing. Gauge is the number of needles per 1½ inches (3.8 cm); the higher the gauge number, the closer the stitches. Sheerness depends on a combination of gauge and denier: 60 gauge, 15 denier is closer knit than 51 gauge, 15 denier and is therefore less sheer and wears better although the yarn is the same denier.

To make the yarn into stockings, the pirns are placed on frames above the knitting machines and the yarn is fed into the machine immediately below. Individual pirns are connected by a method called double tailing—when one reel is exhausted a new full reel is automatically brought into operation. About 4 miles (6 km) of yarn are used for each pair of panty hose.

Machine needles

The two types of machine needle in use are bearded and latch needles. The bearded needle was invented by Lee in 1589, but the latch was not developed until 1849 by Matthew Townsend of Leicester, Britain. The latch needle has a pivoted latch element and makes its loop with a simple up and down movement, as in the needle commonly used on domestic sewing machines.

The bearded needle has a springy elongated hook, called a beard, which has to be closed on each operation of the needle. Although its operation is more complex than that of the latch needle, the bearded needle is still widely used in machine knitting because it can be manufactured in fine gauges and it can be used to knit garment sections that are fashioned to shape on the knitting machine. In bearded-needle knitting, the yarn is linked into loops as a first step, and as the needle moves down, a presser closes the beard so that the new loop is pulled through the old loop, which is cast off.

In latch-needle knitting, the action is continuous, and as the needles move down, the hooks take the yarn and pull loops through the old loops. The deeper the needle moves, the greater the length of stitch created.

Circular-knitting machines

Circular-knitting machines are high-speed production machines that can knit rolls of fabric for cutting and sewing in single jersey, double jersey, or purl stitch according to the type of knitting machine. Single jersey is knitted when there is only one set of needles, usually set vertically around the machine, each in its groove. Cams move the needles up and down, and this movement can be controlled for patterning, so that those lifted knit, and those left down miss the yarn and hold their loops; this process is called floating. Color patterns are made using this system. Alternatively, needles may misknit but still take the new yarn, a process called tucking.

Double-jersey knitting requires two sets of needles. In addition to the vertical needles in the machine, there are horizontal needles, and these pull two faces to the fabric, hence the term double jersey. Purl knitting requires needles with hooks at each end, since some loops are knitted to the back and some to the front. Combinations of needle positioning and selection for floating and tucking can produce some of the well-known structures such as interlock, which consists of two ribbed fabrics locked together.

Flat-knitting machines

The knitting action of a simple flat machine is like double-jersey circular knitting except that the needles are in an inverted V configuration. Latch

◄ After the legs of the panty hose have been knitted, the next step is sewing together the seams in the stocking toes. A separate gusset is sometimes inserted when the two legs are sewn together to form the top of the garment.

One of the final stages in hosiery making is shape boarding. The process is controlled and moved automatically, with the operator supervising. The stockings are then dyed, in a range of colors.

needle flat-knitting machines are slower than circular machines, but because the knitting is carried out with a to-and-fro motion, the fabric has a firm edge on each side called a selvedge. The way in which hosiery is made on this type of machine is similar to traditional machine knitting—back and forth across the fabric (weft knitting) using a straight-bar machine that was invented by an Englishman, William Cotton, in 1864.

Machines with bearded needles are called fully fashioned machines and are capable of manipulating the loops at each selvedge so that the different garment sections are knitted to shape without any need for cutting afterward. Flat machines are extremely versatile.

Warp knitting

The final group covers machines that knit the threads vertically, a process called warp knitting. The terms warp and weft are the same as those used in the weaving industry, where weft describes the threads across the fabric and warp describes those running vertically. In one machine for producing shirting fabric, two yarns are fed to every needle in the machine, and since the machine has 2,500 needles 5,000 ends of yarn are fed to the needles at once.

Hosiery-knitting patterns

The latch needle is a common feature of all hosiery machines, used today for the production of panty hose and stockings. There are about 400 to 430 needles in vertical slots on the outside of a cylinder in the machine. These slots extend far below the needles to provide space for the jacks or patterning devices, which are used when making stitches such as micromesh and runresist. During knitting, the fabric falls down inside the cylinder and is pulled down by a vacuum device, dropping automatically on completion into a collection bag at the side of the machine.

The three basic patterns used for hosiery are plain knit, micromesh, and runresist. In plain knit, the yarn is fed into an open hook, which is lowered in its slot until the hinged latch comes up against a previously formed loop, which acts as a barrier. This action closes the latch as the needle continues to move down, and the new yarn is pulled through the old loop, which passes over the needle head as it continues to move down (known as knockover). Having drawn the new loop through the previous one, the needle rises again, ready to start a new cycle. Shape is introduced by increasing or decreasing the size of the loops.

When producing runresist or micromesh patterns, the needles are raised by the jacks, which are in the same slots as the needles and directly below them. Patterns such as these are made by forming two or more loops together. This is done by taking the needle back to a height at which the yarn does not go around the needle stem, so that at the next cycle when the needle descends with a new yarn in the hook, it collects the previous yarn and both are slipped off the end of the latch together when it is raised to its full height.

In runresist patterns there is a larger number of tuck stitches, and every other row is knitted tighter than usual to strangulate the yarn, thus enabling it to resist the spillage of loops that is commonly known as a run. For stockings, the machine can knit the entire garment in one piece, whereas panty hose may be formed as extra-long stockings, which are then cut and seamed together.

Fully fashioned stockings, however, are knitted flat as described above and then joined by a seam up the back. These stockings are shaped by decreasing the number of stitches over the calf. Modern machines at their most automated take just 70 seconds to complete the whole knitting cycle—a marked improvement on the two weeks that it took a hand knitter to complete a single silk stocking in the 16th century. The job today is both less demanding and less skilled, although the resultant hosiery is considerably cheaper.

▶ A warp knitting machine used to make lingerie and shirting fabrics. Similar machines are used to produce lace and even carpets.

Making up

Products that have not been knitted with a closed-seam toe are now delivered to the toe-seaming section where the open toe is sewn up.

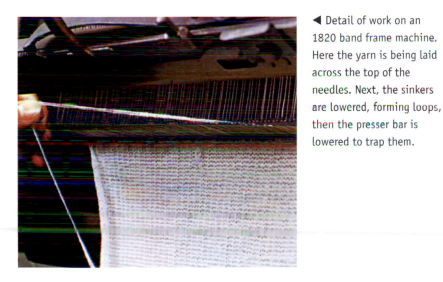

◀ Detail of work on an 1820 band frame machine. Here the yarn is being laid across the top of the needles. Next, the sinkers are lowered, forming loops, then the presser bar is lowered to trap them.

The next operation involves straightening the garment, as the product coming off the knitting machine naturally tends to be quite crumpled. Straightening may be carried out on a heated leg form or on a cold wire frame, somewhat resembling a large hair pin.

The two single legs are now ready to be joined. The operator feeds two halves into an overlocking machine, which first cuts the fabric with a knife and then sews it together. Garments may be joined either without a gusset, joining the two legs to each other to form a simple U seam, or with a variety of gussets, and even full back panels may be used for the larger sizes.

Today, most of this process has been automated. The operator has only to introduce the

▶ Close-up view of a flat-knitting machine showing the yarn being fed to the needles. The machines can be fully automatic or manual.

product to the machine in the required position, and from then on, the machine automatically loads, positions, and clamps the toe before feeding it through a sewing machine head independently of any input from the operator.

Dyeing

Up to this point the garments are plain white in color. They are now ready to be dispatched to the dyehouse, where they are packed in large sleeves, resembling sausages, so that they retain their shape and the dyeing is uniform. During the dyeing cycle, samples are taken and examined to ensure that the garments match the master shades.

The dyed garments are then placed on thermoplastic or wire forms for a final quality-control check to ensure that there are no flaws. Finally, the garments are neatly folded and inserted into individual packets or boxes.

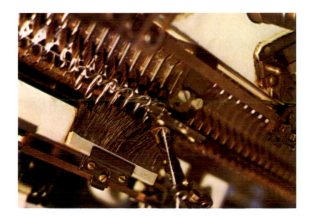

SEE ALSO: CLOTHING MANUFACTURE • DYEING PROCESS • FIBER, SYNTHETIC • LOOM • SPINNING

Hurricane and Tornado

Cyclones are violent circular storms with winds rotating about a calm center of low atmospheric pressure. When they occur in the tropics of the western Atlantic, they are referred to as hurricanes, in the western Pacific they are called typhoons, and if they occur on land they are called tornadoes.

Hurricanes

Near the center, hurricanes are characterized by wind speeds over 73 mph (117 km/h). We know they are spawned over the oceans in a band of latitudes between 5 and 20 degrees on either side of the equator. To grow, they must remain over a sea surface having a temperature of at least 80°F (26°C). They moderate and eventually die, either when they drift northward (in the Northern Hemisphere) over cooler seas or are cut off from their moisture supply by passing over extended areas of dry land. The center of a hurricane is called the eye. This area often experiences only light breezes or even complete calm. The surface pressure generated in the eye by the weight of air in the column above is similar to that found at a height of 3,000 ft. (900 m) in the area near the periphery of the storm.

Air attempts to rush toward the center of the hurricane and fill the void, but because of the rotation of Earth, such a flow is deflected and forms a spiral, which rotates counterclockwise in the Northern Hemisphere but clockwise south of the equator. This phenomenon, called the Coriolis effect, causes the hurricane to develop in a way similar to that of a spinning ice skater who increases his or her speed of rotation by pulling the arms in towards the body—in a hurricane, the inward spiraling air rotates faster and faster.

Peak velocities are reached in a narrow ring surrounding the low-pressure center, with a radial distance of about 20 miles (32 km). The converging air outside this ring, warmed and moistened by the broken sea over which it flows, is forced upward. Water vapor condenses in the ascending air, releasing its latent heat and forming massive cumulonimbus clouds, which in turn generate torrential rain. In the ring of maximum wind, the towering clouds merge into a wall encircling the eye, where cloudiness is minimal and rain is absent.

In its mature form, the hurricane is a self-sustaining heat engine in which the warm core is a result of the heating of the inflowing air by the

▲ This farm in the United States is threatened with destruction by the rapidly moving winds of a tornado. In certain parts of the world, such as central areas of the United States, tornadoes are common and can cause large-scale devastation.

tropical seas. The heat released per day by the condensation of clouds alone is equivalent to about 400 20-megaton hydrogen bombs. Of this, about 3 percent, or the equivalent of 12 bombs, is converted into wind energy. As a result, wind speeds of well over 100 mph (160 km/h) are common in the eye wall. A fully developed hurricane pumps about 2 million tons (1.8 million tonnes) of air per second up and out of the vortex.

Saffir-Simpson scale

The strength of Atlantic hurricanes is measured using the Saffir-Simpson scale developed in the 1970s by the American engineer Herbert Saffir and the former director of the National Hurricane Center, Robert Simpson. This scale uses five categories to indicate the level of damage a hurricane causes: the first category being the least destructive, causing only minor damage to buildings and vegetation, and category five the most destructive, causing catastrophic damage with winds of over 155 mph (248 km/h).

In October 1998, the worst hurricane in 200 years struck the Western Hemisphere. Hurricane Mitch tore across Central America leaving in its wake a trail of disaster, with more than 11,000 people dead and over 3,000,000 left homeless. Reaching speeds of 180 mph (290 km/h) and with gusts of over 200 mph (320 km/h), this hurricane reached category five on the Saffir-Simpson scale, causing billions of dollars of damage. Worse hurricanes than this, however, have been experienced in Bangladesh, where vast areas of low-lying ground make the country vulnerable to the flooding caused by hurricanes. In November 1970, one of the most devastating cyclonic storms in history hit Bangladesh. An estimated 300,000 people died before the storm-driven water receded.

Although the main characteristics and effects of hurricanes can be described, much more must be known before we can predict their behavior in specific instances. The first task is to identify embryo storms at an early stage, and the closest monitoring is essential if their subsequent development is to be forecast with any accuracy. In the North Atlantic, for example, out of approximately 100 seedlings, or cloud clusters, observed each season, about 60 or 70 can be traced to the African coast—the prevailing easterly winds carrying them toward the Caribbean Sea. Of these, perhaps nine or ten become tropical storms, and about seven become fully fledged hurricanes.

Since the 1960s, the development of satellite imagery providing an overview of developing clouds and their movement has allowed much improved monitoring of weather patterns over

▼ Tornadoes arise when severe thunderstorms draw in enough moist warm air to cause rotational motion of the thundercloud. As more warm air is drawn in, the core begins to rotate violently until the whole thundercloud is rotating and touches the ground, forming a tornado. Powerful winds are created at the base of the tornado that can destroy anything in their path.

Cool air descending

Base cloud of thunderstorm

Warm air spiraling upward by updraft

Tornado

Smaller secondary tornado

Warm moist air drawn in

Trees disturbed by wind from tornado

TORNADO FORMATION

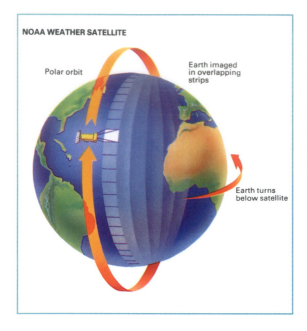

NOAA WEATHER SATELLITE

Polar orbit

Earth imaged in overlapping strips

Earth turns below satellite

◀ A National Oceanic and Atmospheric Administration (NOAA) satellite orbits over the poles. The entire Earth is scanned twice every 24 hours and data are relayed to Earth for analysis of possible weather patterns.

the oceans. Geostationary satellites, locked in orbits that keep them at fixed points over the equator, allow constant supervision of the area beneath them. U.S. research aircraft also fly into storms carrying sophisticated instruments, such as weather radar able to display rainfall patterns and devices for estimating the surface pressure and measuring temperature.

Data are passed via satellite to operation centers responsible for issuing warnings and advice to the public. Reliable forecasts can do much to alleviate the havoc caused by hurricanes, as they make it possible to close down sensitive operations and evacuate areas at risk. Twenty-four-hour landfall forecasts accurate to a few tens of miles are being achieved. It is still not possible, however, to provide adequate evacuation routes capable of handling all the possible demands of major population centers.

Stormfury

The first serious attempts to moderate the effects of devastating storms were made in the 1960s in a series of experiments devised by the American scientists Joanne and Robert Simpson called Project Stormfury. Because the vast energies involved make it unlikely that we will ever be able to dissipate hurricanes, Project Stormfury attempted to find some other way of reducing their force. The method chosen was to transfer the region of maximum up draft and wind outward from the center. The effect was expected to be similar to that of a spinning skater extending his or her arms to slow the rate of rotation. To try to achieve this effect, attempts were made to seed the clouds outside the wall with large quantities of silver iodide. This is a crystalline chemical that promotes freezing of water drops cooler than 32°F (0°C). Provided that

these clouds consist predominantly of such super-cooled water, their conversion to ice (or glaciation) releases latent heat and further invigorates them. The old eye wall was expected to weaken, as its inflow was cut off, and be replaced by a new eye wall where maximum winds would reduce in proportion to the increased diameter of the new circulation. Because of the relationship between wind strength and the damage caused, even a small reduction in wind speed offers the chance of significant reduction in a storm's destructive power.

Mixed results

Three mature Atlantic hurricanes were seeded to test this theory: Esther in September 1961; Beulah in August 1963; and Debbie in August 1969. Peak winds dropped by about 10 percent in Esther and 14 percent in Beulah. The reduction lasted for about eight hours following the seeding. In Beulah, the eye wall decayed and reformed about ten miles outward from the center. The experiment was then redesigned for the more massive seeding permitted by improved aircraft and seeding techniques. Debbie was treated five times every two hours on August 18 and 20. On the first day, wind speed dropped by 30 percent, four to six hours after the last seeding. It recovered on August 19 but dropped 15 percent after the final seeding on August 20.

For the techniques developed by Project Stormfury to work, there must be sufficient super-cooled water in the natural clouds outside the eye wall; if they are mainly ice, seeding cannot initiate further growth. But the probable composition of such clouds is not known. In addition, little information is available on the optimum amount and location of seeding material.

In 1980, Project Stormfury came to an end. No other storms had been seeded and no conclusive evidence had been gained to prove that seeding was responsible for the weakening of the the three hurricanes tested. In the process of researching hurricanes, however, Project Stormfury provided a wealth of information on how hurricanes work.

The future for research in seeding hurricanes is dependent on a number of factors. Legal constraints and concerns about public safety are major influences in determining the nature and pace of hurricane-moderation attempts. Most tropical storms in the Pacific, Atlantic, and Indian Oceans are likely to pass over or near the territorial water and land mass of a number of coastal island nations. Each nation is likely to have a view about the merits of attempted moderation. Present pressures will continue to limit experimentation on hurricanes to the very few storms that have an acceptably low probability of making a landfall.

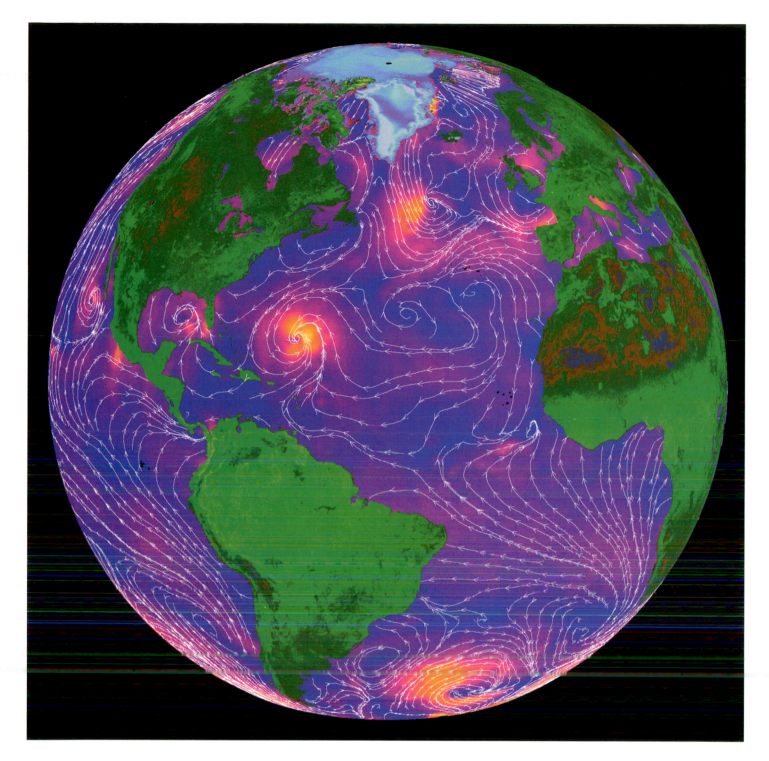

▲ This image of Earth's surface winds was created in a single day using the *QuikSCAT* satellite. The different colors represent different speeds, with blue as the lowest-speed winds and orange as the fastest winds. The orange area to the northeast of Hispaniola is Hurricane Gert.

Tornadoes

A tornado is a violently rotating column of air in contact with the ground that occurs beneath some thunderstorms. Winds of 200 mph (320 km/h) have been inferred, but few instruments survive passage through a tornado, so measurements are rare. A reduction in pressure along the axis of this vortex leads to condensation of moisture so that it takes on the appearance of a funnel protruding through the base of its parent thunderstorm cloud. The area of contact is usually further marked by a mass of lifted debris. A high proportion of embryonic tornadoes fail to develop to ground level but exhibit suspended funnels of rotating air.

Tornadoes are the most ferocious and locally destructive of all wind storms. Hurricanes are usually larger, affect a wider area, and cause more damage to property than tornadoes, but in the United States at least, tornadoes are responsible for more deaths.

A Doppler radar reveals incipient tornadoes by the remote measurement of wind velocity over a wide area. The device uses the Doppler principle that waves emitted or scattered by a moving object increase or decrease in their frequency (or pitch) depending upon the object's velocity toward or away from the observer. The waves in this case are electromagnetic in the centimeter band used by radar, and the objects are particles in the air, such as raindrops or hailstones. A tornado produces a particularly characteristic radar display because the rotation generates a strong motion toward and away from the radar within a very short distance.

Earlier warnings

Doppler radar has demonstrated that the incipient tornado first develops in the lower middle levels of a thunderstorm and thereafter extends both upward and downward, eventually to the top of the storm and to the ground. The fact that the embryonic vortex can be detected before there are any visual signs at the cloud base has obvious implications for improvement in tornado forecasting.

The relative rarity and brief lifetime of tornadoes makes it unlikely that attempts to control them will be successful. However, communities at risk in the United States have well-developed tornado prediction and warning systems. The first

step is to identify and forecast the conditions that are likely to lead to the development of severe thunderstorms. As with all weather forecasts, the process must start from a knowledge of the state of the atmosphere. A network of stations releasing balloon-borne instruments provides this basic data, in the form of measurements of temperature, humidity, and wind as a function of height, although they are unable to describe atmospheric variability with individual storms. A pattern of relatively cool dense air overlying air that is warm and buoyant is typically unstable.

A number of laboratory experiments imitate the structure of tornadoes. The essential features of such experiments are a source of circulation and an induced vertical motion. A cage rotating in air and vented through an axial hole at its top and a rotating cylinder of water into which bubbles can be injected along the axis have both been used. It is found that the updraft does indeed concentrate the vortex until it is balanced by centrifugal forces

▼ This satellite image of Hurricane Floyd, taken as it began to form off the coast of Florida (top right) in September 1999, clearly shows the whirling vortex of clouds with the calm eye of the storm in the center. Hurricane Floyd eventually turned away from Florida but instead hit the coast of North Carolina, resulting in massive flooding.

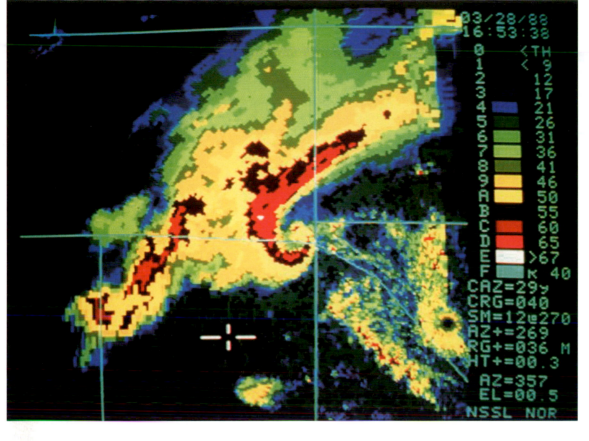

◀ The curved red area of this satellite image shows the development of a hook echo, which is often an indicator of a tornado forming.

acting on the spinning fluid. If this balance cannot be struck, or is established at too large a diameter, no tornadolike feature is generated. However, if a concentrated vortex begins to form, it acts only through the lower end. Fluid drawn inward toward the open end must increase its rate of rotation until a new balance is achieved. In this way, the vortex grows downward until at the base of the tank, friction between the fluid and surface disrupts the balance achieved aloft and ensures that the inflow is concentrated close to the surface of the tank.

Tornado forecasts

Insofar as such experiments are able to reproduce conditions in the atmosphere, they demonstrate that a rather narrow range of conditions is necessary for a tornado to form. Recognition of these conditions is expected to allow further improvement in tornado forecasts. However, in spite of our present understanding of hurricane and tornado origin and behavior, little can yet be done to prevent or lessen their effects. They are among the most complex manifestations of a highly complex weather system.

Fujita tornado scale

Like the Saffir-Simpson scale for hurricanes, the strength of tornadoes also has a system of measurement—the Fujita scale. This scale, devised in 1971 by the Japanese meteorologist Dr. Theodore

Fujita while working at the University of Chicago, classifies tornadoes into six different strength categories beginning with F0, for those tornadoes that cause only minimal damage and reach maximum speeds of up to 72 mph (115 km/h), to F5, for tornadoes that cause devastating amounts of damage with maximum speeds reaching 318 mph (508 km/h). At this speed, a tornado is capable of lifting automobiles for distances of more than 300 ft. (100 m) and totally destroying frame houses. In contrast, the strongest wind speeds of Atlantic hurricanes reach only to F3 or a weak F4 in the Fujita scale, showing how much faster the wind speeds of tornadoes can be.

One particularly severe set of tornadoes hit Oklahoma and Kansas on May 3, 1999. The strongest of these reached F5 on the Fujita scale, and tore across central Oklahoma destroying any buildings and vegetation in its path. A total of 54 people died as a result of these related tornadoes, and it is estimated that more than 9,000 homes or businesses were destroyed with over $1 billion of damage. This central region of the United States is sometimes called "tornado alley" owing to the frequency with which it experiences tornadoes. Unique geographical conditions make this area ideal for the formation of cyclones.

SEE ALSO: AIR • CLIMATOLOGY • METEOROLOGY • PRESSURE • THUNDERSTORM

Hydraulics

▲ The excavator is controlled by hydraulics. The rubber pipes contain pressurized oil, used to direct the jacks that control the movements.

Mechanisms that are operated by liquid under pressure are called hydraulic mechanisms. In order to understand the working of hydraulic mechanisms, it is necessary to consider two basic principles. The first is that liquids are virtually incompressible, even when subjected to very high pressures, and the second, which was discovered by the 17th-century French scientist Blaise Pascal, is that pressure applied to an enclosed liquid is transmitted with undiminished force in every direction. For example, if a cylinder containing a piston 1 sq. in. (6.45 cm²) in area is connected by a pipe to a cylinder containing a piston 10 sq. in. (64.5 cm²) in area and a 10 lb. (4.5 kg) weight is placed on the smaller piston, then a 100 lb. (45 kg) weight will need to be placed on the larger piston to balance the smaller one. It follows that the bigger the larger piston is made, the greater the weight, proportionately, that the 10 lbs. on the smaller piston will support.

Although some research into the principles of hydraulics was carried out by Archimedes as early as 250 B.C.E., it was not until 1795 that the earliest known industrial hydraulic mechanism was made. This was a hydraulic press, designed by the English locksmith and inventor Joseph Bramah, that consisted of a large cylinder containing a piston with a ramrod that was applied to the material to be pressed. Pressure was built up by a hand pump with a small piston, and water was used as the working fluid. This system enabled 19th-century engineers to lift huge bridge girders. Since that time the use of hydraulic machinery has expanded rapidly to every branch of engineering, chiefly because of the simplicity of the components required and also the fact that the liquid can be carried through small-bore piping to operate mechanisms far removed from the source of pressure—aircraft and ships, especially tankers, use hydraulics extensively.

Hand pumps have now been generally superseded by power-driven pumps as a source of pressure, although they are still used on aircraft for servicing the system and in case of emergency. They are also used on simple mechanisms, such as lifting jacks, where they form part of the unit. The lower part of the jack is used as a reservoir for the liquid; the pump is usually at the side and transfers the liquid into the jack cylinder to extend the piston that performs the lifting. A needle valve with a threaded spindle can be unscrewed to let the liquid escape back to the reservoir when the jack is lowered.

Present-day hydraulic systems generally use oil as the working fluid because it offers a good combination of properties, including a wide working-temperature range, typically –40 to 212°F (–40 to 100°C), good lubricating properties, and an anticorrosion action. Where very large quantities of fluid are required oil-in-water or water-in-oil emulsions are used, and synthetic fluids are finding increasing application.

Maximum system pressures vary between 1,000 and 5,000 lbs. per sq. in. (68–340 bar) but are usually about 2,500 lbs. per sq. in. (170 bar). The section of the hydraulic system concerned with the pressurizing and supply of the liquid is the power system, and it is sometimes supplied by manufacturers as a separate unit, called a power pack, that can be made in various sizes to suit the pressure and volume of liquid required to operate the mechanisms.

A power system, or pack, in addition to supplying sufficient liquid at the correct pressure, should not be subjected to undue shock caused by the sudden increases in pressure that can occur when an actuator reaches the end of its operation. Another requirement is that the delivery should be off-loaded when not needed to operate the mechanism, in order to prevent overheating.

A typical power system consists of a reservoir, a power-driven pump (several may be used), a filter, a relief valve, an accumulator, a cut-out valve

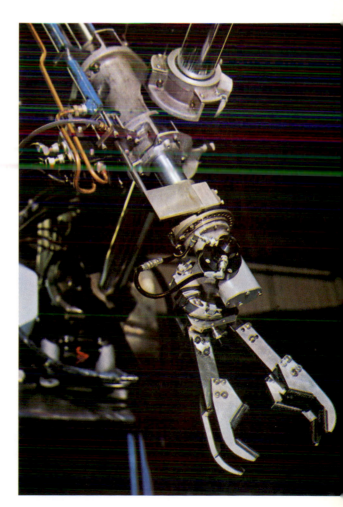
▶ A mechanical arm is operated by means of hydraulic jacks. The feed pipes are at the top left.

(pressure regulator) or a pressure switch, and a nonreturn valve (check valve). The reservoir contains a supply of liquid for the pumps and accommodates the returning liquid from the system, the pumps build up the pressure, and the filter ensures a steady buildup in addition to storing liquid, under pressure, for emergency or supplementary use. The cut-out valve automatically bypasses the liquid from the pumps back to the reservoir when the maximum pressure is reached; the nonreturn valve prevents the pressurized liquid from leaking back when the cut-out valve operates, and the relief valve is incorporated as an additional safeguard if the cut-out valve fails.

From the power system, the liquid is piped to a selector valve (there may be several) that is usually manually controlled and then to a jack, actuator, or hydraulic motor that operates the particular mechanism. A return line is taken from the working element back to the reservoir.

Reservoirs

Reservoirs are tanks, usually of metal, with the pump-feed lines taken from near the bottom and the fluid-return line entering at the top. There is a filler cap at the top and some form of level indicator, such as a sight glass. Tanks are normally sealed to prevent contamination and fitted with a combination breather and air filter. In some cases, the pump is fitted to the reservoir, eliminating the suction line. For some applications, such as military airplanes that are subjected to rolling and aerobatics, the reservoir is a sealed cylinder containing a piston that exerts a slight pressure on the liquid to ensure that the pump is kept primed irrespective of the position of the aircraft.

Pumps

Pumps may be driven directly by the engines on aircraft and vehicles, but on stationary equipment, they are normally driven by electric motors. Two commonly used types are the gear pump and the radial cylinder pump. The gear type is very simple and comprises two meshed gears, one of which is driven. The gears are enclosed in a casing with very small clearances between the gears and case to ensure the minimum of internal leakage. The inlet port enters the case at a point where the gear teeth separate, and the outlet port is taken from the opposite side where they mesh. Liquid is carried around the case from the inlet to be expelled at the outlet. Other rotary-pump designs include the vane type—generally similar to the vane motor described below—and the screw pump.

Cylinder pumps are made in a number of different arrangements but share the common feature that the fluid is compressed by the action of a piston working in a cylinder, while most designs also use self-seating valves. The cylinders may be arranged in line, with the piston movement provided by an eccentric drive; radially, with the pistons driven from a common eccentric; or axially, with a swashplate (an obliquely mounted disk) drive. These pumps normally give a constant delivery but variable stroke versions allow control of the delivery rate.

Accumulators

Accumulators typically consist of a cylinder containing a floating piston. One end of the cylinder is charged with air or nitrogen to a pressure of one-third to half the maximum system pressure, forcing the piston toward the end of the cylinder—the opposite end is connected to the system pressure line. As the system pressure builds up, it is applied against the piston in the accumulator until it is equal to the air pressure. The increasing pressure then forces the piston into the cylinder, the air pressure rising with the liquid pressure.

When the liquid pressure reaches its maximum and the pumps are off-loaded, the pressure is maintained in the system by the air in the accumulator. This reserve of liquid can be used to operate the units until the liquid pressure drops to

◀ A self-propelled hydraulic boom platform, useful for working in intricate building structures where space for maneuvering is limited. The boom itself consists of two or three steel or aluminum sections, each designed to telescope one inside the other. The boom is extended by hydraulic cylinders. The hydraulic pump also powers small motors for turning the chassis in any direction.

a level at which the pumps cut in. However, in many systems, the use of variable-delivery pumps means that accumulators are not needed. On aircraft, additional accumulators are used to maintain a liquid supply to operate the brakes, undercarriage, and flaps (or air brakes), in case of failure of the main supply.

Cut-out valves vary in design but the principle of operation is similar. They consist of a cylinder that houses a spring-loaded piston at one end and has a chamber containing a nonreturn valve at the other. Nonreturn valves are small loaded valves, inserted in the pipelines to allow liquid to pass in one direction only. Liquid from the pumps is introduced into the valve chamber and also passes through an external nonreturn valve into the piston end of the cylinder and into the accumulator and the pressure lines. An additional port, which is between the piston and the internal valve, is connected to the reservoir-return line.

As pressure builds up, it is exerted against the piston, which moves in the cylinders against the spring until an extension on it contracts the nonreturn valve and unseats (opens) it. The liquid from the pumps passes beneath the valve and leaves the cylinder at the return-line port, completing an idling circuit. The system liquid pressure is maintained by the external nonreturn valve, which is now seated (shut). When the system pressure falls below a certain level, the piston is forced back by the spring, the valve becomes unseated, and the liquid from the pumps is again delivered into the system.

Where pumps are driven by electric motors, a pressure-operated switch may be used to stop the motors when the maximum pressure is reached, instead of running the motors continuously and bypassing the liquid. The switch automatically cuts the motors back in when the pressure has dropped to a certain figure.

Relief valves, more heavily spring loaded than nonreturn valves, are inserted between the pressure line and the return line and are set, usually by an adjusting screw, to open at a pressure slightly higher than the cut-out pressure. They protect the system if the cut-out valve or pressure switch fails.

Selector valves

Selector valves are the means by which the operator controls the actuator, or jack, that operates the mechanism. Their function is to transfer the pressure to one side or other of the actuator cylinder and bypass the opposite side to the return. The most common type is one that has a waisted plunger sliding in a ported bore. Four ports are usually employed, one each for pressure and

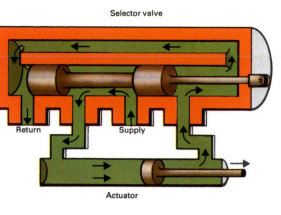

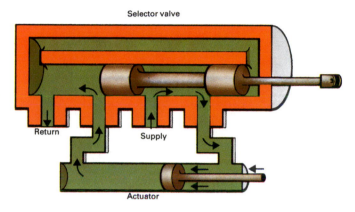

◄ The selector valve and actuator of a hydraulic system. The position of the selector valve piston determines whether the actuator will move right (top) or left (below). Arrows show the flow of hydraulic fluid.

return liquid and one for each side of the actuator. In one position of the plunger, one of the waists forms a passage between the pressure port and an actuator port, the other waist joining the return and the other actuator port, causing the actuator to move in a particular direction. Moving the selector plunger to its other position changes the pairing of the ports and reverses the movement of the actuator. Where the hydraulic mechanism is some distance from the control point, the selector valves may be operated electrically by a solenoid, thus saving lengthy pipe runs and associated problems.

Actuators are sometimes called jacks and consist of a cylinder containing a ramrod and piston. The cylinder is fixed to the structure, and movement of the ramrod operates the mechanism, usually in a reciprocal movement. Hydraulic jacks can also be used to operate semirotary mechanisms such as butterfly valves, which are used extensively on oil tankers.

Hydraulic motors

Whenever a hydraulic system is required to provide continuous rotary power, it is connected to a hydraulic motor rather than an actuator. Hydraulic motors are similar in construction to rotary pumps, two common types being gear motors and vane motors. A gear motor, like a gear pump, consists of two intermeshing gearwheels in a closely fitting housing having both an inlet and

▲ Implements such as plows, cultivators, and disk harrowers are controlled from the tractor by means of two-way hydraulic systems, which can exert pressure in either direction, and so lift or lower the implement as required.

an outlet port. Hydraulic liquid under pressure is fed to the inlet port and passes between the gear teeth and the motor housing to the outlet, thus driving the gearwheels, which are coupled to the mechanism, to be driven. A vane motor has a rotor fitted with a number of movable, radially extending vanes that are spring loaded to press against the motor housing. The rotor is eccentri-cally mounted in the housing. Hydraulic liquid under pressure is introduced through an inlet on one side of the rotor, passes between the rotor and the housing, thus driving the rotor around, and then leaves the motor through an outlet on the other side of the rotor.

To give some indication of the extent to which hydraulic components are used, a modern oil tanker of 250,000 tons (225,000 tonnes) employs some 22 miles (35 km) of piping and over 100 actuators. The selector valves are mounted on a huge console, and each valve has an indicator that shows whether it is opened or closed, enabling the cargo to be discharged with a minimum of personnel.

An increasing use of the hydraulic torque converter, especially for automotive transmission—to replace the mechanical clutch—provides a more efficient and lasting mechanism. Mounted between the engine and the transmission, the torque converter provides a fluid coupling to achieve drive, which is sheared to enable gears to be changed.

The torque converter has proved to be of increasing benefit the larger the engine installation, particularly in earthmoving machinery and road-going trucks with engine outputs of 60 horsepower and upward to 1,000 horsepower.

FACT FILE

- Sophisticated hydraulic automata were employed in ancient Greece in the theater to power special-effects machinery. By opening and closing valves to regulate water flows, statues of gods were moved, doors opened, and singing models of birds appeared to fly into the air.

- By the beginning of the 17th century, there were so many public and private fountains in operation in Paris that normal water supplies were dangerously reduced. Henri IV's Samaritaine pump employed a 17 ft. (5 m) diameter wheel in the Seine that raised 24,705 cu. ft. (700 m³) of river water each day to distribution pipes 75 ft. (22 m) above river level.

SEE ALSO: COMPRESSOR AND PUMP • FLOWMETER • FLUIDICS • HYDRODYNAMICS • HYDROELECTRIC POWER • PRESSURE GAUGE

Hydrocarbon

Hydrocarbons are organic compounds that contain only carbon and hydrogen atoms. They can be divided broadly into two groups, saturated and unsaturated hydrocarbons. Saturated hydrocarbons contain only single bonds whereas unsaturated hydrocarbons contain one or more double or triple bonds. Unsaturated hydrocarbons are generally more reactive than saturated hydrocarbons, for example, they can readily be hydrogenated (combined with hydrogen atoms) to give their saturated counterparts.

Because carbon has a valency of four and hydrogen has a valency of one, each carbon atom has four bonds to it and each hydrogen atom only one. Hydrocarbons, such as ethyne, that contain triple bonds are called alkynes, those containing double bonds, like ethene, are called alkenes or olefins, and those that contain only single bonds, in other words, saturated hydrocarbons, such as ethane, are called alkanes or paraffins. The following compounds are simple examples of alkynes, alkenes, and alkanes:

Alkynes:	$CH{\equiv}CH$	$CH_3{-}C{\equiv}CH$	
	ethyne	propyne	
Alkenes:	$CH_2{=}CH_2$	$CH_3{-}CH{=}CH_2$	$CH_3{-}CH{=}CH{-}CH_3$
	ethene	propene	but-2-ene
Alkanes:	CH_4	$CH_3{-}CH_3$	$CH_3{-}CH_2{-}CH_3$
	methane	ethane	propane

Of the three simplest hydrocarbon compounds containing only two carbons (ethyne, ethene, and ethane), ethyne is the most reactive, because triple bonds are easily broken. Two of these three bonds will readily open to allow the carbons to combine with other atoms and molecules, resulting in a more stable formation. The double bond in ethene is less reactive, but one of these two bonds is also quite readily broken. Ethane, possessing only one bond between its carbons, is the most stable and therefore the least reactive of the three.

In some alkanes and alkenes, the carbon atoms are linked together to form rings rather than open chains; they are called cycloalkanes and cycloalkenes. Cyclohexane and cyclohexene are examples of hydrocarbon rings.

Benzene (C_6H_6) is a special type of hydrocarbon and can be represented by a hexagonal ring structure with three double bonds; it is not normally regarded as an alkene. Although the ring structure does show the atomic constitution of benzene, it is not a very satisfactory representation because the double bonds are not localized

◄ A wide range of household products is based on many aliphatic compounds: (1) wool (a type of protein known as keratin), (2) butterscotch essence, (3) linseed oil, (4) red beans, (5) methylated spirit, (6) olive oil, (7) carboxylic acid, (8) acetic acid, (9) soap, (10) skin perfume, (11) lighter fuel, (12) butane gas, (13) cheese (over 50 percent protein and fat), (14) meat, (15) melamine formaldehyde plastic, (16) starch, (17) sugar. All of these either contain aliphatic compounds, or else they rely on the action of them in a manufacturing process.

between particular pairs of carbon atoms, but the electrons forming the bonds flow around the ring, giving each bond a partly single and partly double bond character. As a result, benzene is much less reactive than might be expected. Hydrocarbons that contain benzene rings are called aromatic compounds.

Production of hydrocarbons

Hydrocarbons, also known in industrial use as petrochemicals, were traditionally produced from coal tar and later, after the great oil discoveries in the early decades of the 20th century, from oil. After the 1940s, when oil was cheap, it became the major source of hydrocarbons. Today, alternative sources are again being developed because of the increases in oil prices following the 1973 and 1979 oil crises. Natural gas is now a major source of hydrocarbons, and coal is again being used.

To produce usable hydrocarbons, crude oil is processed in very large chemical plants known as refineries. First it is distilled to separate it into light and heavy fractions, each having different boiling points. These fractions correspond to mixtures of hydrocarbons with short and long chain lengths, respectively. These fractions are then further processed by distillation and by thermal, catalytic, and hydro cracking, and sometimes catalytic reforming, to give the desired hydrocarbon products.

Alkanes

The lower alkanes, those having from one to four carbon atoms, are gases at room temperature. The simplest, methane (CH_4), is the major constituent of natural gas and as such is used in domestic cooking and heating as well as in the firing of industrial furnaces. Ethane, also a constituent of natural gas, is converted industrially into ethene (ethylene) by a cracking operation and is thus an important starting material for a very wide range of plastics and other petrochemicals. It is found in large quantities in the North Sea off the coasts of Britain and Norway, in the Middle East, and in Canada and the United States. It is a cheaper source of ethene than oil and its exploitation in recent years has put many oil-based processing facilities out of action.

Gases at room temperature, propane (C_3H_8) and butane (C_4H_{10}), are easily liquefied

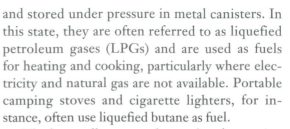

▼ The structure of the benzene ring. Its useful chemical properties are due to the complicated bonding between its carbon atoms.

H
C
H — C — H
C
Double bond   Single bond
C   C
C
H   H
C
H – Hydrogen
C – Carbon
H

and stored under pressure in metal canisters. In this state, they are often referred to as liquefied petroleum gases (LPGs) and are used as fuels for heating and cooking, particularly where electricity and natural gas are not available. Portable camping stoves and cigarette lighters, for instance, often use liquefied butane as fuel.

The lower alkanes are also used as the starting materials in the manufacture of other industrially useful chemicals. Methane can be chlorinated to give such products as dichloromethane (CH_2Cl_2), an industrial solvent, and carbon tetrachloride (CCl_4), an intermediate in the manufacture of aerosol propellants. The chlorination of ethane yields ethyl chloride (CH_3CH_2Cl), which is used in the production of tetraethyl lead ($Pb(C_2H_4)_4$), an antiknock additive in gasoline. Butane also finds further uses and can be dehydrogenated to give the alkene butadiene ($CH_2=CH–CH=C_2$), used in the manufacture of synthetic rubbers and plastics. The cycloalkane cyclopropane (C_3H_6) is sometimes used as an anesthetic gas, although great care must be taken since it forms explosive mixtures with air.

Gasoline is composed of a large number of different hydrocarbons mostly containing from 4 to 12 carbon atoms per molecule. For use in internal combustion engines, it is important that gasoline should have good antiknock qualities, in other words, the fuel-air mixture must not ignite prematurely in the cylinder, and these properties are measured by the fuel's octane number. The alkane isooctane ($CH_3C(CH_3)_2CH_2CH(CH_3)_2$) has very good antiknock properties and is the standard against which other fuels are rated; it is arbitrarily given an octane number of 100. Fuels having octane numbers lower than 100 have antiknock properties inferior to isooctane, while fuels with octane numbers greater than 100 have better antiknock properties. The octane number of a low-grade gasoline can be increased by incorporating additives such as tetraethyl lead, although legislation in the United States and Europe is limiting the amount of lead that is used in this way.

Kerosene is a mixture of hydrocarbons having from 10 to 16 carbon atoms per molecule. It is used as a jet engine fuel and for domestic heating. Lubricating oils, waxes, tars, and bitumen are also mixtures of hydrocarbons with other organic compounds.

Alkenes

The most important alkene is ethene (C_2H_4), which is derived by the cracking of either ethane from natural gas or naphtha from oil refineries. Work is now in progress to develop other large-scale routes to remove the reliance on oil and avoid the political problems of the Middle East: one possibility is ethanol, which can be produced by a variety of fermentation reactions from corn and sugar. Ethene is the starting point for many of industry's basic chemicals and today's modern plastics. It is used in the manufacture of benzene, toluene, styrene, and propene, another alkene; together these chemicals represent the starting materials for 75 out of the top 100 chemicals produced in the United States, including plastics such as polyethylene, polypropylene, and polystyrene.

Ethene can be converted into ethylene oxide (C_2H_4O), an intermediate in the manufacture of ethylene glycol, used as antifreeze in car radiators, and ethanol (CH_3CH_2OH), a widely used industrial solvent and the base for perfumes. Ethene dichloride (CH_2ClCH_2Cl) can be converted into vinyl chloride ($CH_2{=}CHCl$), the starting material for yet another plastic, PVC, which is used in packaging and window frames.

Alkynes

Ethyne (acetylene), a gas at room temperature, is by far the most important of the alkynes. It is prepared either by the action of water on calcium carbide (CaC_2), made by heating together lime and coal, or from petroleum feedstocks under severe cracking conditions. From calcium carbide, it is written

$$CaC_2 + H_2O \rightarrow CH{\equiv}CH + CaO$$

calcium   water   ethyne   lime
carbide

Because of its high reactivity, ethyne is a useful starting material for making other organic compounds. For example, it reacts with hydrogen chloride (HCl), to give vinyl chloride, the starting material for PVC:

$$CH{\equiv}CH + HCl \rightarrow CH_2CHCl$$

ethyne   hydrogen   vinyl
chloride   chloride

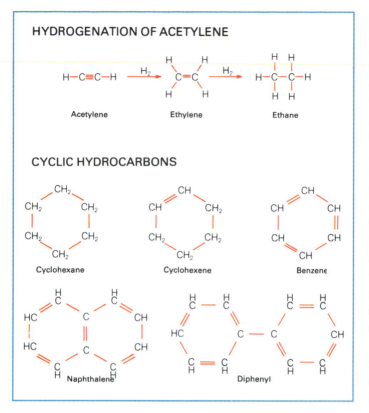

HYDROGENATION OF ACETYLENE

Acetylene   Ethylene   Ethane

CYCLIC HYDROCARBONS

Cyclohexane   Cyclohexene   Benzene

Naphthalene   Diphenyl

▲ How hydrocarbons are hydrogenated (top) to give their saturated counterparts. In cyclic hydrocarbons (bottom), the carbon atoms are linked in rings.

Aromatics

Aromatic compounds are an important group of substances in organic chemistry, all based on the cyclic hydrocarbon benzene. The word *aromatic* is apt because many of these compounds have a pleasant smell. This applies particularly to the essential oils that give plants their fragrances, such as vanillin, oil of bitter almonds, and eugenol, which is found in clove oil. Common aromatic solvents, such as toluene, xylene, and even benzene itself, also have agreeable odors, which unfortunately make them attractive to solvent abusers.

Important sources of aromatic compounds include coal and crude oil. When coal is heated to around 1800°F (1000°C) without any air being present, various volatile products are given off, and the coal is converted to coke. Some of these products are naturally gaseous, such as coal gas and ammonia, but the rest condense on cooling and are collected. The condensed mixture includes crude benzole, crude tar, and naphthalene and is a useful source of benzene, as well as various other principal aromatic compounds, such as xylene, toluene, and phenol.

Toluene, ($C_6H_5CH_3$), is a benzene ring with one hydrogen replaced by a $-CH_3$ group, and xylene ($C_6H_4(CH_3)_2$), is a benzene ring with two hydrogen atoms replaced by $-CH_3$ groups. There are three different types of xylene, depending on the relative positions of the two $-CH_3$ groups on the benzene ring. Benzene, toluene, and xylene are flammable liquids at room temperature.

Benzene is used in the manufacture of several useful compounds: styrene, the starting material for polystyrene; cyclohexane, used in the production of Nylon-6; dodecyl benzene, used in detergents; aniline, used in the manufacture of dyestuffs; and phenol, (C_6H_5OH), the starting material for a number of plastics.

Toluene can be nitrated using a mixture of nitric and sulfuric acids to give the explosive TNT (trinitrotoluene). It is also used to make toluene diisocyanate (TDI), a starting material for plastic foams.

The xylenes are used as solvents in paints, lacquers, and insecticides. Terephthalic acid, which is used to make polyester fibers such as Terylene, is derived from one of the xylenes.

Useful benzene derivatives

Most households contain numerous products made from aromatic compounds. There are disinfectants based on phenol, (C_6H_5OH), better known as carbolic acid. Unlike phenol, which is very corrosive and therefore dangerous, its derivatives, chlorophenolic products such as chloroxylenol and TCP, are effective antiseptics. Phenol is also used for making various phenol formaldehyde resins, the best known being the plastic Bakelite. The cresols, which are methylated derivatives of phenol, are widely used in the Lyso type of disinfectant. Aminophenols are important starting materials for many dyes, and they can undergo modifications to give two different but very useful compounds: phenacetin, a painkiller, and dulcin, which is a sweetening agent. Polyhydric phenols contain more than one hydroxyl (–OH) group. The hormone adrenaline, used as a heart stimulant, is synthesized from one of these phenols, catechol. Other important members of the group are hydroquinone, which is a photographic developer, and resorcinol, which is the basis of the powerful antiseptic n-hexylresorcinol, the active constituent of Listerine.

When phenol is nitrated with nitric acid, it forms the bright yellow crystals of picric acid, which is sometimes used to relieve pain on bad burns. Picric acid is also used to make dyes and a high explosive known as lyddite. Toluene, $C_6H_5CH_3$, is a liquid that closely resembles benzene, probably best known for its pale yellow, crystalline derivative trinitrotoluene, the explosive TNT. It is also the starting point for many aromatic compounds, among them the painkiller novocaine, the sweetener saccharine, and various dyes.

Another aromatic solvent similar to toluene and benzene is xylene, $C_6H_4(CH_3)_2$. The synthetic fiber Terylene (Dacron) is made from xylene and ethene. The xylene is converted to terephthalic acid, $C_6H_4(COOH)_2$, and the ethene to the alcohol ethylene glycol. These products condense to form a polymer fiber (polymers have long chainlike molecules from which their strength is derived). One well-known plastic derived from benzene is polystyrene, a light and strong material made from dehydrogenated ethyl benzene, which gives vinyl benzene—the basis of the links in the polystyrene chain.

Benzene is also found as a constituent of many useful drugs, especially those used to treat tropical diseases. Paludrine, for example is a useful drug against malaria. One of the forms of penicillin (penicillin G) contains the benzene ring, and the benzene-based drug sulfanilamide is effective against pneumonia.

◄ As the basis of a vast range of aromatic compounds, benzene can have any or all of its hydrogen atoms replaced by other atoms or radicals to form compounds with widely differing properties: polyester netting is a typical example.

FACT FILE

■ The structure of benzene was discovered in 1865 by the German chemist Friederich August Kekulé. He had been working to discover how the carbon atoms in benzene were arranged when in a dream he saw the carbons dancing before his eyes. The carbons formed themselves into snakes and proceeded to seize their own tails. Kekulé immediately woke and used this dream to work out that benzene must have a ring structure.

■ Some of the simplest forms of plants—algae—are capable of producing hydrocarbons such as methane, which can be used as a fuel. In the United States, several large-scale plants have been built to treat domestic sewage using microscopic green algae. The algae produce oxygen gas, fermentable material, and useful animal foodstuffs. The oxygen released is used to treat the sewage, and about 50 percent of the solar energy trapped by the algae can be obtained as methane—a very high ratio. This sewage-treatment process saves energy and reduces costs, since much less oxygen has to be supplied from outside the system.

SEE ALSO: ATOMIC STRUCTURE • CARBON • CHEMICAL BONDING AND VALENCY • CHEMISTRY, ORGANIC • HYDROGEN • OIL REFINING

Hydrodynamics

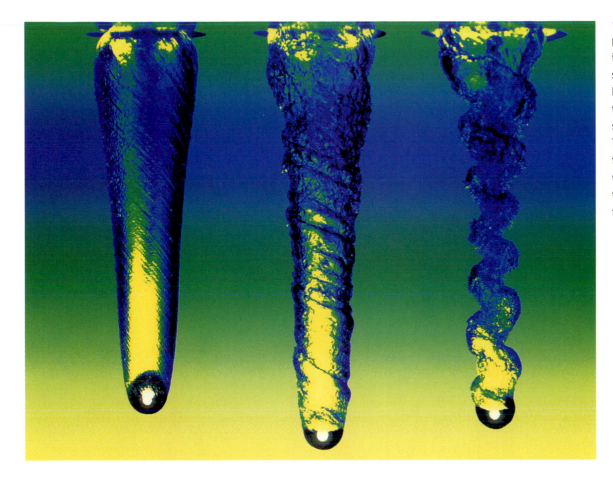

◄ High-speed photography of whirlpools in water caused by rapidly spinning balls. The balls have been dropped from the same height, but are spinning at different rates. Their spin rate increases from left to right. The whirlpools, or vortices, they produce depend on their speed of rotation.

Hydrodynamics is the study of the forces and pressures of fluids in motion and can be taken to include hydrostatics, which is concerned with the study of the forces and pressures in a liquid at rest.

The analysis of a fluid at rest is much simpler than that for a moving fluid, and it is possible to obtain precise solutions. An essential feature of liquids is that applied pressure is evenly distributed through the fluid, so the pressure at any depth is given by $P = Pa + \rho gz$, where P is the pressure, Pa the applied pressure, ρ the density of the fluid, g the gravitation constant, and z the depth in the fluid.

Because the pressure in a fluid increases with depth, the fluid will produce a force on a body submerged or floating in it. This force is the buoyancy, which acts upward and is equal to ρgV, where V is the immersed volume of the floating body: this is the principle of Archimedes.

Fluid flow

Analysis of the flow of a liquid is considerably simplified by considering an ideal fluid that has no viscosity and is incompressible. The flow pattern of the fluid can be described by the use of a set of streamlines, which are noncrossing, imaginary curves drawn along the direction of flow. If the streamlines are drawn so that the same quantity of fluid flows between all adjacent pairs of streamlines, the way the streamlines bunch up or move apart gives an indication of the flow.

For any fixed region in a fluid, the mass of fluid entering the region must be the same as the mass leaving—this is the continuity equation: ρAU = constant, where A is the cross-sectional area of the flow region and U the flow velocity. For incompressible fluids, this equation becomes AU = constant. As the area decreases, the mean velocity increases.

As a fluid moves along a streamline, its velocity may vary, and because by Newton's First Law of Motion, such variation must be accompanied by a force, the pressure in the fluid can be assumed to change. Analysis of the changes associated with a particle of fluid in motion led to Bernoulli's theorem (named after the Swiss mathematician who published one of the first analyses of fluid flow in 1783):

$$P + 1/2\rho\, U^2 + \rho gz = \text{constant}$$

Alternatively,

$$P/\rho g + U^2/2 + z = \text{constant}$$

This shows that the total energy—the sum of the pressure, kinetic energy, and potential (static) energies per unit volume—of the fluid is constant, providing an explanation of the phenomenon by which a stream of water from the end of a pipe can be converted into a strong jet by constricting the end of the pipe. Such constriction increases the pressure in the pipe, and as the water comes out past the constriction, the pressure energy is released and converted into kinetic energy—the jet.

If a jet is directed against a surface, it will exert a force on the surface. Similarly, a force can be produced by a change in the fluid velocity or direction, and the effect of such changes is given by momen-tum theory, which shows that the force is equal to the change of momentum (mass times velocity) of the fluid. This effect is of importance in the design and operation of hydrodynamic machines.

Real fluids

Although analysis is simplified by the assumption of an ideal fluid, all real fluids have viscosity that tends to oppose fluid motion. Experiments carried out in the 1880s by the English engineer Osborne Reynolds showed that the flow of a fluid in a pipe altered as the flow velocity changed, the type of flow depending on the relationship between the inertial and viscous forces in the fluid.

▼ Moving fluids are affected by a large number of factors, such as density, velocity, pressure, compressibility, and viscosity. These drawings illustrate general concepts of flow.

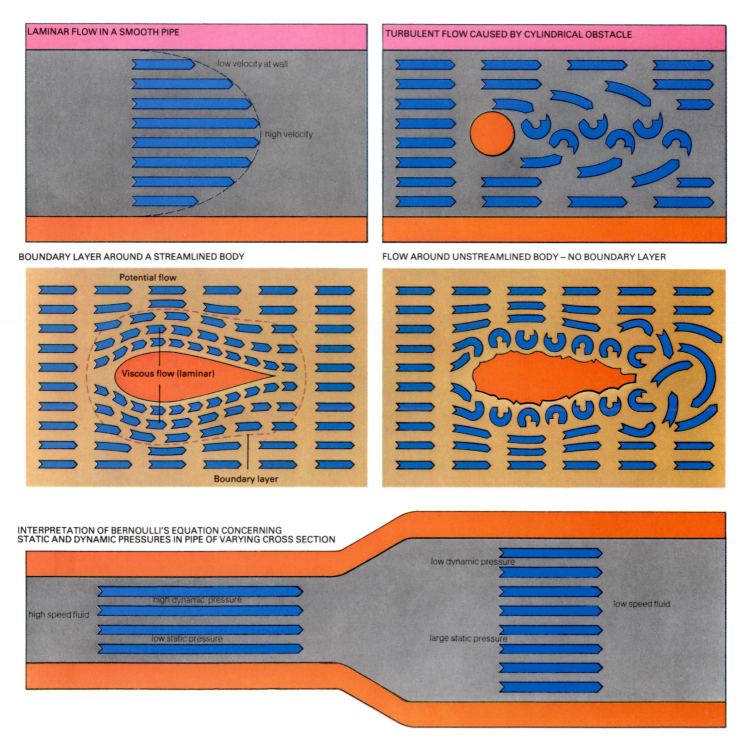

LAMINAR FLOW IN A SMOOTH PIPE

low velocity at wall

high velocity

TURBULENT FLOW CAUSED BY CYLINDRICAL OBSTACLE

BOUNDARY LAYER AROUND A STREAMLINED BODY

Potential flow

Viscous flow (laminar)

Boundary layer

FLOW AROUND UNSTREAMLINED BODY – NO BOUNDARY LAYER

INTERPRETATION OF BERNOULLI'S EQUATION CONCERNING STATIC AND DYNAMIC PRESSURES IN PIPE OF VARYING CROSS SECTION

high dynamic pressure

high speed fluid

low static pressure

low dynamic pressure

low speed fluid

large static pressure

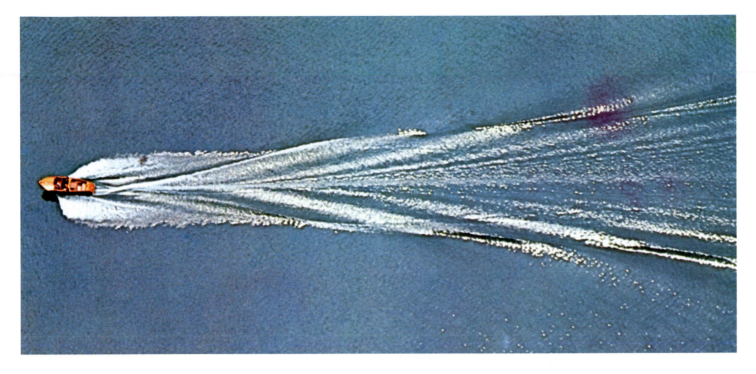

From his experiments, Reynolds derived the non-dimensional Reynolds number: $R = Ul\rho/\mu$, where U is the fluid velocity, l a characteristic dimension of the system (the diameter for pipe flows), ρ the fluid density, and μ the fluid viscosity. From his experiments, Reynolds identified two main types of flow: laminar and turbulent. Laminar flow is smooth, the liquid closely follows the surface it is flowing through or over, and it occurs at lower fluid velocities with Reynolds numbers of up to 20,000.

At higher speeds, the flow starts to break up as individual fluids move in a complex and erratic manner. This effect occurs with Reynolds numbers over 40,000, the transition from laminar to turbulent flow occurring at Reynolds numbers in the range 20,000 to 40,000.

If the liquid flow has a free surface, as with the flow in an open channel or past a ship's hull, gravity forces also come into consideration, and the flow characteristics are given by the Froude number (after the English naval engineer William Froude):

$$Fr = U/(gl)^{1/z}$$

These dimensionless numbers are used in dynamic modeling of hydraulic flows, for example, in model tests to predict the drag of a ship. Provided the Reynolds number and Froude number of the model correspond to those calculated for the ship, the drag coefficient obtained from model tests will also apply to the full-size ship and can be used in performance calculations. Dimensional analysis of this type can be applied to a range of other flow problems.

▲ This motorboat is traveling faster than the surface waves it produces—giving them their characteristic and familiar shape.

Unsteady flow and cavitation

Although much of the analysis of fluid dynamics is concerned with steady flows, there are a number of important cases of unsteady flow, where the momentum of the moving fluid is a major factor. Such unsteady flow can result from the sudden opening or closing of a valve, which generates a shock wave that travels through the fluid. A common example is the knocking sound sometimes heard from a faucet when it is shut off quickly. This effect is known as water hammer, and the forces associated with the pressure wave can be considerable and lead to damage of the faucet and pipework. The problem is particularly severe with pipelines running from a reservoir to a turbine. Such systems often include surge tanks to absorb the shock waves.

In rotodynamic machinery and with high-speed flows, the dynamics of fluid motion sometimes result in cavitation, which is the production of low-pressure areas in regions where the fluid velocity is high. If the local pressure falls below the vapor pressure of the liquid, vaporization occurs, giving small bubbles in the liquid. These bubbles can be carried in the fluid flow to areas of higher local pressure, where they collapse. This collapse may result in high local pressures, which can cause severe damage to nearby solid surfaces. Cavitation also produces additional noise and vibration and may cause a reduction in the efficiency of such machines as marine propellers, water turbines, and centrifugal pumps.

SEE ALSO: Fluidics • Hydroelectric power • Magnetohydrodynamics • Newton's laws • Propeller • Viscosity • Water

Hydroelectric Power

The cycle of evaporation, rainfall, and runoff set in motion by the Sun's heat and Earth's gravity is ceaseless. By harnessing the energy of water as it flows back to the sea, water wheels, and turbines convert this natural, renewable resource into usable power. In fact, falling water is the source of a quarter of the world's electricity.

To construct a hydroelectric plant, it is necessary to dam a river. The result is a vast reservoir of water extending many acres in a floodplain. Electricity is generated by converting the kinetic energy of the water as it flows down pipes and through turbines. Dams are usually one of three types: gravity, built of timber, earth, or rock fill, where the weight of the dam alone gives stability; buttressed or hollow, made of reinforced concrete and inclined toward the upstream; and arched, used in narrow gorges.

Two main types of hydroelectric plants can be seen around the world, although no two are exactly alike. First, there are the high-head projects used in mountainous areas, which have drops of 500 to 5,000 ft. (150–1,520 m)—the head is the distance through which the water falls onto the turbines. Second are the low-head projects of up to 100 ft. (30 m).

The theoretical amount of energy available from a hydroelectric plant is given by the volume of water in the dam multiplied by the head. The continuous power than can be supplied is determined by the minimum flow. If the turbine can be shut down for periods of low energy demand, the water can be conserved and then used later during periods of high demand. This is called pondage.

It is common to take this idea further and use electricity from conventional and nuclear power stations to pump water from the bottom to the top during the night, when power demand is at its lowest. Some projects use the electricity generated by the plant itself to return water to a higher level during off-peak hours. In this way, the reservoir acts as a kind of storage battery, because the energy from the falling water can be used again during peak-demand periods. The high efficiency of hydroelectric plants makes this economical, and it is the practice used in the two massive hydroelectric "hollow mountain" plants in Britain—Dinorwic in Wales and Ben Cruachan in Scotland—where the plants were constructed within mountains and artificial lakes were hollowed out of the mountain tops to hold the water.

The turbine

Two main types of turbine have been developed: the impulse turbine, with buckets arranged at the perimeter onto which a high-pressure jet of water

◀ Construction of a hydroelectric power station near Viluisk in Russia. The river on which the station is being built has been diverted to allow construction of the dam. It will hold back a large reservoir of water. To generate electricity, sluice gates are opened to allow the water to flow through turbines. Hydroelectric power does not emit any damaging pollutants and can respond very quickly to changes in demand for power.

▲ The vast power of Niagara Falls is tapped by a number of hydroelectric projects that send the water down tunnels into turbine halls. The plants are so unobtrusive they cannot be seen on this infrared photograph.

is directed, and the reaction turbine, which consists of a vaned wheel inside a curved outer casing.

Both types of turbine are used in hydroelectric plants. A development of the impulse turbine, called the Pelton wheel—after Lester Pelton, a Californian engineer—is used where there is a high head and a low volume of water flow. Efficiencies of over 90 percent have been achieved, and Pelton wheels delivering over 60,000 kW have been built.

Various designs of reaction turbine have been used, but they are generally more suited to high-flow situations than the impulse type. With a high head, efficiencies can exceed 90 percent. Despite the highest efficiencies being available from higher heads, the reaction turbine is much better suited to low-head schemes than the Pelton wheel.

In a hydroelectric plant, the turbine or turbines are connected to conventional electricity generators, as found in ordinary coal- and oil-fired power stations.

Planning hydropower

There are many planning considerations before a hydroelectric project can be built. There are certain locations that, although they appear to offer a suitable fall in a river, may not make a successful project. Water flow is crucial, not only to supply the reservoir but also to ensure there is a sufficient amount of water left to supply areas downstream of the dam. Evaporation losses may reduce the river flow farther down the river, and the opposite may also be true—the plant may not be able to cope with seasonal flooding because the flow exceeds its capacity.

The power output from hydroelectric plants is progressively reduced as the reservoir silts up. Although silting is inevitable, the site must be surveyed so that the expenditure involved in the

▶ The force of water is used to power turbines that generate electricity. Hydroelectricity is a clean source of power, but it can have environmental drawbacks if the water source has to be dammed to provide sufficient flow.

plant is not wasted because the dam has silted up within a few years.

The land that is going to be flooded must be considered. It may simply not be surplus or it may be of high quality, in which case the economic advantage of hydropower must be balanced against the loss of farming land. Countries with large areas of barren, mountainous terrain have few troubles siting hydroelectric schemes, although social and environmental considerations are of increasing importance. The November 2000 report of the World Commission on Dams concluded that while hydroelectric dams came closest to fulfilling expectations, most dams fail to bring all of their predicted benefits.

Hydroelectric power and the world

The hydroelectric power potential of the world is very large. Some rivers are particularly notable for their potentials. The Yenisey-Angara in Russia is estimated at some 64,000 MW, and India's Bramaputra at some 20,000 MW.

If completed, the Three Gorges Dam on the Yangtze will be the largest hydroelectric dam in the world. It will be 6,342 ft. (2,150 m) wide and 3,327 ft. (185 m) high, across the world's third longest river. Its reservoir will be over 335 miles (600 km) long. Construction began in 1994 and is scheduled to take 20 years; the project is expected to cost over $24 billion.

Areas of the world that are poor in coal and oil, such as South America, Africa, and Southeast Asia, are notable for their great hydropower resources. At present, only about 20 percent of their resources have been exploited. This situa-

▶ A Kaplan-type reaction turbine being installed at a hydroelectric plant.

tion is in stark contrast to the 80 percent exploitation of hydropower resources in Europe and 60 percent exploitation in the United States.

The overall figure for world exploitation of hydropower is about 16 percent—some 372,000 MW—and output is growing by about 3 percent a year. This power output would take around 600 million tons (540 million tonnes) of coal to achieve if conventional power plants were used, so hydropower is making a major contribution to conserving the world's fossil energy resources.

Full utilization of the world's hydropower resources is extremely unlikely for several reasons, including loss of land. For example, the Cabora Bossa scheme in Mozambique, giving an output of some 2,000 MW, required an area of 1,042 sq. miles (2,700 km²) to be flooded. Such an area of land would not be available in many highly urbanized European countries.

The enormous cost of hydroelectric plants is just one factor. More crucial is the health of a country's economy. Hydroelectric plants are suitable for an economy that has a high demand for electricity. Therefore, there must be enough people who can purchase electrical appliances to pay for the scheme. A poor country may simply have insufficient demand for electricity to enable hydropower to be an economical alternative to oil.

Hydroelectric power can never provide the world with all its energy needs, but exploitation of the world's reusable energy looks certain to expand. As conventional energy sources, such as oil and coal, dwindle and become more expensive, hydroelectric power will become more attractive.

◀ The pumped storage hydroelectric power plant at Dinorwic in north Wales, Britain, consists of four 75 MW turbogenerators. During off-peak periods, they serve the additional function of pumping water 4,500 ft. (1,370 m) back to the storage reservoir. This drawing shows a sectional view of the plant's generator, a Francis-type turbine and storage pump. The technician at the bottom indicates the plant size. (1) Transformer, (2) valve controls, (3) gantry crane, (4) valve pits, (5) No. 1 generator, (6) access hatch, (7) No. 2 generator, (8) bearing, (9) cooling fan, (10) heat exchanger, (11) rotor windings, (12) stator windings, (13) turbine inlet, (14) inlet valve, (15) reaction turbine, (16) guide-vane servo, (17) relief-valve servo, (18) relief valve, (19) guide vanes, (20) turbine governor, (21) oil coolers, (22) oil pumps, (23) coolant system, (24) governor oil pump, (25) water outlet, (26) discharge pipe, (27) pump coupling, (28) discharge valve, (29) valve servo, (30) storage pump, (31) impeller, (32) pump inlet, (33) pump-inlet gate, (34) oil filter.

SEE ALSO: Dam • Electricity • Energy resources • Energy storage • Tidal power • Turbine • Water supply • Wave power

Hydrofoil

The speed that can be achieved by a conventional displacement ship is limited by the power needed to overcome resistance to motion. This resistance has two main components. One is the skin effect, by which friction between the hull and the water increases with speed. The other is the resistance of waves produced by the movement of the ship increasing with the speed of the vessel.

Various approaches have been adopted to reduce these factors. In the planing hull, for example, the front of the vessel rises out of the water at high speeds, and there are surface skimmers, which lift the vessel clear of the water surface. Included in this broad classification are hovercraft, ground-effect craft (essentially very low-flying aircraft that rely on ground effects to provide lift), and hydrofoils.

The hull of a hydrofoil is lifted out of the water and supported by the lift from a set of water wings, or hydrofoils, which are basically similar to the aerofoils that give an aircraft lift. Because water is more than 800 times denser than air, however, a hydrofoil can be made much smaller to give the same amount of lift. As the craft gathers speed, the hydrofoils start to provide lift, the amount increasing with the speed until it is sufficient to lift the main hull clear of the water. The first working hydrofoil was built in 1900 by an Italian, Enrico Forlanini, but hydrofoils did not come into common use until the 1950s.

Foil types

Essentially, there are two main types of foil in general use—the surface-piercing system and the fully submerged system. A third type, the semisubmerged system, is used for calm-water applications. There are also hybrid designs that use a combination of foil systems. With all foils, the aim is to achieve stable operation, allowing the main part of the vessel to ride evenly above the water.

The surface-piercing system gains stability by the design of the foils themselves. As the name suggests, the foils pierce the surface of the water with V-shaped tips beneath the hull, one on each side of the craft. The lift provided by a foil system increases with the speed through the water, lifting the vessel higher out of the water, but with a V foil, the upward movement reduces the amount of the foil that is submerged. This reduction in submerged foil area reduces the amount of lift, so the vessel ends up riding at a stable height.

Similarly, if the craft is subjected to a forward-pitching movement so that the bow moves down, the forward foil will be pushed deeper into the water, producing more lift and causing the bow to move up again. Rolling of the vessel to one side causes the foil section on that side to move deeper into the water, giving extra lift that counteracts the roll. Although this design is effective and widely used, it is restricted in the amount of wave clearance that can be achieved to a maximum of

▼ A hydrofoil leaves Piraeus, Athens' busy port, carrying tourists to the Greek islands. The hydrofoil reduces the journey time by more than two-thirds.

around 10 ft. (3 m) and so is not suitable for really rough conditions.

This limitation is overcome by the fully submerged foil design, which has the further advantage that it can be made lighter and smaller than a surface-piercing V foil of the same lift. A fully submerged foil, however, is not stable on its own, so a control system has to be fitted to sense the motion of the vessel and adjust the action of the hydrofoils accordingly. The lift produced by a foil can be varied by tilting it to alter the angle of attack or by the use of flaps on the trailing edge of the foil. Sensing can be carried out with a mechanical system fitted to the bow of the vessel. The sensor rides on the waves and drives a linkage to control the foils.

Alternatively, hydraulic actuators can be linked to an electronic sensor system to control the foils. With such a system, there is an acoustic sensor at the bow to measure the wave height, along with a system of gyroscopes to measure pitch, roll, and yaw. Information from these various sensors is processed and used to control hydraulic actuators, which adjust the foil action to maintain stability.

The performance of all types of foils is dependent on the smooth flow of water over the foil to give lift. A smooth flow is not always possible because of the mechanics of fluid flow, and practical foil design has to take such factors into consideration. For example, at high speeds, the

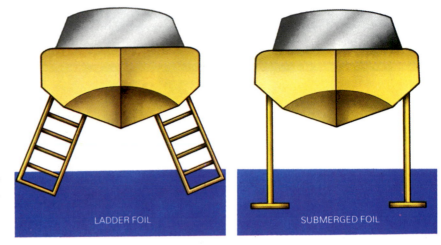

LADDER FOIL   SUBMERGED FOIL

pressure drop (necessary for lift) caused by the flow over the foil surface can be great enough to reduce the pressure below atmospheric pressure, and ventilation can occur. As a result, air is sucked down along the foil, destroying the flow and the lift. Local reduction in pressure over the foil can lead to cavitation effects with bubbles of dissolved air or water vapor forming in the low-pressure areas. Cavitation destroys the lift and can also lead to severe erosion of the surface.

Hydrofoils are limited to only moderate sizes and ranges. One design that attempts to avoid the problem of limited range is the U.S. Navy's Extended Performance Hydrofoil (EPH). This craft has a combined fuel/buoyancy tank that remains fully submerged when the main hull is foilborne. The tank is streamlined to give minimum drag and provides about half of the total foilborne lift requirement. This arrangement gives the craft a range well beyond that of any other comparable hydrofoil.

Drives

When a hydrofoil is foilborne, the hull is fully out of the water, so the normal arrangement of propeller shaft is impracticable. A number of different arrangements have been used. Screw propellers are normally powered through a Z drive, passing from the hull down to the propeller mounting on the submerged hydrofoil (or hydrofoil support). A less-conventional arrangement is used in the Boeing jetfoil, which uses a jet of water to provide drive thrust. Sail and even pedal-powered hydrofoils have also been produced. A pedal-powered hydrofoil has a maximum speed of about 15 mph (24 km/h) as opposed to the 12½ mph (19.5 km/h) that can be achieved with a racing single-scull rowing boat.

▲ The hydrofoil below the hull acts as a wing in water, providing lift in the same manner as an aircraft's wing. In some designs, the foil is submerged in the water. The amount of lift is controlled by altering the angle of the foils by jacks, which are rods moved hydraulically. They press down on or pull back from the hydrofoil to change its angle of inclination.

SEE ALSO: HYDRODYNAMICS • SAILING • SHIP

Hydrogen

There are two other isotopes of hydrogen. Deuterium, symbol D, has one neutron and one proton in its nucleus (the nucleus of ordinary hydrogen is a single proton) and is known as heavy hydrogen because it is twice as heavy as ordinary hydrogen. Tritium, symbol T, has one proton and two neutrons in its nucleus and so is three times as heavy as ordinary hydrogen. Tritium is radioactive—its half life is 12.5 years. Being radioactive, it can be used for labeling hydrogen-containing compounds and is used in radiobiology. Deuterium is used to produce lithium deuteride, which is an essential part of the hydrogen bomb.

Manufacture

In the United States, about 75 percent of all hydrogen is manufactured from natural gas, which is mainly methane (CH_4). Refinery gas, produced during oil refining, is a mixture of methane, propane (C_3H_8), and butane (C_4H_{10}) and can also be used for hydrogen production. The natural or refinery gases are treated with steam at about 1292 to 1472°F (700–800°C) in the presence of a nickel catalyst. The gases react with the water, forming carbon monoxide and hydrogen:

$$CH_4 + H_2O \rightarrow CO + 3H_2$$
methane   water   carbon   hydrogen
monoxide

Separation of hydrogen and carbon monoxide is achieved by treating the gas mixture with steam in the presence of a catalyst at high temperatures, giving carbon dioxide and hydrogen. The carbon dioxide is then removed by absorption in a suitable solution to form a carbonate.

The other main method uses electrolysis, which offers the advantage of providing pure hydrogen. In the electrolytic decomposition of brine during the manufacture of caustic soda, one of the by-products is hydrogen. Where electricity is cheap, it is economic to obtain hydrogen from the electrolysis of water. The plant consists of a series of cells, each cell containing water in which some sodium hydroxide is dissolved to make it conductive. Two electrodes in plate form, one of iron and the other of nickel-plated iron, are immersed in the water. The electrodes are separated by an asbestos diaphragm or metal mesh, which keeps the gases produced apart. When a current is passed, the water decomposes, hydrogen going to the cathode and oxygen to the anode, where they are collected, respectively.

Hydrogen is the lightest element, one liter weighs only 0.0032 oz. (0.0898 g) at 32°F (0°C) and one atmosphere pressure, and it forms a diatomic molecule: H_2. This colorless, odorless gas is highly flammable, burning vigorously and often explosively in air or oxygen when ignited by a flame or even a single spark and, in the process, forming water. Because it is highly reactive, hydrogen is found combined with other elements in Earth's crust. It occurs widely in compounds such as water, rocks, and petroleum, as well as in many other organic compounds, that form the basis of all vegetable and animal life. The element hydrogen exists in air in negligible amounts but is a major component of stars and the Sun—90 percent of the atoms in the Universe are hydrogen.

▲ The main propulsion system for the space shuttle uses liquid hydrogen as a fuel and liquid oxygen as an oxidizer, carried in separate tanks and supplied to the rocket engines under pressure.

Applications of hydrogen

The main uses of hydrogen include ammonia manufacture (probably the largest volume use), hydrofining and hydrocracking in the oil industry, methanol production from hydrogen and carbon monoxide, the hydrogenation of vegetable oils and fats and the manufacture of hydrochloric acid (HCl). Hydrofining is used to remove sulfur from petroleum products where it is undesirable, for example, in diesel oil, while hydrocracking is used to introduce more hydrogen during the breaking down of wax distillates to make the lighter hydrocarbons found in gasoline.

Because of its great heat of combustion, hydrogen is also used for cutting and welding, and the oxyhydrogen flame can reach temperatures above 3600°F (2000°C). In electric arc welding, atomic hydrogen (H rather than H_2) is formed, resulting in exceptionally high temperatures of around 7200°F (4000°C). Hydrogen is a strong reducing agent and will reduce metal oxide ores to the pure metal. Compressed hydrogen is used for cooling dynamos because of its low density and high heat conductivity and the fact that coronas (electrical discharges) cannot produce ozone, which destroys the insulating material. Hydrogen lowers the winding temperature more than air cooling, thus reducing winding resistance and losses and improving output power.

Hydrogen compounds

Water (H_2O) is undoubtedly the best-known hydrogen compound, but the common acids, such as hydrochloric (HCl), sulfuric (H_2SO_4), nitric (HNO_3), and acetic (CH_3COOH) acid, and the common alkalis, sodium hydroxide (NaOH), potassium hydroxide (KOH), and ammonium hydroxide (NH_4OH), are also familiar. Hydrogen peroxide (H_2O_2), a thick syrupy liquid with strong oxidizing properties usually sold as a solution in water (3 percent), is used for bleaching and as a disinfectant. Pure hydrogen peroxide is very unstable, readily decomposing into water and oxygen. Strong 90 percent hydrogen peroxide is used for military and technical applications, especially as an oxidant in rocket fuels.

Hydrogen sulfide (H_2S) is a poisonous gas with a smell of rotten eggs. The pungent colorless gas hydrogen chloride (HCl) dissolves readily in water to form the corrosive acid, hydrochloric acid, with the same formula, HCl. Hydrogen bromide (HBr) is also a gas and closely resembles hydrogen chloride but gives a weaker acid when dissolved in water. Hydrogen iodide (HI) is a heavier gas that dissolves in water to give hydriodic acid, the basis of many iodide salts, while hydrogen fluoride (HF) is a liquid that dissolves in water to give an acid. It is used as a catalyst in organic reactions and as a reagent in the preparation of fluorides, hydrofluoric acid, and uranium. The highly poisonous liquid hydrogen cyanide (HCN) dissolves in water to form hydrocyanic acid (prussic acid) with a faint smell of bitter almonds. It is used as a fumigant, in electroplating and in the synthesis of organic compounds.

Most of the above compounds can be termed hydrides, that is, compounds formed by combining hydrogen with other elements. Those formed with nonmetallic elements are usually gases or liquids, for example, ammonia (NH_3). Alkali and alkaline earth metals form crystalline compounds with hydrogen, such as lithium hydride (LiH), sometimes used as a hydrogen carrier. Lithium aluminum hydride ($LiAlH_4$) is used as a reducing agent in organic chemistry for adding hydrogen atoms to molecules, such as when a carboxylic group (–COOH) is turned into an alcohol (–CH_2OH).

FACT FILE

- ■ Hydrogen may be the fuel of the future. Many car manufacturers are experimenting with prototypes for hydrogen-powered cars, and some vehicles are already on the road. Buses in Vancouver and Chicago are powered by hydrogen, and Reykjavik in Iceland hopes to have hydrogen-powered buses on its streets by 2002.

- ■ Fears over using hydrogen as a fuel go back to the destruction of the Hindenberg airship in 1937. Hydrogen was blamed for the catastrophic fire that killed most of the airship's passengers and thus people have been reluctant to use hydrogen to power cars and other motor vehicles. Some scientists, however, have argued that the airship did not in fact explode and that the deaths were caused by burning diesel fuel and by people falling from the airship rather than by burning hydrogen. It is also argued that although hydrogen may be highly flammable, so is gasoline, and that what matters is finding a way to store hydrogen safely.

SEE ALSO: ATOMIC STRUCTURE • AUTOMOBILE • ELECTROLYSIS • ELEMENT, CHEMICAL • ENERGY RESOURCES • NUCLEAR WEAPON • ROCKET AND SPACE PROPULSION

Hydroponics

Hydroponics is a water-working process—the name derives from two Greek words, *hydro* (water) and *ponos* (work). It is a form of crop technology in which crops grow entirely in water, fed on substances dissolved in a watery bed.

The word was coined in the 1930s by William Gericke of the University of California, who was the first to see the technique's commercial potential although people had been growing plants in water for centuries, as the floating gardens of the Aztecs testify. Mustard and cress raised on blotting paper are a humbler demonstration.

Plant nutrition

Hydroponics works because growing plants gain all their weight by taking in water. Experiments conducted by a Belgian, Jan van Helmont, as long ago as 1600 showed that as a plant grew, it took hardly any weight from the soil in which it was planted. He therefore concluded that the plant gained all it needed to grow from water. Although the plant does gain weight almost entirely by taking in water, it is not correct to say that it gains all its nutrition from water—the various chemicals needed to promote growth come from the soil via the water. So a plant will not necessarily grow in tap water, it needs other chemicals as well.

It was originally believed that water was adequate provided it contained salts of phosphorus, potassium, nitrogen, calcium, sulfur, and magnesium. These elements, now known along with hydrogen, oxygen, and carbon as the macroelements are required in relatively large quantities.

In further studies of plant nutrition, it was discovered that plants also need seven elements in smaller quantities. Known as the microelements, these are boron, chlorine, iron, manganese, copper, zinc, and molybdenum. Photosynthesis could not occur, many enzymes would not be activated, and nitrogen would not be fixated without them.

These elements account for a tiny proportion of a plant's initial weight, 85 to 95 percent of which is water. Of the weight that remains once the water has been extracted, 90 percent is made up of oxygen, hydrogen, and carbon. The remaining essential elements constitute only 1.2 percent of the plant's initial weight. Apart from the carbon and some oxygen, which is absorbed from the atmosphere, all the elements—along with others that are nonessential—enter the plant through its roots. Each root is covered by hairs that have semipermeable cell walls through which water and certain minerals can pass. When the cell sap contains a greater concentration of minerals than

the solution within the soil, water will pass into the cells so that the concentrations might become even. Provided there is always an ample supply of water, this process—called osmosis—will never result in water passing out of the roots. Such an occurrence, which produces wilting and the eventual death of the plant, cannot take place in a normal-running hydroponic plant.

This is just one of the many advantages of soilless cultivation. Another is the lack of need for fertilizers, both chemical and organic. Only occasional wind-blown weeds have to be dealt with by a labor force kept to the minimum by the use of growing mediums that require no digging or raking. It is easy to revitalize and start plants whose yield will always be predictable, large, and of high quality. Large yields are due to the relatively short time it takes for plants to mature from seedling to fruit producer in an environment where there is no competition for nutrients. Tomatoes can mature in four months and produce four to five times the usual amount of fruit. As a result, a 10 acre (0.4 ha) site is able to provide about 3 million lbs. (1.4 million kg) of tomatoes annually. The fact that all necessary nutrients are supplied ensures high quality; soil-produced fruit is often soft or puffy when fully ripe because of potassium and calcium deficiencies.

Nutrient film technique

The nutrient film technique (NFT) was invented by Allen Cooper of the Glasshouse Crops Research Institute in Britain in the 1960s. The main difference between NFT and other forms of hydroculture is that plants draw water and nutrients from a continuously circulating film supplied by a central reservoir instead of the more conventional stationary source. Instead of rooting in a bulky inert medium, plants grow on a thin polyethylene mat in troughs. This process means

▲ Better understanding of the versatility and vigor of natural desert plants, such as New Mexico's soapbush yucca, is leading to the establishment of gene banks of wild plants as a source for new hybrid crops of the future, suitable for growing in the desert under hydroponic or other systems.

that it can be used for a much wider range of plants than normal. It is now possible to grow virtually anything by NFT, although economic considerations restrict the range. Most multi-stem crops, such as cereals, are unlikely to be grown by NFT, although it is an ideal means of growing grass since the turf can be lifted up and rolled on its light capillary matting for easy and efficient transportation.

Commercial viability also varies from place to place. While it is economical to grow cabbages, peas and many other vegetables in the tropics, it is generally only worth growing crops like tomatoes, lettuces, peppers, and the like in the temperate European countries because cabbages grow just as well in soil.

Acidity

Not only the supply of nutrients but also the acidity of the water must be controlled. A solution's acidity is expressed by its pH value. Pure water, with a pH number of 7, is neutral: below 7 is acid, above 7, alkaline. Most plants grow best in media with a pH between 5.0 and 6.5. If any alteration of the pH is required, it can be lowered either manually or automatically by the addition of sulfuric acid or phosphate solution and raised by the addition of calcium hydroxide.

NFT, like all hydroponic systems, uses water as a growth medium for the plants. The main difference is that the water, instead of being held in a large tank or in the interstices of some inert medium such as gravel, is continuously circulated around the roots of the plants in a thin film.

Circulation is achieved by gently sloping the beds so that the water drains down through the bed under the influence of gravity and is collected at the far end to be pumped back to the top again. A reservoir containing the water and the dissolved nutrient supplies the water beds in which the plants root.

In earlier systems, the bed is made from narrow sheets of polyethylene laid over strips of hardboard, and the plants are put into sterile peat pots or stonewood cubes placed at intervals along each sheet. The edges of the sheets are turned up and fastened between every other plant to form a gully, allowing greater ventilation than a more solid structure. Unfortunately, the roots quickly grow through the pots or cubes to form a thick mat that slows down the flow of water and consequently creates an oxygen shortage.

In the latest systems, the bed is a long rigid polyethylene trough or hydrocanal in which the plants are grown free of any solid rooting medium. As long as the nutrient film is thin but flowing constantly, a thick root mat develops in and above the solution so that roots are kept moist and have a good supply of oxygen all the time.

Growth media

It is important that the flow of nutrients is even and constant. The flow is made possible by an even but fairly steep slope to the hydrocanal of over 1 in 100 and by a special capillary matting. Plastic surfaces, although cheap, light, and waterproof, are notorious for creating uneven flow, and the capillary matting ensures steady, constant

◀ These soybean plants are being grown hydroponically in pots. Virtually any single-stem crop can be grown using the nutrient film technique, even trees like the ones being grown in the next greenhouse.

flow at the optimum depth of about 1 mm. The capillary matting also encourages good aeration and provides a good base for the plants to root in during the early stages of growth.

Although NFT seems to have most possibilities for the future, there are a number of other forms of hydroponic cultivation, and each of these has had its successes. Much more expensive than NFT, though once widely used, is a system known as gravel culture. This system uses a solid but inert growth medium that sits in the water and provides something for the roots to hold onto.

Gravel culture can be used with many types of crops. Among these is "fresh green fodder," a sprouted grain fed to animals six to seven days after germination when it is about 6 to 8 in. (15–20 cm) high. The fodder can be grown in a wooden and plastic shed with no temperature control, but for best results, it needs control of temperature, light, and irrigation. Provided good quality seed is used, 1,100 lbs. (500 kg) of fodder can be obtained from 110 lbs. (50 kg) of seed; it is a particularly valuable foodstuff because it contains the basic protein and unidentified growth factors that many natural grasses lack.

Even more extensively employed than gravel culture is sand culture. The sand is either put into plastic-lined beds or spread over an entire greenhouse floor lined with polyethylene. A drip-irrigation system is used, which unlike both the sub- and drip-irrigation systems employed with gravel, does not involve the recycling of the solution. In sand this open system results in the loss of only 8 to 10 percent of applied nutrients. If used in gravel, the loss would be greater.

Several other mediums can be used in soilless culture: each, of course, has particular advantages and disadvantages. Vermiculite, a mica mineral found naturally in very thin plates, is used in soilless culture after treatment in a furnace at nearly 1800°F (1000°C) to turn it into a lightweight granular material. Perlite, a siliceous mineral mined from lava flows, is similarly processed in a high-temperature furnace.

Both vermiculite and perlite are ideal materials for raising seedlings and for use on a small scale by home gardeners, particularly apartment-dwellers who have to grow plants in pots. In fact, a wide variety of mediums can be used in the home by those interested in hydroponics and many have achieved very satisfying results with home hydroponics.

Artificial light

In a greenhouse, the degree of control over the environment is such that it seems possible that NFT crops could be grown virtually anywhere

there is daylight. In these circumstances, it would be quite feasible to grow tomatoes in Alaska or lettuces in Lapland. The only barrier would be the cost of keeping the plants at the required temperature. In these areas, it is soil deficiencies as much as climate that prevent wide-scale horticulture; it would be prohibitively expensive setting up normal greenhouses in these areas because of the problems of obtaining soil and moving it to the required site. Wherever the soil is inadequate or the climate unsuitable, NFT could be the answer—crops could be grown on rocky ground, on roofs, and even perhaps, one day, on hydroponic farms out in space.

Over the past decade, experiments have been conducted to see if crops will grow in artificial light, with encouraging results. If artificial-light farming should prove feasible, NFT would be an ideal system to take advantage of the possibilities. Crops could be grown underground, under the sea, or virtually anywhere, provided the energy is available, and energy is a large obstacle. Farming using artificial light may even produce bigger yields, but this result is some way off in the future.

At the moment, NFT and all forms of hydroponics are largely daylight projects confined to relatively favorable financial and climatic environments. Noticeably, all the major desert developments are in the Middle East, where sunshine and money are plentiful. Other large developments in hydroponics are in the United States, Mexico, and Russia.

Hydroponics is still a young science and has considerable potential for further development. With further refinements in growing techniques, the quality and quantity of crops might surpass those already attained. It is, therefore, one source of hope for the future in a world faced with the problem of feeding an ever-increasing population.

▲ Strawberries are just one of the crops being grown in the orchard house of the Hydroponicum, a special greenhouse that has been built in the far north of Scotland. Despite its location, vines, sweetcorn, grapefruit, and even banana trees have been grown successfully using hydroponic techniques. The growing houses are triple-glazed with polycarbonate, which lets in light and warmth while giving the insulation of a 9 in. (23 cm) thick brick wall.

 SEE ALSO: AGRICULTURAL SCIENCE • BOTANY • HORTICULTURE • IRRIGATION TECHNIQUES • SOIL RESEARCH • WATER

Hygrometer

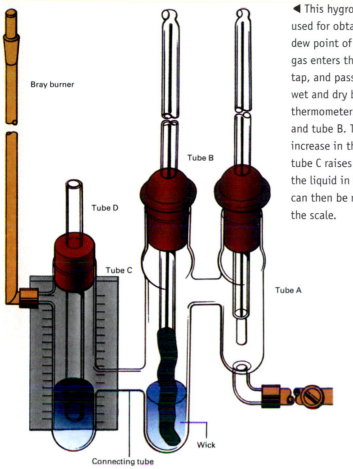

Bray burner

Tube B

Tube D

Tube C

Tube A

Wick

Connecting tube

◀ This hygrometer is used for obtaining the dew point of gases. The gas enters through the tap, and passes over the wet and dry bulbs of the thermometers in tube A and tube B. The resulting increase in the pressure in tube C raises the level of the liquid in tube D, which can then be read against the scale.

A hygrometer is a device for measuring the humidity, that is, the amount of water vapor in the air. The word comes from Greek words meaning "wet measure." The first hygrometer was built by the Italian inventor Leonardo da Vinci and measured the weight of a ball of wool, which absorbed moisture according to the humidity. Since then several types of instrument have been developed.

The most common designs are based on the same principle as da Vinci's hygrometer—certain organic substances absorb moisture readily. Such substances are called hygroscopic; human hair is the most commonly used. The length of a hair changes as it absorbs moisture, and the change can be easily magnified and recorded.

A psychrometer uses evaporation to calculate humidity from the difference in the readings of two thermometers. The bulb of one of the thermometer is kept wet by means of a thin wet wick, and the other is kept dry. Evaporation causes the wet bulb to cool more than the dry bulb, resulting in a temperature difference that can be used to measure humidity. The condensation, or dew-point, device also utilizes two thermometers, one of which has its bulb submerged in ether. Air is bubbled through the ether to accelerate evaporation, and the temperature at which condensation forms on the outside of the container is compared with the temperature of the other thermometer.

Several more elaborate designs are used for certain purposes. An instrument used for observing the upper atmosphere measures the changes in electric resistance of certain substances, such as lithium chloride, as they absorb moisture. At temperatures below freezing, where condensation or evaporation methods cannot be used, a spectrographic instrument can be used to measure the absorption of radiation by water vapor at different places in the electromagnetic spectrum. Devices are under development for measuring the low humidity thought to exist at other places in the Solar System by means of an electrolytic moisture cell; the conductivity rather than the resistance of the medium is measured. The most accurate method is by weighing a chemical that extracts moisture from air.

Other methods commonly employed measure the varying thermal conductivity of a gas, the varying impedance of a capacitor, or the change of frequency of a piezoelectric crystal.

Hygrometers are used to regulate the humidity in air-conditioned atmospheres and industrial control processes, as well as in meteorology and the study of outer space.

Humidity measurements

The humidity of the atmosphere is usually defined in terms of relative humidity, which is the ratio of the pressure of water vapor actually present in the atmosphere at a given time to that of the saturated (maximum possible) water vapor pressure at the same temperature, expressed as a percentage. Alternatively, the weight of water vapor in unit volume of saturated air at the same temperature may be used. The dew point (the temperature at which water condenses out of the atmosphere at a given atmospheric pressure) may also be used to calculate relative humidity, because the saturated vapor pressure at the dew point is equal to the aqueous vapor pressure at the temperature of the experiment. The dew-point hygrometer measures the temperature at which dew forms. By using tables that give the saturated vapor pressure at various temperatures, it is possible to obtain the relative humidity.

SEE ALSO: Air • Electrolysis • Electromagnetic radiation • Temperature • Vapor pressure • Water

Ignition System, Automobile

In gasoline engines, the energy to ignite the compressed fuel–air mixture in the cylinders has to be supplied by an external source, normally a high-voltage electric spark. In applications where complete independence from other systems or very high performance is required, such as for some motorcycles, stationary power units, and aircraft piston engines, the spark is usually provided by a magneto system. In automobiles, however, a storage battery is fitted to supply power to other electric equipment, and so a battery-powered ignition system is used.

Some early engines used "hot tube" ignition in which a metal tube screwed into the top of the cylinder was heated to red hot by an external flame. The outer, heated end of the tube was sealed, and on the engine compression stroke, some of the fuel–air mixture was forced into the glowing tube where it ignited, causing the rest of the fuel–air mixture in the cylinder to also ignite. The amount of control available with this system was very limited, though, and reliable electric ignition systems were developed in the 1890s by several car makers with both battery-powered and magneto types being used.

Conventional system

A conventional battery-powered ignition system consists of three main elements: a distributor, an ignition coil, and spark plugs. These components are connected in two electric circuits with the low-tension circuit being supplied with current from the automobile battery through the ignition switch. The current passes through a contact

breaker in the distributor to the primary winding of the ignition coil, which consists of a few hundred turns of heavy-gauge insulated copper wire, and sets up a magnetic field in the laminated iron core of the coil.

As the distributor shaft turns, a cam mounted on it opens the contact breaker points, so interrupting the current in the primary coil. The magnetic field then collapses, causing a high voltage to be induced in the secondary winding, which is made up of 15,000 or more turns of very fine insulated copper wire around the iron core (the primary winding is wound over the secondary winding). The induced voltage pulse flows along a lead to the central contact of the distributor, through the rotor arm and from there to the appropriate spark plug—this is the high-tension circuit. When the voltage across the spark plug electrodes is sufficiently high, the fuel–air mixture ionizes, and the energy stored in the ignition coil discharges across the gap as a spark that ignites the mixture.

The magnetic field owing to the induced secondary voltage will in its turn induce a voltage (the back emf) of up to 500 V in the primary winding. This voltage can arc across the contact breaker points, dissipating some of the energy stored in the coil and burning the points, so to prevent arcing, a capacitor is connected across the points.

Distributor

The distributor is quite a compact unit, housed in a cylindrical aluminum casing about 1 in. (2.5 cm) across at the bottom end, belling out from the

▲ The Ferrari T4 Formula One racing car. Its ignition system must run with perfect accuracy.

middle upward to about 3 in. (7.5 cm) across. A typical unit about 7 in. (18 cm) long is clamped to the side of the cylinder block so that it can tap the rotary motion of the camshaft. This is the shaft that operates the pushrods to open and close the valves, rotating once for every firing sequence of the engine. This connection therefore mechanically locks the movement of a central drive spindle in the distributor to the motion of the engine. Changes in the timing of the spark plugs can be altered coarsely by twisting the distributor around the drive spindle and, more precisely, by a screw thread.

The distributor shaft is driven at half engine speed through reduction gearing, and the contact breaker cam has lobes on it that correspond to each engine cylinder. This arrangement supplies a spark to each cylinder every second cycle, as needed by the four-stroke engine design. The cam arrangement is set so that the contact breaker opens as the piston is approaching the top of its compression stroke, when the ignition stroke is required. At this point, the rotor arm on the top of the distributor shaft points to the appropriate contact in the distributor cap, so directing the high-tension pulse to the correct cylinder. The precise time at which the spark has to be applied to the fuel–air mixture varies according to the

speed and loads on the engine, and centrifugal timing weights in the distributor body act to give ignition advance at the higher engine speeds, while a vacuum advance mechanism comes into play under low-load conditions.

Electronic ignition

While conventional ignition systems can give good service, increasing demands for performance, fuel economy, and reduced pollution has led to a need for more precise control of the ignition process and the introduction of electronic systems. In the simplest arrangement, the contact breaker is retained, but its output is used to trigger a power transistor that switches the primary current, so reducing the load on the contact breaker contacts and giving a longer life. The power transistor also has a very rapid switching action, which helps to give a stronger spark.

Greater benefits are obtained by completely replacing the contact breaker, using a sensing circuit to sense the distributor shaft position and supply a signal to operate the primary-circuit power transistor. A number of different position sensors are used in ignition systems, for example, one optical system uses a shutter to interrupt a light beam falling on a light-sensitive transistor. More common are magnetic-pulse generators,

▲ A distributor with a magnetic transducer instead of a contact breaker. This unit is for use on a four-cylinder engine.

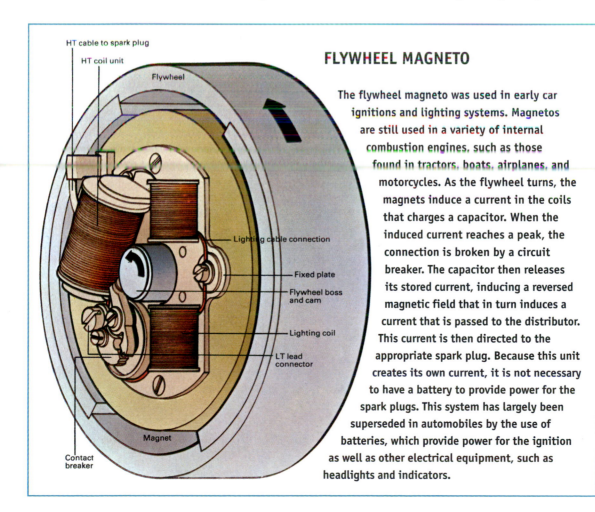

HT cable to spark plug
HT coil unit
Flywheel
Lighting cable connection
Fixed plate
Flywheel boss and cam
Lighting coil
LT lead connector
Magnet
Contact breaker

FLYWHEEL MAGNETO

The flywheel magneto was used in early car ignitions and lighting systems. Magnetos are still used in a variety of internal combustion engines, such as those found in tractors, boats, airplanes, and motorcycles. As the flywheel turns, the magnets induce a current in the coils that charges a capacitor. When the induced current reaches a peak, the connection is broken by a circuit breaker. The capacitor then releases its stored current, inducing a reversed magnetic field that in turn induces a current that is passed to the distributor. This current is then directed to the appropriate spark plug. Because this unit creates its own current, it is not necessary to have a battery to provide power for the spark plugs. This system has largely been superseded in automobiles by the use of batteries, which provide power for the ignition as well as other electrical equipment, such as headlights and indicators.

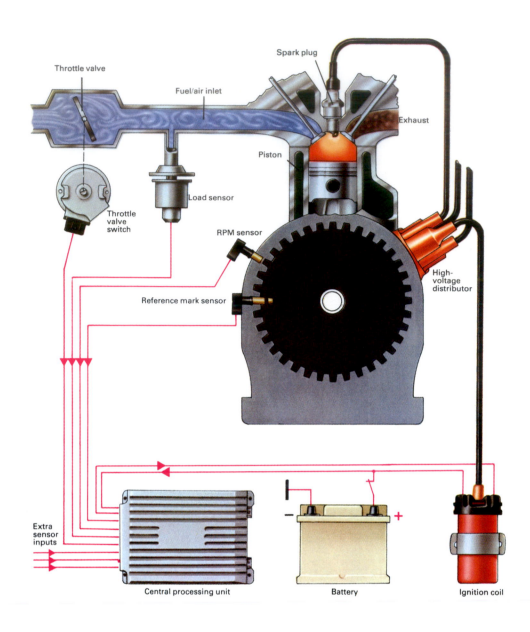

Throttle valve

Fuel/air inlet

Spark plug

Exhaust

Piston

Load sensor

Throttle valve switch

RPM sensor

Reference mark sensor

High-voltage distributor

Extra sensor inputs

Central processing unit

Battery

Ignition coil

◄ Bosch's computerized ignition system. Sensors measure engine load, speed, temperature, crankshaft position, throttle position, and air pressure. The information is fed to a central processing unit that then fires the spark.

where the cam on the distributor shaft is replaced by a soft iron trigger wheel with teeth corresponding to the cam lobes (one for each cylinder). Rotation of the trigger wheel is sensed by a coil and magnet detector unit that gives a voltage output. This output is processed in the control unit and used to operate the power transistor.

The power transistor works in a similar manner to the contact breaker, supplying current to the ignition coil primary winding and interrupting the current when a spark is required. The high-voltage pulse produced is fed to the appropriate spark plug in the same manner as a conventional system.

These electronic ignition systems are usually built into the distributor body and use timing weights and vacuum-advance mechanisms to adjust the ignition timing to suit engine requirements. Electronic sensors can also be used in conjunction with a microprocessor control system to set the ignition timing, leading to the development of engine management systems.

Capacitive systems

With the ignition systems considered above, the spark energy is stored in the coils, but there is an alternative design in which a capacitor is used to store electric energy that is then rapidly discharged through an ignition coil to give a very high intensity spark of short duration. This type of spark is effective with spark plugs that have become fouled with oil or carbon deposits but suffers from the drawback that it does not work as well with the weak mixtures favored in lean-burn engines.

Another system is the Saab Direct Ignition. In this system, the 12 V supply is boosted to 400 V in a control unit and used to charge capacitors, which are then discharged into individual ignition coils positioned above the plugs to give 40,000 V across the plug points. The spark timing is carried out by a microprocessor in the control unit connected to piston speed and position sensors. The spark is said to be produced some 20 times faster than is the case with a conventional system.

Engine management systems

With electronic ignition systems it is possible to carry the control a stage further to give an engine management system. Such systems are often integrated with electronically controlled carburetors or fuel-injection systems to ensure optimum performance, economy, and emission control.

Magneto

The magneto is an ignition device for spark-ignition internal combustion engines, and it combines most of the features of a coil ignition system into a single unit. Driven directly from the engine, it performs the same functions as the coil and distributor of a conventional system, and in addition, it generates its own electric energy, thus eliminating the need for a battery to power the ignition system.

Battery ignition systems are standard on most automobile and many motorcycle engines today, but magneto ignition is still in common use on lightweight motorcycles (particularly those with two-stroke engines), aircraft piston engines, stationary engines, and lightweight engines such as those used for lawn mowers and small pumps.

The three main types of magneto are the rotating-coil, rotating-magnet, and inductor magnetos. The rotating-coil magneto has a rotating armature wound with two coils: the primary, which consists of a few hundred turns of thick insulated copper wire, and the secondary, which has many thousands of turns of fine copper wire and is wound around the primary. The armature rotates between the poles of a permanent magnet, and the magneto also has a contact breaker to switch the primary current and a distributor unit that delivers the high-tension secondary current to the spark plugs.

As the armature rotates, the coils pass through the magnetic flux between the pole pieces of the magnet, and with the contact breaker closed, an alternating current is induced in the primary winding. The maximum induced current flows when the coils are at 90 degrees to the lines of flux between the pole pieces. When the armature is in this position, the contact breaker points open, interrupting the current flow in the primary. The magnetic field associated with this current collapses rapidly, and a high voltage is induced in the secondary winding. This voltage is discharged to the distributor part of the magneto, which delivers it to the appropriate spark plug for ignition.

An improvement on the rotating-coil magneto is the rotating-magnet type, in which the coils are wound around a stationary core. The core is mounted across the ends of a pair of pole pieces,

forming a U-shaped magnetic circuit, and a permanent magnet, fixed to a shaft driven by the engine, is rotated between the pole pieces. This action produces a changing flux in the core, inducing an alternating current in the primary. When this current is interrupted by the opening of the contact breaker a high voltage is induced in the secondary and passed to the distributor.

In the inductor magneto, both the coil assembly and the magnet are stationary, the flux changes being created by the action of a soft iron inductor. The inductor has four lobes, and the magnetic circuit is completed through them. As the inductor rotates, the lobes move in and out of the magnetic flux, causing flux changes and creating a current in the primary coil.

The current in the primary is interrupted by a contact breaker operated by a cam on the drive shaft, and the resulting secondary current is passed to the spark plugs by means of a distributor unit at the end of the magneto.

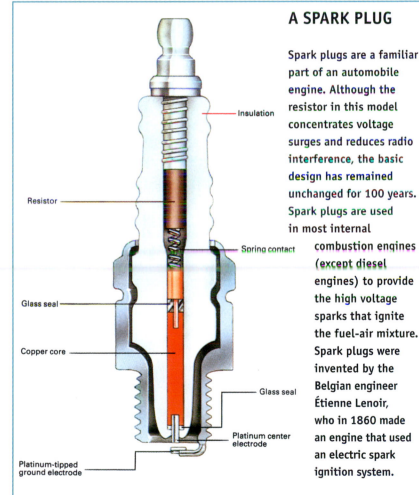

A SPARK PLUG

Spark plugs are a familiar part of an automobile engine. Although the resistor in this model concentrates voltage surges and reduces radio interference, the basic design has remained unchanged for 100 years. Spark plugs are used in most internal combustion engines (except diesel engines) to provide the high voltage sparks that ignite the fuel-air mixture. Spark plugs were invented by the Belgian engineer Étienne Lenoir, who in 1860 made an engine that used an electric spark ignition system.

Labels on diagram: Insulation · Resistor · Spring contact · Glass seal · Copper core · Glass seal · Platinum center electrode · Platinum-tipped ground electrode

SEE ALSO: Automobile • Cam • Capacitor • Carburetor • Governor • Induction • Insulator, electric • Internal combustion engine • Solenoid

Image Intensifier

An image intensifier is a device used to amplify the intensity (or brightness) of images at low light levels so that they can be readily viewed or recorded. The amplification is achieved by electronic means, and the image intensifier is a passive device that relies only on the very low levels of light coming from the object being viewed. Typical applications include the amplification of X-ray images in medical diagnosis, in astronomy for recording very faint telescopic images, and for night viewing—this aspect being particularly useful for military and security applications.

Light amplification

Light energy from a scene comes in the form of photons, which can be considered as packets of light energy. While the energy of these photons is sufficient to affect the retina of the eye, it is quite low in electronic terms. In addition, photons cannot be directly amplified or accelerated, and so to amplify light, it is first necessary to convert the photon energy into a form that can be amplified.

The normal way to accomplish this goal is to allow the photons to fall on a photoemissive surface that absorbs the light and gives out electrons. Different photoemissive materials are used to suit the frequency of the radiation involved, which can range from X rays through visible light to infrared. The materials normally include elements such as cesium, which has large atoms with a single electron in the outermost shells, these electrons being rapidly dislodged by a photon. A typical photoemitter material used for the visible-light range is a compound of sodium, potassium, cesium, and antimony. The electrons produced by the photoemitter can readily be accelerated and focused by electric and magnetic fields to give the required amplification. Following amplification, the "electron image" is converted back into a light image that can be viewed by the eye.

Image tube

In its simplest form, an image intensifier consists of a sealed glass cylindrical tube about 1 in. (2.5 cm) in diameter and length, evacuated of air and with electrodes at either end. A photoemitter layer (the photocathode) is deposited on one of

► This image has been taken with a camera that can detect the infrared light given off by objects. Hot objects generate more infrared and so appear brighter. Image intensifiers can only work with the available light and so are ineffective in very low light or smoky conditions. In these cases, infrared cameras are more suitable.

the flat end plates (the faceplate). The other end plate (the anode) is coated with a fluorescent material. Between them is a photomultiplier tube that carries out the amplification.

Light from the scene to be viewed is focused onto the faceplate photoemitter by a conventional lens system. Around 10 percent of the photons in the incident image stimulate the emission of electrons from the photoemitter layer, with the intensity of the electron emission corresponding to the brightness of the optical image. The electrons from the photoemitter are accelerated down the photomultiplier tube by a potential difference of several thousand volts and focused onto a secondary emission electrode, or dynode. The dynode gives off a number of electrons for each one hitting it. These secondary electrons are in turn accelerated to a further dynode and the process is repeated. A series of dynodes can be used in a single photomultiplier tube, greatly increasing the amplification. The electrons resulting from this process are then focused on the fluorescent screen at the other end of the tube. At this screen, the accelerated electrons excite the fluorescent coating so that it glows to give an image. Around 30 percent of the energy in the electrons is converted into light, but since the energy of the electrons is considerably increased by the acceleration along the tube, there is a net amplification of the light.

Tube arrangements

There are a number of different ways in which the electron image can be focused onto the fluorescent screen. In the simplest arrangement,

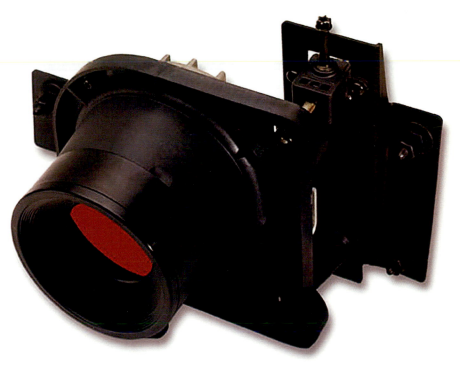

▲ Image intensifiers and infrared cameras (like the one above) are finding uses in cars, as they allow drivers to see up to five times farther than with headlights alone. The image from the camera is projected onto a head-up display inside the car.

proximity focusing, the photoemitter and fluorescent screens are positioned close together so that the electron image travels straight between them without spreading or scattering. However, with this arrangement, the amount of acceleration given to the electrons is limited by the maximum potential difference that can be maintained across the narrow gap. Larger gaps—and hence higher accelerating potentials and an increased image brightness—can be used if the electron image is focused using electric and magnetic fields.

Even higher levels of light amplification can be achieved by connecting several intensifier stages in series (cascaded) with the output of one stage feeding the next. For example, a cascaded set of four stages can achieve a final light amplification of around 10,000 times.

In the cascade tube, the electron image is focused with a cylindrical electromagnet or permanent magnet positioned around the intensifier tube, giving a flat image on the fluorescent photocathode that is deposited on a very thin transparent membrane of glass, mica, or similar material. The photoemitter of the next stage is deposited on the other side of the membrane, and the close coupling achieved results in a very good light-transfer efficiency between the stages.

When electrostatic focusing is used, the photoemitting and fluorescent screens have to be curved to minimize image distortion. Coupling between stages is achieved by the use of fiber-optic faceplates. These fiber-optic plates are made up of an array of microscopically narrow optical fibers fused together along their length to form a

solid block of parallel fibers. Each fiber acts as a separate "light pipe," and high-definition images can be transmitted through such plates, each image element being carried by a different fiber.

In the fiber-optic coupled multistage tube, the flat optical image is coupled to the curved photoemitter inside the tube by a fiber-optic plate. The electron image is accelerated and focused onto a curved fluorescent screen deposited on another fiber-optic faceplate that completes the first tube. The flat output face of this faceplate is placed in optical contact with the input face of a second tube to give efficient image coupling.

▲ The L1A2 night-image intensifier (known as the Starlight Scope) can be fitted to a variety of weapons. It picks up moonlight or starlight that is reflected from the target and then amplifies it to give a clear-sight picture.

◄ An image intensifier is central to this forgery detector. The operator looks through the eyepiece at the top and can detect flaws in banknotes that would not be visible with ordinary eyesight.

Channel plate intensifiers

Another way of achieving amplification in image intensifiers is by the use of a microchannel plate multiplier. It is based on the continuous-channel electron multiplier consisting of a very fine glass tube (or channel) coated on the inside with a secondary electron emitter. An accelerating potential is applied along the length of the tube, so the tube acts in a similar manner to a dynode photomultiplier. When a primary electron enters the tube, it collides with a secondary emitter on the tube walls to release several secondary electrons. These secondary electrons are accelerated along the tube by the applied potential and in turn collide with the tube walls to release more electrons. This process is repeated several times along the tube, resulting in an electron gain—the number of electrons leaving the tube for each electron entering—of approximately 10,000 times.

In the microchannel plate, a large number of such tubes are formed into a disklike array resembling a honeycomb. Typically, a plate 1 in. (2.5 cm) across will have as many as three million individual microchannels and will be around 1 mm thick. Microchannel plate multipliers are used to intercept the electrons produced by the photoemitter in an image intensifier, the output from the plate passing to the fluorescent layer for viewing. The high amplification produced by the plate multiplier can equal the combined amplification of a series of simple intensifier stages. In the simplest arrangement, the channel plate is used in a proximity-focused arrangement with the plate separated from the photoemitter and fluorescent screens by a gap.

Alternatively, the channel plate can be incorporated in an electrostatically focused intensifier.

In this case, the incident light image is transferred to a curved photocathode by a fiber-optic faceplate, and the resultant electron image is electrostatically focused onto the microchannel plate, where the electrons are amplified and passed to the fluorescent screen. With this arrangement, the image is inverted and so is suitable for use with optical systems that also invert the image, the combination giving a noninverted image. It is also possible to magnify the image size by altering the focus of the beam.

Microchannel intensifiers are known as second-generation devices as opposed to the first-generation cascade-type intensifiers. The latest image intensifiers are referred to as third generation. Although they use the same microchannel plates for the amplification as second generation intensifiers, they use the more light-sensitive gallium-arsenide for the photocathodes.

Digital imaging

Increasingly, charge-coupled devices are replacing fluorescent screens as the mediums to view and record the amplified images. Charge-coupled devices are light detectors made mainly of silicon and manufactured using the same technology as conventional computer chips. The silicon is covered with a grid of electrodes, the pattern of the the grid defining the pixels (picture elements) of the image. When a photon hits the grid, it is absorbed and releases an electron from the silicon. The charge-coupled device stores these free electrons, with the charge on each pixel being proportional to the amount of light it has received. As the charge-coupled device can be readily integrated with conventional electronics, the charge can be transferred (coupled) to the electronics, allowing a digital representation of the individual pixels to be built up.

Recording the intensified image digitally enables it to be easily manipulated with computer software. The software can be used to minimize the "blooming" effects that occur when a particularly bright light source produces a blinding effect on the image intensifier. Blooming occurs because the light from a bright source can spill over into neighboring pixels, causing a loss of contrast, or even a complete whiteout.

Another advantage of digital imaging is that infrared cameras can be used in conjunction with an image intensifier. Although infrared cameras are not as high-resolution as image intensifiers, they do have certain advantages over them. They can be used in conditions where there is not enough light for an image intensifier to work, and they can also see through smoke and fog. Devices that use software to combine the images from

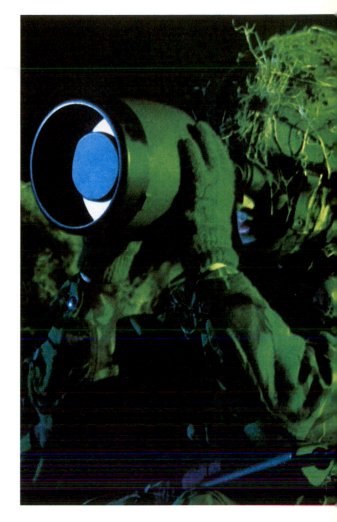

▶ The Eagle is a lightweight, hand-held, long-range, passive night-vision device. It features a catadioptric lens configuration and houses a second-generation microchannel plate intensifier tube.

infrared cameras and image intensifiers can provide a night-vision system that can perform in even the poorest light conditions.

Applications

Image intensifiers find widespread use in military or security night surveillance where being able to see in poor light is essential. Visible-light image intensifiers are also used for wildlife night photography. Image intensifiers are an essential part of many telescopes. The faint object camera on NASA's Hubble space telescope uses a three-stage photomultiplier tube to view far-off galaxies.

Intensifers also play an important role in scientific laboratories. They are used in microscopes, in spectrometers that measure the light given off by molecules, and to view low levels of fluorescence from "tagged" strands of DNA, allowing them to be tracked and monitored.

X rays can be intensified in a similar manner to light. By using an image intensifier in place of the screen usually used for fluoroscopy, it is possible to use much lower X-ray doses.

SEE ALSO: ATOMIC STRUCTURE • CHARGE-COUPLED DEVICE • LIGHT AND OPTICS • PHOTOMULTIPLIER TUBE

Immunology

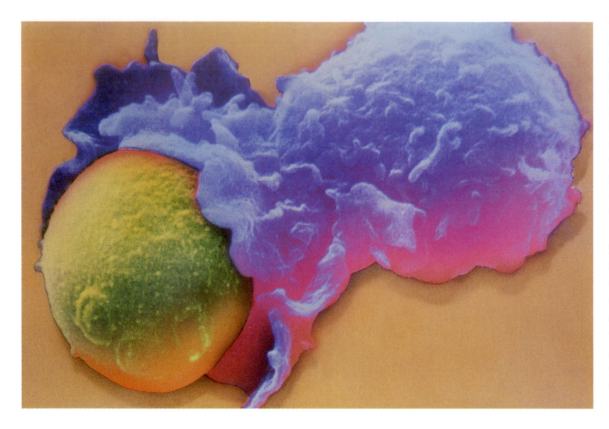

◀ A colored scanning electron micrograph image of a lymphocyte cell engulfing a yeast cell in a process called phagocytosis. The lymphocyte white blood cell (here colored blue) is using pseudopodia projections of its cytoplasm to extend towards the yeast spore (colored yellow). The yeast cell will be swallowed up and digested. Lymphocytes circulate in the blood and play an essential role in the immune response, collecting at sites of infection to repel foreign invaders.

Immunology is the study of immunity—the body's ability to resist harmful substances, among them such disease-producing organisms as bacteria and viruses. The term *immune response* refers to the body's production of disease-fighting cells.

Immunity to a particular infectious disease can be given via injections of small quantities of certain parts of the microorganism that causes the disease. They mobilize the immune response, and the body builds up its defenses to that particular disease. The first advances in immunology were due to the English surgeon Edward Jenner, who in 1778, started his investigations into smallpox. He produced the first vaccine. It is ironic that Jenner had no knowledge of viruses, let alone the mechanisms of the immune system, but was still able at least partly to achieve his aims of making his patients immune to the killer disease.

Today, the scope of immunology runs from the study of organs, cells, and molecules in the immune system (those responsible for recognizing alien molecules and disposing of them) to the study of how they respond and interact, the consequences of the immune system's activity, and ways of controlling the responses of the immune system.

Natural and adaptive immunity

The immune system has two kinds of resistance—natural (sometimes termed nonspecific), and adaptive (sometimes termed specific). Both kinds of resistance consist of cellular elements and humoral elements (those that are free in blood serum or other body fluids). Natural resistance is older in evolutionary terms than the adaptive mechanisms of immunity, but many elements of these two different systems interact.

Natural immunity mechanisms

Natural immunity mechanisms are largely indistinguishable from the mechanisms that cause inflammation in reaction to tissue damage. It is because of these mechanisms that natural immunity has been labelled nonspecific, but there are some parts of natural immunity that have specific targets among nonself cells—those cells that do not belong to the host organism.

Almost all cells involved in mammalian immunity have their origins in bone marrow. These cells come from the so-called stem cell, from which all types of blood cell are derived. Those involved in natural immunity include macrophages, large tissue cells that remove damaged tissue and cells, as well as recognizing and disposing of bacteria in a limited capacity. A series of enzymes in blood serum, known collectively as complement, and lysozyme (also known as muramidase), an enzyme secreted by macrophages, also have this limited ability to recognize and dispose of bacteria. Finally, among the specifically acting agents of the natural immunity mechanisms is interferon, a family of proteins that is produced by a variety of cells as a response to virus infection. Different cells each produce their own type of interferon.

Adaptive immunity mechanisms

Adaptive immunity mechanisms are quite different. The keys to these mechanisms are lymphocytes and antigens. Lymphocytes are cells found in the bloodstream; their function is to detect all foreign substances. Detection is through specialized and specific surface receptors. There are two kinds of lymphocytes—B, which secrete antibodies, and T (thymus-derived), which interact with B lymphocytes to kill virus-infected cells.

Antigens are often defined as substances that stimulate any kind of adaptive immune response, but more correctly, they are substances that stimulate the production of antibodies. Antigens are normally foreign molecules, but sometimes the body's own materials act as antigens—this situation may occur when body cells have been infected and need to be disposed of.

When a lymphocyte is stimulated to produce antibodies by an antigen, the antibodies bind to, and thereby neutralize, the bacterial toxins. They also bind to specific bacteria, viruses, or other parasitic material. When this happens, myeloid cells are able to recognize and engulf these parasites. This process, known as phagocytosis, occurs in natural as well as adaptive mechanisms, but antibodies are the agents that identify the specific intruder and speed its disposal.

Antibodies in detail

Antibodies—also known as immunoglobulins—are protein molecules. Specific antibodies can be made against almost any antigen. When antibodies interact with antigens, antigen-antibody complexes are formed.

The antibody that is produced in response to an antigen has binding sites that are specific to and complementary with the structural features of that antigen. It is usual for the antibody to have two binding sites. If this is the case, long chains of alternating antigens and antibodies can be formed, known as precipitins.

There are five major classes of immunoglobulins in human blood plasma. These are known as IgG, IgA, IgM, IgD, and IgE, of which the IgG immunoglobulins are the most common. Structurally, they are built from four polypeptide chains—two identical heavy (H) chains and two identical light (L) chains. The terms heavy and

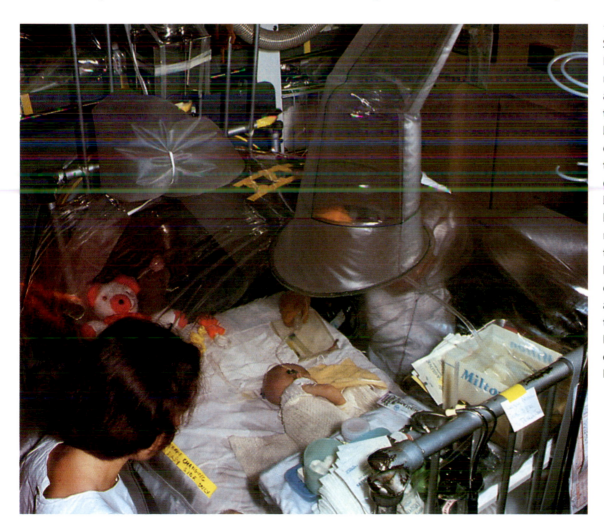

◄ Babies suffering from Severe Combined Immune Deficiency (SCID) do not naturally produce antibodies. The medical team has to care for the baby from the other side of its polyvinyl tent. The tents are known as gnotobiotic environments, because the doctors have a knowledge of the microorganisms inside the tent (*gnosis* is Greek for knowledge). The aim is for controlled rather than absolute sterility. These tents are also used to keep infection in—for example, when a patient has Lassa fever.

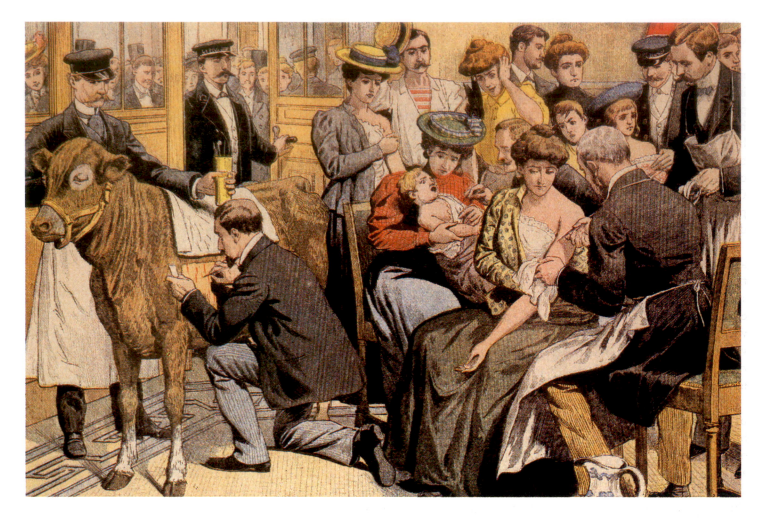

light refer to the number of amino acid residues to be found in the chains. Variations in these chains are responsible for the differences in antigen binding—the specific binding—and biological activity, which determines the exact function of the antibody in question. Some people can produce antibodies faster than others.

How lymphocytes learn

The B lymphocyte population can make millions of different antibody molecules capable of recognizing all pathogens (harmful disease-causing bacteria or viruses). But there is not enough room in the genetic material, the cells' DNA, for the number of genes necessary to make so many molecules.

In fact, genetic diversity is generated by splicing and rearranging the DNA in each B cell. This extraordinary process is called somatic mutation, which means that the rearranged DNA is not transferred to future generations. For example, just because our mothers had measles, we are not ourselves immune to it. In 1988, Mark Davis and his group at Stanford University in California discovered that genetic diversity in the T-cell population is generated in the same way.

There are two types of T lymphocytes: cytotoxic T cells and helper T cells. Cytotoxic T cells constantly monitor the proteins on cells, and those

that are different, such as virus-infected or cancerous cells, are killed directly. Helper T cells help B cells to make antibodies and encourage the cytotoxic T cells to kill. Without this action, the killing and antibody production would be minimal.

To respond correctly and to our benefit, our immune system must learn to be tolerant of our own proteins (self proteins) and cells yet respond to foreign harmful ones (nonself proteins). This education takes place in an organ above the heart called the thymus.

In 1987, Philippa Marrack and John Kappler from the Howard Hughes Medical Institute in Denver demonstrated that for a cell to develop into a T cell, it must pass through the thymus. There, the T cells interact with all the proteins they are likely to see in the body. Marrack and Kappler showed that if the interaction is too strong, the cells die, and if they do not interact, the cells still die. Thus, we end up with a population of T cells that are able to recognize self proteins.

When these cells circulate in the blood and lymph and through the organs of our bodies, they see again all the self proteins and they know that all is well. Both types of immune cells must recognize nonself proteins to generate an immune response. This usually ensures that no response is mounted against self. If, however, they see some-

▲ Inoculation in 1905. On the premises of a Paris magazine, free doses of cowpox, which provide smallpox immunity, are dispensed to all comers.

thing foreign, then they respond with speed and vigor and eliminate the intruder.

Because of the remarkable process of somatic mutation by which antibodies are generated, our immune system has the potential to respond to all pathogens, both known and unknown. We each have approximately a billion lymphocytes in our bodies at any one time. There will, however, be only a few (between one and ten) of each B or T cell that are specific to any individual pathogen. Once these cells encounter their bacteria, virus, or parasite, they divide rapidly so that within a few days there will be many thousands of specific cells.

It takes a few days for an antibody response to an influenza virus, for example, to reach levels that can slow down the spread of the virus. As soon as these levels are high enough and there are enough cytotoxic T cells to kill infected cells, the virus is rapidly cleared from the body. If the same virus tries to invade the same person a second time, there will now be many hundreds of immune cells ready to respond immediately.

The immune system adapts and will "remember" that it has seen the particular pathogen before. It will then respond much more vigorously when the same pathogen tries to invade again. This ability of the immune system to adapt and remember is why a person will rarely get chicken pox twice, and it is how immunization works. By injecting inactive forms of the pathogens that cause polio, diptheria, tetanus, measles, whooping cough, or rubella, each of these populations of cells will be expanded.

The viruses that cause influenza and colds, however, have developed the knack of rapidly changing their appearance, thus causing epidemics of, say, Russian flu or Hong Kong flu among the human population. In the 1980s, Andrew McMichael and his group at the John Radcliffe Hospital in Oxford, England, showed that evolutionary pressure on influenza viruses has given them a cunning way of avoiding the adaptive nature of our immune systems. Variants of the virus develop with mutations in the DNA that code for the proteins on their outer coat, thus having the effect of tricking the immune system, because although it is the same influenza or cold virus, it looks different from the outside. Our immune system has to go through the same process of expanding the few reactive cells up to a level that can once again repel the unwanted invader.

Genetic control of immunity

The ability of any animal to mount any immune response is determined by a large variety of genes. Many of the details of the genetics involved in immunology are still unknown, but the best-understood area is called the Major Histocompatibility Complex (MHC), which regulates the family of responses involving T-lymphocytes. In humans, the MHC is known as HLA (human leucocyte antigen).

Tolerance and autoimmunity

One unwanted side effect of a highly adaptive immune system is that antibodies to almost any molecule can be made. It is therefore very important that the immune system does not seek out and destroy self as well as nonself material, because as far as the antibody-producing mechanisms are concerned, one molecule is much like another.

As a safeguard, several protective mechanisms against self-reactivity have evolved. When under certain circumstances, these safeguarding mechanisms are triggered by nonself materials, the immune system will ignore their presence by treating them as self materials. In most people, for example, the immune system treats harmless pollen as a self material, but in people who suffer from hayfever, the immune system reacts to the pollen as nonself material, causing an unnecessary and unpleasant allergic response. This ability of the immune system to treat harmless nonself material as self material is called tolerance.

The reverse side of the tolerance coin is autoimmunity. This is a state where tolerance to self material breaks down. In circumstances where antigens and self material display certain similarities, the immune system may fail to distinguish between the two, and antibodies are produced that destroy both types of molecule. This response is the cause of such autoimmune diseases as multiple sclerosis, rheumatoid arthritis, and diabetes.

Immunity as protection

There are several kinds of nonself materials that the immune system needs to dispose of. They include bacteria, viruses, protozoa, worms, fungi,

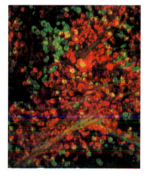

▲ Tissue from a mouse spleen magnified x 1,000. The sample has been treated to reveal two separate types of cell, colored red or green, each of which produces one sort of antibody protein. No cell is both red and green, indicating that the immune response is highly specific.

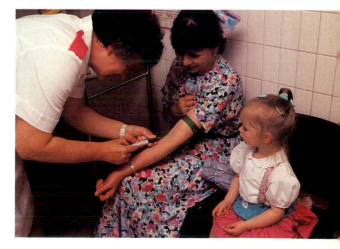

► Many of the tests that are done during pregnancy to make sure that the developing baby is healthy depend on recognizing specific antibodies.

and tumors. Each involves slightly different mechanisms, but in general, the natural immunity mechanisms come to bear immediately, whereas the adaptive mechanisms need several days to react against new nonself material.

Bacteria are usually disposed of by the body by phagocytosis. In order to avoid this fate, bacteria produce different capsule and cell wall materials, which have little effect because they tend to be strongly antigenic in themselves and are disposed of easily by the immune system. They also produce exotoxins—material that poisons phagocytes. Fortunately, the body can normally produce antibodies to exotoxins. In addition to the phagocyte-based mechanisms, lysozyme (a natural antibiotic with some things in common with penicillin) will also kill bacteria.

Viruses are simpler organisms than bacteria, but they come in a huge range of different types, a fact reflected by the range of different naming schemes that have been adopted by scientists. Virus infection is through intracellular replication, which may lead to cell death. Interferon provides rapid protection by adopting a natural

antibiotic role, but via a very different mechanism from that adopted by lysozyme during bacterial invasion. The antibody system is not so effective against viral infection. Instead, adaptive immunity comes from the T-cell system, which recognizes certain MHC antigens.

Less than 20 protozoa infest humans, but among them are four parasites that are both dangerous and extremely widespread—those causing malaria, American and African trypanosomiasis, and leishmaniasis. These organisms usually display a combination of the strategies found in bacteria and viruses, making them very difficult for the immune system to tackle, and complete resistance to protozoal infections is extremely rare. The result is usually that the immune system keeps the number of protozoa in the body down—this state is called premunition. The state of premunition is usually to the advantage of the parasite because as long as the host remains alive with some protozoa present, the continued existence of those protozoa is assured.

Worm-borne infections are sometimes very unpleasant for the sufferer, causing problems in a

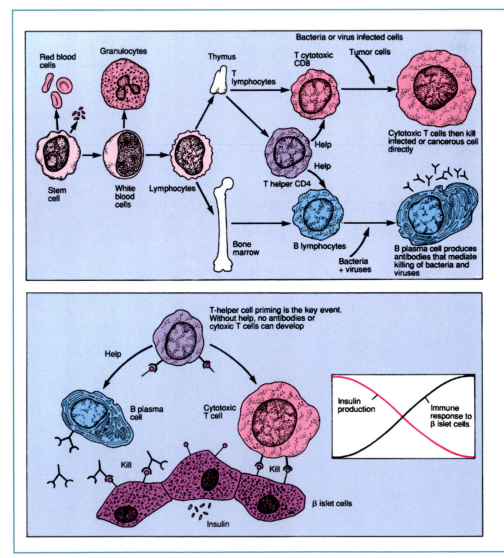

THE IMMUNE SYSTEM

When the immune system swings into action (top), stem cells can turn into lymphocytes, red blood cells, granulocytes, or platelets. Lymphocytes become either B cells or T cells—that is, in the bone marrow or thymus. Two types of T cell come from the thymus—T-helper cells and T-cytotoxic cells. T-helper cells help cytotoxic cells to kill bacteria, virus-infected, or tumor cells. They also help B lymphocytes to make antibodies that mediate killing bacteria and viruses.

In diabetes (bottom), T-helper cells wrongly recognize molecules on the surface of ß-islet cells, which make insulin in the pancreas, as foreign. They then help cytotoxic T cells to kill these ß-islet cells and help B cells to make antibodies that also mediate killing of the ß-islet cells and so prevent the production of insulin. This reaction stops the body from utilizing glucose sugar, and so levels of blood sugar increase, causing an increase in the volume of urine, itching, weakness, hunger, weight loss, and thirst.

number of different organs—the lungs, liver, eyes, bladder, muscles, and so on. The immune responses against these infections are complex, and some are not well understood, but evidence suggests they have a predominance of IgE- and IgG-based reactions. Fungal infections tend to be comparatively rare and not serious, although there are some notable and serious exceptions.

Immunity to tumors may seem impossible to achieve, but some immunologists are looking forward to the day when they may be able to claim the credit for conquering cancer. There is much debate as to whether this goal will be reached, but basically the argument in favor of this outcome compares the role of a tumor to the role of a conventional parasite. However, there are probably just as many fundamental differences as similarities.

Transplant rejection

The various immune mechanisms are very efficient at recognizing nonself materials, but problems can occur when the immune system reacts to foreign materials such as transplanted organs. In most cases, it seems that these nonself MHC molecules fall foul of T cells, which confuse them with self plus antigen or self plus virus, although some B cells also have a role to play in rejection. Successful transplantation depends on matching the donor's and the recipient's MHC antigens as closely as possible—close relatives and siblings are usually the best source of transplant organs.

Another avenue open to transplant surgeons is immunosuppression. This can be extremely problematic and dangerous, because, unless the suppression is very specific, the patient may become open to all kinds of infection and to cancer. Fortunately, drugs have been developed that enable the immune system to learn not to reject the transplant. Immediately after the transplant, the patient is given a large dosage of the drugs, but after several months, this dosage may be reduced or in some cases stopped altogether.

Immunostimulation

Despite the effectiveness of the immune system, there are still shortcomings—the existence of death through disease is all the evidence needed in support of this statement. The answer in many cases is immunostimulation.

The main area of interest is the adaptive immune mechanisms because they can be slow to respond to invasion and sufficient antibodies may arrive too late to prevent death or disability, for example, in the case of tetanus or polio. There are two main kinds of selective immunization: active and passive.

▲ Electron micrograph of *Haemophilus influenzae* bacteria (light blue in this false-color image), which can cause pneumonia and bronchitis, on human nose tissue. This image is magnified x250,000.

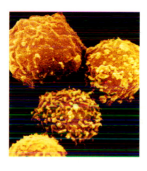

▶ B lymphocytes, here magnified x2,000, play a crucial role in the human immune system as their surface membranes bear antibodies, called immunoglobulins, that act as receptors to specific antigens on foreign substances.

Active immunization is usually known as vaccination. An antigen is used to safely generate immunological memory to reduce the effects of any subsequent infection. Vaccines are given as soon as the immune system is fully developed—usually at about six months, with carefully timed boosts at intervals. In passive immunization, the antibody is injected preformed. Although the effect is very rapid, it is relatively short-lived.

AIDS—immunodeficiency

People infected with the HIV-1 AIDS virus have shown us how necessary our immune system is to us. This virus infects and kills helper T lymphocytes, thus removing the very cells that would have led to its own destruction. The AIDS sufferer is therefore more prone to common infections, such as colds, influenza, and pneumonia, and has no mechanism to prevent cancerous cells from growing.

Manufacturing antibodies

Manufacturing human antibodies has been a problem for many years. The old method of purifying blood serum was very time-consuming and expensive. Instead, in 1975, a way of manufacturing monoclonal antibodies was developed. The technique relies on the fact that every antibody is produced by one cell (or family of cells) only.

Using spleen cells (or lymphocytes) and cancer cells, a special cell called a hybridoma is produced. These cells are grown in a culture medium, and those cells that produce the desired antibodies are cloned or injected into mice, where they produce tumors that secrete the antibodies.

Interferon

Interferon, produced naturally in cells to combat viruses and bacteria, can now be artificially produced. Though not the wonder drug for treating cancer that scientists initially hoped, interferon is currently used in the treatment of Kaposi's sarcoma—a form of cancer that frequently affects people with AIDS. It is also used to treat hairy-cell leukemia, hepatitis B, hepatitis C, and relapsing-remitting multiple sclerosis, a disease of the nervous system.

SEE ALSO: Cancer treatment • Cell biology • Enzyme • Pharmaceuticals • Transplant • Vaccine

Induction

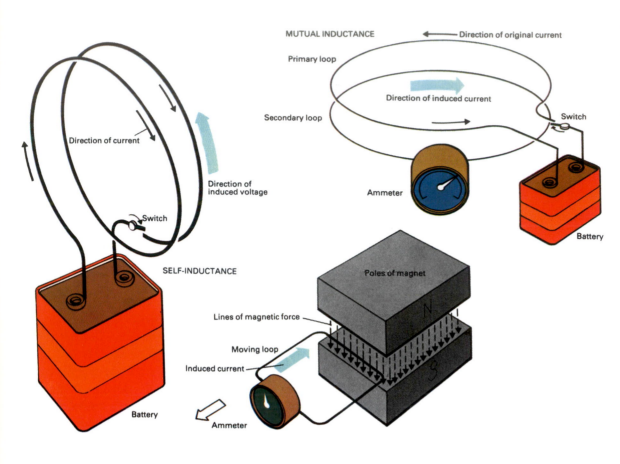

MUTUAL INDUCTANCE

Primary loop

Direction of original current

Direction of induced current

Secondary loop

Ammeter

Switch

Battery

Direction of current

Direction of induced voltage

Switch

SELF-INDUCTANCE

Poles of magnet

N

S

Lines of magnetic force

Moving loop

Induced current

Battery

Ammeter

◀ An electromagnetic field is generated in a loop of wire when it moves through a region of changing magnetic field. Mutual inductance occurs in a loop near to a changing electric current. Self-inductance is generated within the circuit itself against the battery's current.

The word inductance comes from *induce*, meaning "to bring about" or "to give rise to." In electromagnetism, it refers to the ability of a changing current to give rise to a voltage.

In an electrical circuit, currents arise in conductors that connect points of different electrical potential, or voltage. The voltage is generally established by a device that converts another form of energy into electrical energy. A battery, for example, converts chemical energy into electrical energy; a solar cell converts light energy into electrical energy; and a generator converts motional energy into electrical energy by forcing a conductor to move through a magnetic field.

The moving charges that constitute an electric current set up a magnetic field in the space around them. As long as the field is unchanging it will have no effect on a second, nonmoving conductor placed in it. If, however, the second conductor is moving or the magnetic field around it is changing, a voltage is induced in it, and if it is part of a complete circuit, a current will flow in response. The magnitude of the induced electromotive force will be proportional to the rate at which the magnetic flux (field strength x area measured perpendicular to the field direction) is changing.

Inductance and changing current

Potential differences give rise to currents, which in turn create magnetic fields. Any change in the current will create a change in the field, which induces a voltage in any neighboring circuits and in the original circuit as well.

The induction of a voltage in one circuit by the changing current in another is termed mutual inductance. The additional voltage induced in a circuit by changes in its own magnetic field is termed self-inductance. According to a principle known as Lenz's law, the voltage induced in any circuit by a changing magnetic flux will produce currents that resist the change in flux. Self-inductance is therefore a factor that resists any change in current.

Because the magnitude of induced voltage is proportional to the rate of change of current, high-frequency (fast-changing) current signals will produce larger induced voltages than low-frequency (slow-changing) signals. Furthermore, as these induced voltages always try to impede the current that produced them, they will impede higher frequencies more than lower frequencies. Steady currents are not affected by inductance.

In many situations self-inductance can be a nuisance. For example, when transmitting a signal along a wire, the self-inductance of the wire will impede the higher frequencies more than the lower ones. Inductors, on the other hand, are devices that are designed to have a specific self-inductance and are useful for their frequency-dependent properties. An inductor will allow DC to flow through unhindered but will progressively restrict higher and higher frequencies of alternating current (AC).

When a capacitor is combined with an inductor, they form tuned circuits that are of fundamental importance in oscillators. Capacitors have reverse frequency characteristics to inductors—that is, they impede low frequencies and DC more than high frequencies. Together, capacitors and inductors impede both the low and high frequencies. At a particular frequency, determined by the values of the inductance and capacitance, the impedances compensate each other exactly. A tuned circuit is just one example of a frequency filter, and inductors are generally used in such applications.

Mutual inductance

Mutual inductance—the ability of a changing current in one conductor to induce a voltage in a second (and separate) conductor—forms the basis of the transformer.

Here, two coils of wire are mounted on a common magnetic circuit (usually a laminated iron ring or core). An alternating current produced by an alternating voltage across the terminals of the first (primary) coil sets up an alternating magnetic flux in the magnetic circuit. This alternating flux threading the secondary coil induces a voltage in it. The size of the secondary voltage in relation to that of the primary voltage is the same as the ratio of the number of turns in the two coils.

Apart from this particular application, mutual inductance is usually a hindrance. It means, for example, that a signal in one wire will affect the voltage-current relationships in a second and totally separate wire where no such effect was required. Again, this becomes a more important problem at higher frequencies, where the effect is greater. For example, underground cables can interfere with telephone lines.

In electric circuits, care must be taken in the design to minimize stray self- and mutual inductance because these will be important factors in determining the highest frequencies that can be handled by the circuit. Also, it will affect the speed with which the device can operate.

Unit of inductance

The unit of inductance is the henry (symbol H), named for the U.S. physicist Joseph Henry, who first discovered the phenomenon of self-induc-

tion. When a rate of change of current of one ampere per second induces a voltage of one volt, then the inductance is one henry. Inductance therefore has the units of volts per amp per second or volt-seconds per amp. One henry is a large inductance, and normally inductors are measured in millihenrys (thousandths of a henry).

Induction coil

The induction coil is another instrument for producing a high voltage from a low one—this time using DC current. The first principles of the induction coil were discovered by the English physicist Michael Faraday, and the design was improved during the 19th century by, among others, the French physicist A. H. L. Fizeau and the London company of Apps. By the early 1900s, induction coils were being used to produce electric discharges in low-pressure gases. This application in its turn led to the subsequent discovery of X rays and cathode rays.

The basic instrument comprises two coils: a primary winding of approximately 200 turns of thick insulated wire wrapped around a secondary winding of about 20,000 turns of fine insulated wire wrapped around a laminated iron core.

A low-voltage DC source provides current for the primary and is switched rapidly on and off by means of an iron armature similar to that of an electric bell. Current passes through an adjustable screw, on which the flat steel spring supporting the armature rests, and into the primary coil. This magnetizes the soft iron core of the coil, which attracts the iron armature toward it. As the armature moves, it breaks the electric contact at the screw, cutting off the current flow and thus demagnetizing the core. The steel spring pulls the armature back to its original position, conse-

▼ Electromagnetic induction. A cogwheel in a transmission undergoes heat treatment: the current from the coil induces current in the transmission and thus heats its interior.

◀ This picture, published in 1883, shows an induction coil being used to give therapeutic shocks to a patient in a bath. Induction coils create large voltages from the small DC voltage of a battery.

quently restoring the current flow, and the cycle of operations begins again and is repeated many times a second.

The magnetic flux produced by the current in the primary winding links with the turns of the secondary, and when the current stops flowing, the magnetic field collapses, and a high electromotive force (or emf, measured in volts) is induced in the secondary winding.

As with the transformer, the magnitude of the induced emf in an induction coil depends upon the ratio between the number of turns on the primary and the number of turns on the secondary. For example, if there are 1,000 times more turns on the secondary than on the primary, then the induced emf in the secondary is approximately 1,000 times the emf in the primary.

Self-induction in the primary coil slows the rate at which the primary current builds up and also causes arcing across the armature contacts, thus prolonging the duration of the primary current. This phenomenon reduces the magnitude of the induced secondary emf because this value is dependent on the rate at which the primary flux changes. Placing a capacitor (typically of about one microfarad) across the contacts is one way of reducing this effect. Instead of arcing across the gap, the primary current charges the capacitor, which then discharges through the primary coil, opposing the self-induced emf and giving rise to an increased secondary emf.

Losses

The efficiency of a coil is dependent on the sharpness of the break made by the armature, and in larger instruments, the armature is replaced by a

rotating jet of mercury. Energy losses are created in the iron core by hysteresis, caused by the interaction between the fields of the core molecules and the induced magnetic fields.

Further losses are caused by eddy currents (described below) induced in the core material by the changing flux cutting through it. These losses can be reduced by laminating the iron core and insulating the laminations from each other. This can be achieved by making the core from lengths of soft iron wire insulated from each other or by making the core out of ferrite (a ceramic compound with ferromagnetic properties).

Ferrite cores are made of materials such as nickel–cobalt ferrite, nickel ferrite, and magnesium–manganese ferrite, and they have extremely low losses even with very-high-frequency currents.

The induction coil finds its greatest application in gasoline engine ignition systems, where it converts the 6- or 12-volt supply from the battery to as much as 30,000 volts to operate the spark plugs, the make-and-break action in the primary circuit being produced mechanically by a contact-breaker set or electronically by a semiconductor-switching circuit. A variation of the basic induction coil is the Tesla coil, a more elaborate device that produces high voltages at high frequencies.

▶ When a permanent magnet is moved across the surface of a metal—for example, magnesium—strong electrical currents with magnetic fields called eddy currents are produced in the metal.

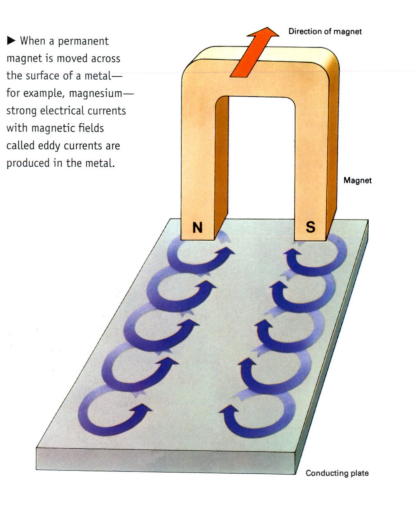

Direction of magnet

Magnet

N   S

Conducting plate

Eddy current

The term *eddy current* is used to describe a phenomenon of electromagnetism that has many features similar to the original usage of the term to describe movement in water. Water-flow patterns in streams may be divided into progressive currents, which flow steadily downstream, and eddy currents, which circulate with little overall movement.

The basis of electrical transformers is that a changing current flowing in a loop of wire will produce a magnetic field, and vice versa. If a metal cycle wheel rim is laid flat on a table with an AC-powered electromagnet underneath its center, an alternating current will flow around the wheel rim even though all points on the rim are at the same voltage. If the spokes and hub are now added, the current flow will remain unaltered since there is no force driving current along the spokes. If the wheel is now replaced by a metal disk, current will flow in a similar pattern—around the center in concentric circles with no radial movement. This phenomenon applies to all conductors, not just ferromagnetic ones such as iron, which can be strongly magnetized. Neither is the circular outline important—a sheet of any shape will suffice. Finally, the AC-powered electromagnet can be replaced by anything that will produce a varying magnetic field, such as a mov-ing bar magnet. Thus if a bar magnet is moved across the surface of a metal plate without touching it, a pattern of circulating electric currents will be set up in the plate behind it. Eventually, the energy in these currents will be converted to heat by the resistance of the plate material. These currents circulating within conductors are called eddy currents. The energy to drive them comes from the magnetic field. If this was produced by a moving magnet, the magnet will experience a dragging force that resists its movement, just as water-current eddies will act to slow down a boat. Eddy currents are almost invariably unwanted in boat design, but they can be either a hindrance or a useful mechanism in electrical machines.

When designing transformers, metallic cores are normally used to provide a low reluctance path for the flux around the desired magnetic circuit. If these cores were to be made from solid metal, large eddy currents would circulate within them, resulting in unwanted heating and power wastage. Eddy currents in transformers can be greatly reduced by making the cores from a pile of thin metal sheets called laminations. Each lamination is insulated from its neighbor, and consequently the paths that the eddy currents would otherwise have taken are broken by a series of insulating bands.

▼ Induction coils operate on the principle that a fast-changing current in one coil (the primary coil) induces an extremely large voltage in an adjacent, or surrounding, coil (the secondary coil). Performance is improved by using a few turns of thick wire in the primary (that is, low self-inductance) coil and many turns of thin wire in the secondary coil.

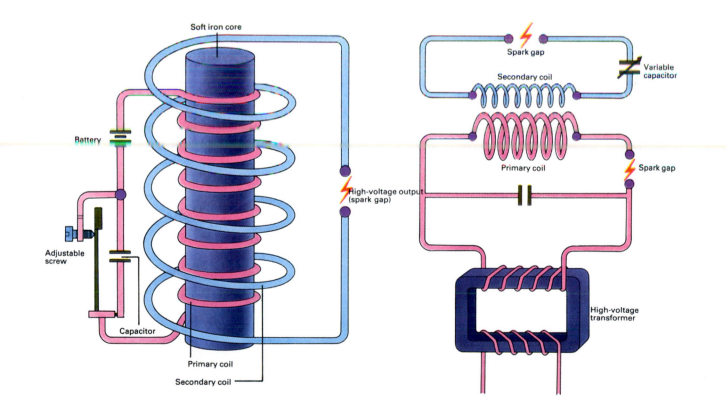

| Soft iron core | Spark gap | Variable capacitor | Secondary coil | Battery | High-voltage output (spark gap) | Adjustable screw | Primary coil | Spark gap | Capacitor | Primary coil | Secondary coil | High-voltage transformer |

Inertia

It is a matter of everyday experience that it requires effort to start objects moving, to change their direction of movement, and to stop them again. This resistance to changes in speed and direction of movement is called inertia.

Even if all resisting forces, such as friction, were absent, the inertia of a truck, for example, would limit the rate at which an applied force would accelerate it. The truck's inertia becomes apparent in the force that its brakes must apply to slow it and that its tires must exert on the roads at curves. If free of all such forces, the truck would keep moving in a straight line at a constant speed indefinitely. This generalization about the behavior of moving bodies is the first of Newton's laws.

The inertia of a body is proportional to its mass. Although the weight of an object varies depending on the strength of the gravitational field it is in, its mass and, consequently, inertia will remain unchanged wherever the object is—its inertia will still manifest itself as a resistance to any applied force.

The tendency of a rotating body to continue rotating about an axis passing through its center of mass is termed rotational inertia. The rotational inertia in this case equals the body's angular momentum, which is the product of its rotational speed and its moment of inertia. The moment of inertia depends not only on the mass of the body but also on its distribution about the axis. A body's moment of inertia can be increased by placing its mass farther from its axis of rotation. For example, if two wheels have the same mass but different diameters, the larger wheel will roll downhill more slowly because of its larger moment of inertia. If a steel disk is melted down and recast as a wheel with the bulk of its mass at its rim, its moment of inertia will be increased, but there will be no change in the body's resistance to nonrotational motion. How difficult it is to throw a discus depends on its mass, not on its moment of inertia.

Every moving object is a store of kinetic energy, or energy of movement. A massive object moving at a certain speed, such as a railroad locomotive, for

▼ Racing motorcyclists know and exploit the limitations of their machines—and how the forces of inertia and gravity will affect them.

example, has more energy than a less massive one such as an automobile at the same speed.

In the case of a rotating body, kinetic energy depends on moment of inertia and rate of rotation in revolutions per second. A classical illustration of the effect of changes in moment of inertia is given by a spinning ice skater. Throwing out his or her arms will increase the moment of inertia (by redistributing his or her mass farther from the axis of rotation). Since the kinetic energy is unchanged, the rate of rotation falls to compensate for the increase. When the arms are pulled in again, the moment of inertia is reduced and the skater spins faster.

Use of inertia

Many kinds of engines deliver power unevenly through their working cycle. The moment of inertia of a flywheel can be a means of smoothing this energy supply. For example, the crankshaft of an automobile receives impulses from the firing of the engine cylinders. When the crankshaft is disengaged from the road wheels—that is, when the automobile is in neutral gear—it would be liable to turn jerkily. A flywheel bolted to the crankshaft keeps it turning smoothly.

Conversely, a smoothly working engine may power a process that requires energy discontinuously. Looms, mechanical hammers, shears, and presses all require bursts of energy that electric motors in particular are ill fitted to deliver. In these cases, the motors drive flywheels, and the flywheels are coupled to the machines by engaging a clutch when needed. The greater the moment of inertia of the flywheel, the smaller the drop in speed of revolution caused when it delivers a burst of energy.

Frames of reference

In 1851, the inertia of a massive pendulum was used by the French physicist Jean-Bernard-Léon Foucault to demonstrate the rotation of Earth. While Earth turned beneath it, the pendulum tended to keep swinging in the same direction in space. The result was that the pendulum's line of swing over the ground seemed to change in the course of a day. The same effect gives rise to the Coriolis force, which makes cyclones blow in circular motions.

Even if the stars were never visible from Earth's surface, we could infer Earth's rotation by observing the behavior of pendulums and of the winds. It might seem easy to go further along this line of reasoning. Even if the stars did not exist and Earth were alone in space, surely the existence of Coriolis forces and other inertial effects would reveal Earth's rotation.

◄ This skater uses the distribution of her mass to affect inertia. By drawing her arms into her body she redistributes her weight closer to the axis of rotation and so reduces her moment of inertia, causing her to spin more quickly. Conversely, by throwing her arms out, her moment of inertia increases, and so the speed of spin slows down to compensate.

Such an idea was a scandal to the Austrian physicist Ernst Mach, who worked at the turn of the 20th century. If no distant celestial objects existed by which a standard of rest could be defined, it seemed to Mach that the idea of motion of Earth would be meaningless. This speculation led him to suppose that if the stars did not exist, the effects of Earth's rotation that we observe would not occur. In short, the inertia of objects on Earth, however minute, is caused by the existence of the rest of the Universe. Astronomers have found that even though our own galaxy or star system is turning, the inertial frame of reference against which we measure such rotation depends on even more distant matter at the limit of the observable Universe. If the celestial bodies were to vanish, we should find ourselves living in a world of objects as light and as unresisting to pushes and pulls as thistledown.

Bizarre as these ideas sound, they bore fruit in the work of Einstein. In ways not dreamed of by Mach, Einstein's general theory of relativity established a link between the inertia of each piece of matter and the distribution of all other matter in the Universe.

SEE ALSO: EARTH • ENERGY, MASS, AND WEIGHT • FRICTION • NEWTON'S LAWS • PENDULUM

Inertial Guidance

Inertial-guidance systems use devices such as accelerometers and gyroscopes to measure changes in the position, velocity, and attitude (orientation) of a vehicle. Such measurements form the basis of a technique, sometimes called inertial navigation, whereby the course of a vehicle is planned without recourse to external navigation aids, such as stars or a global positioning system. Inertial-guidance systems are used in missiles, space vehicles and satellites, aircraft, ships, and submarines; they also have applications in land and deep-sea surveying.

The first inertial-guidance system was developed during World War II for the German V-2 missile, first launched in September 1944. The V-2 design used gyroscopes to stabilize the attitude of the missile in flight and a single accelerometer to measure acceleration along the flight axis. The rocket engine extinguished once the required speed had been achieved. Engineers in the United States developed a complete inertial-navigation system based on accelerometers and gyroscopes by 1948. Ten years later, the efficiency of such a system was proved by its success in accurately navigating the nuclear submarine USS *Nautilus* under the Arctic ice cap.

Measuring acceleration

Devices that measure acceleration—one of the fundamental measurements in inertial guidance—are called accelerometers. A simple accelerometer consists of a mass suspended between two taut springs. By Newton's Second Law of Motion, an accelerating mass experiences a force (F) that is related to the product of its mass (m) and the rate of acceleration (a) by the equation $F \propto ma$.

When an accelerometer is in an accelerating vehicle, the force that accelerates the mass in the accelerometer arises from the compression and extension of the springs that support the mass. By Hooke's law of elasticity, the amount of extension or compression of the springs is proportional to force, so such an accelerometer can be calibrated to measure acceleration in terms of the displacement of the mass from its rest position.

Another type of accelerometer uses transducers that produce an electrical signal in response to the pressure—and therefore the force—that an accelerating mass exerts on them. The output voltage of such a transducer is generated by the piezoelectric effect. The magnitude of the voltage increases with increasing pressure in a predictable manner so that this type of accelerometer measures acceleration in terms of voltage.

▲ A Harrier jet uses a miniature inertial-guidance platform that weighs only 25 lbs. (11 kg). The output from this platform feeds a guidance system that calculates the position of the aircraft at any given time and produces a map display at the center of the pilot's control panel.

Components of acceleration

An accelerometer is sensitive to acceleration in one dimension—along the axis of the springs of a mass-and-spring accelerometer, for example. For this reason, an inertial-guidance system must have three accelerometers mounted along three perpendicular axes, which are typically North–South, East–West, and vertical. The outputs from the three accelerometers are combined to give acceleration in three dimensions and corrected to eliminate acceleration owing to gravity.

Velocity and displacement

If an object accelerates at a constant rate for a given period of time, its change in velocity can be calculated by multiplying the rate of acceleration by the duration of the acceleration. A mathematical procedure called integration, which performs such a calculation for each instant in a given period of time, calculates velocity changes even when the rate of acceleration varies. Modern inertial-guidance systems have microprocessors that perform this type of integration. A second integration with respect to time converts the plot of velocity against time into a plot of displacement, or distance travelled, along the axis of measurement of the accelerometer.

Inertial platforms

One type of inertial-guidance system has accelerometers mounted on an inertial platform—sometimes called a stable platform—that moves so as to maintain the orientations of the accelerometers regardless of the orientation of the vehicle that carries them. Such platforms are mounted in gimbals, which are sets of bearings with three mutually perpendicular and intersecting axes of rotation. These bearings allow free rotation of the platform in any direction.

An inertial platform carries three spinning gyroscopes, whose axes of rotation are aligned to the axes of the accelerometers. The principal characteristic of a gyroscope is that it produces a restoring force in response to any attempt to change its axis of rotation so that the three gyroscopes of an inertial platform act to maintain the platform in a fixed alignment. Many inertial platforms have servomotors that act in concert with the gyroscopes so as to minimize the amount of energy expended by the gyroscopes in maintaining the platform level. This approach ensures that the gyroscopes suffer the least possible disturbance and thus maintain their position to the highest possible accuracy, thereby optimizing the accuracy of the guidance system.

▼ When a mass-and-spring accelerometer is mounted in an accelerating vehicle, the force that makes the mass accelerate with the vehicle is provided by compression and tension of the trailing and leading springs respectively (top left). Acceleration owing to gravity causes a similar effect in a vehicle at rest on an incline (bottom left) and must be eliminated from calculations. Motion relative to Earth's surface can be measured using two accelerometers that are maintained on East–West and North–South axes by a stable platform (right).

An inertial platform measures the components of acceleration—and therefore velocity and displacement—along axes that are fixed in space. Consequently, their measurements must be modified to take into account Earth's spin and its motion through space. When these factors are included, an inertial platform describes the motion of a vehicle relative to Earth's surface. When the measurements are related to a known starting position, they can be used to calculate the vehicle's position without any external input. Motion sensors can be mounted in a platform's gimbals to measure the vehicle's pitch, roll, and yaw. These measurements can be converted into displays of a vehicle's attitude in space, particularly useful for air and space vehicles.

Strap-down systems

In contrast to an inertial-platform system, a strap-down system has a platform that is rigidly mounted to the vehicle that carries it. Three accelerometers provide acceleration data along axes fixed relative to the vehicle, while pressure sensors on a set of three gyroscopes—also rigidly mounted to the vehicle—measure changes in the vehicle's attitude relative to three absolute axes. A microprocessor calculates the vehicle's attitude at

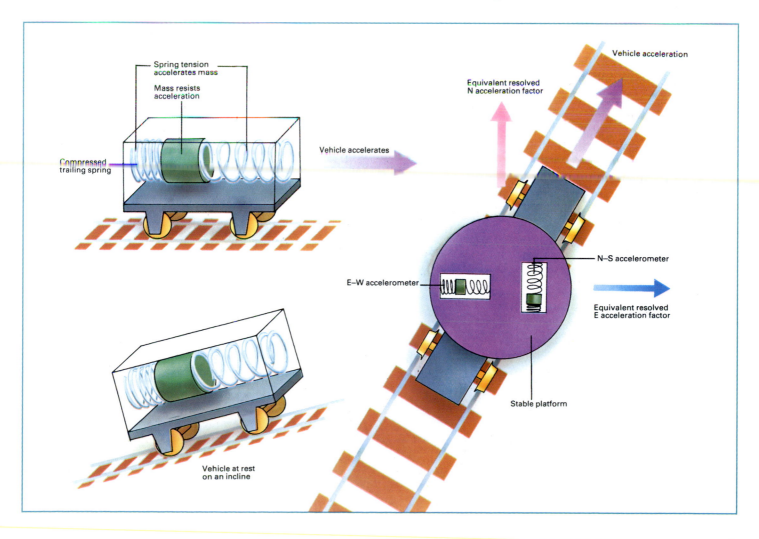

intervals of 0.01 seconds, for example, and modifies the outputs of the three accelerometers accordingly. In effect, this process uses the output from sensors on the gyroscopes to calculate the position of an equivalent inertial platform and then calculates what the accelerometers readings would be for such a platform. The constant recalculations of orientation call for significant computing power, and strap-down systems became practical and then more widely used as adequate microprocessors became available.

Ring lasers

A development of gyroscope-based strap-down systems uses ring lasers to provide accurate measurements of attitude changes. A ring laser uses two laser beams of the same frequency that travel within a solid glass block in opposite directions around a closed path, which is usually triangular.

Ring lasers rely on the Doppler effect to measure attitude changes. If the block rotates around an axis perpendicular to the plane of the laser path, the beam that travels in the opposite direction to the rotation of the block will be detected at a slightly higher frequency than the beam that travels in the opposite direction (the average of the two frequencies is equal to the original frequency of the beams). A microprocessor then uses the frequency difference to calculate an accurate value of the rotation of the block.

Alignment

Alignment is the process whereby the position and orientation of an inertial-guidance system is recorded as a basis for calculations of position and velocity. The accuracy of the alignment process is therefore a vital factor in the accuracy of all subsequent calculations. The procedure entails the entry of longitude, latitude, and altitude data, which are most conveniently obtained from a global positioning system (GPS). Military systems usually have a rapid-alignment option, whereby alignment can be achieved in less than two minutes—at some detriment to accuracy—when a hostile attack is imminent, for example. Some civilian devices can take up to 30 minutes for the system to achieve complete alignment.

Guidance accuracy

The accuracy of an inertial-guidance system is normally given in terms of the position error as a function of time. Typical values for aircraft systems are better than one nautical mile per hour; higher accuracies are achieved by some military systems. The main source of errors lies in the sensitivity of the gyroscopes. Factors such as friction and manufacturing imperfections lead to drift,

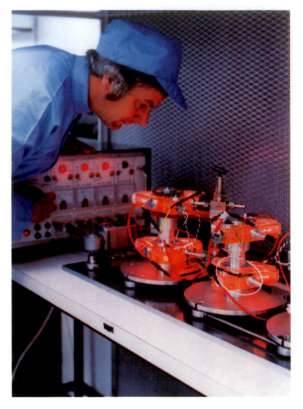

◀ This picture shows the testing of ring lasers, which are high-accuracy alternatives to gyroscopes. Three such devices are mounted along mutually perpendicular axes to measure rotational motion in three dimensions.

which results in the inertial platform being moved slightly away from its desired position. This movement in turn leads to an error in the calculated position of the vessel, since the accelerometer readings no longer lie along the assumed axes.

Accuracy can be increased by periodic reference to external positioning systems, such as GPS. With land-based surveying systems, high accuracy can be achieved by the use of periodic velocity updates, the vehicle being stopped for a few seconds to give a reference.

Advantages over other systems

The advantages of inertial-guidance systems over other types of navigation systems stem from the fact that they are self contained. They do not depend on signals from external systems, such as satellite networks or radio beacons, which are prone to jamming or system failures. A further advantage for military applications is that inertial-guidance systems do not emit signals, such as radar pulses, that make a ship or aircraft prone to detection by hostile observers.

As is the case for other high-accuracy navigation systems, inertial-guidance systems can be integrated with other subsystems of civilian and military craft. Examples of such applications include bomb-aiming and autopilot devices, as well as head-up displays for manual flight.

SEE ALSO: Bomb-aiming device • Global positioning system • Gyroscope • Navigation • Servomechanism

Information Technology

Information assumes a variety of guises: numbers, text, sounds, and images are all expressions of information—they are fodder for the decision-making and perceptive functions of the brain or for the control processes of machinery. Information technology is a combination of applied computer science and telecommunications technology that caters to the manipulation, storage, retrieval, and transmission of such data.

The information revolution

As early as the 1960s, some large organizations started to use huge mainframe computers to process information and store it on reels of magnetic tape. However, it was only by the 1980s that the cost and size of computers had diminished sufficiently for the computerized handling of information to become a viable prospect for small companies and home users.

Also in the 1980s, manufacturers of desktop computers introduced GUIs, or graphical user interfaces. The main elements of a GUI are pictorial menus and icons that represent tasks and instructions. A computer user moves a cursor or arrow across the screen of a monitor using a rolling device such as a mouse or trackball, then selects an icon or menu item by clicking a button when the cursor is in place over the appropriate object. In this way, a few movements of a hand and finger create an instruction that would have required the input of several lines of computer code in earlier systems. The use of GUIs is

▲ Tape archives at the Ogden, Utah, Service Center of the U.S. Internal Revenue Service (IRS). From the 1960s onward, some large corporations and government organizations started to replace their archives of written and typed files with such racks of magnetic tapes. Data are retrieved from archives using tape-reading machines similar to reel-to-reel tape players.

largely intuitive and requires little training, so their adoption eased the retraining of members of clerical staff who had previously typed or written accounts, reports, and other documents.

At first, information technology was mainly concerned with numbers and figures, which can be converted into digital code by simple software (computer programs). Sound, static images, and then movies became an integral part of information technology with the introduction of sound and graphics cards—microprocessors dedicated to processing audio and video data—and with the development of powerful main processors and storage media. Such advances gave rise to desktop publishing and multimedia presentations.

A major improvement in the ease of transfer of information occurred in 1989, when the British computer scientist Timothy Berners-Lee developed software that would form the basis of the World Wide Web. His programming enabled previously incompatible computers to communicate with one another, making them able to gain access to the Internet and exchange electronic mail through telephone links. This advance in interconnectivity, together with the capacity for moving images and sound, promoted home use of the Internet for electronic communication, research, work, and leisure. The launch of WAP (wireless access protocol) cellular phones at the end of the 1990s further extended Internet access and the ability to send electronic mail to users of suitably equipped mobile telephones.

Information theory

Information theory is a collection of formulas, laws, and theories that describe or govern the processing, storage, and transmission of information. As such, it is directly relevant to various aspects of information technology, or IT.

Many IT specialists credit the founding of information theory to the U.S. mathematician and electrical engineer Claude Shannon. In 1940, Shannon published his masters thesis *A Symbolic Analysis of Relay and Switching Circuits*, in which he described how certain electrical circuits can be used to apply the operations of Boolean algebra—a mathematical theory of logic—to electrical signals. Since relay and switching circuits were the predecessors of transistors and eventually microprocessors, the relevance of Shannon's findings extends to the workings of computers.

From 1940, Shannon worked at the Bell Laboratories of American Telephone and Telegraph (AT&T) in New York. There, he applied himself to the study of data transmission through telephone lines. In 1948, Shannon published the results of his work, *A Mathematical Theory of Communication*, in which he coined the term "*bit*," a contraction of *bi*nary digi*t*.

▼ If the information content of a typical DVD (digital versatile disc) were in printed format, it would occupy several thick volumes. The storage density of this medium is so great that the text and illustrations of a major reference work fit on a pocket-sized disc. In addition, a DVD can carry data that computers can convert into sounds and moving images—an option that is not possible for printed publications.

Many of Shannon's proposals have relevance to the transfer and storage of information within computers and through networks. An example is his model for the progress of information through the sequence source, encoder, channel, decoder, and destination. According to that model, a computer modem (from modulator demodulator) can be considered as a combined encoder and decoder for transmitting data between computers as electrical signals that pass through the channel of a telephone line. Extending the same model to data storage, a CD-ROM, DVD, or magnetic disk—floppy or hard—can be considered as the channel, while the devices that write on and read such storage media are the encoders and decoders.

Shannon went on to devise decision-making programs that enabled a computer to play chess (1949) and a robot "mouse" to find its way out of mazes (1952). Such programs later evolved into the programs that control robotic assembly and paint-spraying machines that revolutionized the automobile industry, for example.

A second person to have a profound influence on the development of information technology was the U.S. mathematician Richard Hamming. In 1947, Hamming devised an error-correction technique to help preserve data during transmission and in storage. In Hamming code, a four-bit binary number is protected from corruption by the inclusion of three check bits, whose values of 0 or 1 are determined by algorithms based on the original number. An inconsistency in the check digits not only indicates a corrupted number but also provides a means of calculating the original number and restoring its correct value. Such error-correction techniques enable CD and DVD readers and players to reproduce recorded data from scratched or dirty disks, provided the surface markings are not so extreme as to corrupt several bits of each number.

Data processing

Commerce was one of the first arenas to adopt information technology. The ability to store, retrieve, and manipulate data found use in the control of customer accounts and in the analysis of market data. The two principal tools in data processing are the database and the spreadsheet.

A database is a collection of records that has a common format of data fields (a data field is an item such as "first name," "age," or "country," in which the appropriate value is stored for each record). Data are usually keyed into on-screen forms that have a space for each data field. Database programs can be instructed to restrict or automatically modify the information of individual fields to conform to a standard format. An

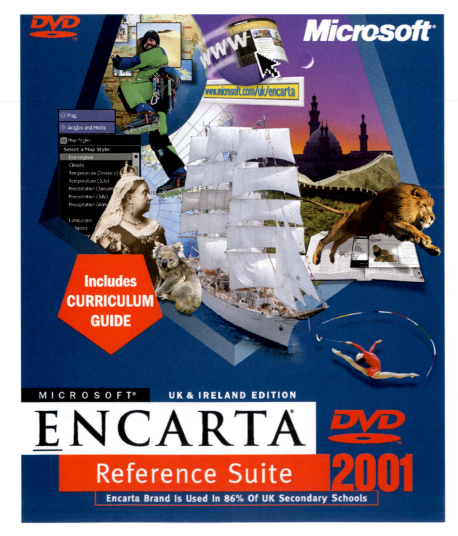

LIBRARY SYSTEMS

For centuries, libraries were the most important reserves of data for individuals, communities, and institutions alike. Although now largely overshadowed by the convenience and speed of information retrieval provided by the Internet, libraries continue to house vast volumes of information, much of which may never be included in Web pages. For this reason, an astute researcher should occasionally take some time away from the computer screen to make sure he or she does not overlook vital facts that can be found only in conventional print.

Several types of libraries exist. Some are personal collections that reflect the interests and chance purchases of the individual or family that assembled the library. Community lending libraries tend to house collections of books that span a wide range of topics to a depth that is dictated mainly by the space and funds available to the library; the libraries of specialist institutions, on the other hand, focus in great depth on a narrower subject range. A few reference libraries are charged with the duty of collecting at least one copy of every copyright work published in a given country.

Of the various coding systems used to catalog the contents of a library, the code that is most specific to a particular publication is its International Standard Book Number, or ISBN. Each format of any given book—hardback or paperback, for example—has a separate and unique ISBN, and every edition of the same book has its own set of ISBNs. The ISBN has the standard format *ISBN-1-234-56789-X,* where the first number or group of numbers indicates the country where the book was published, the second number identifies the company that published the book, the third number is a serial number, and the final character is a check digit that takes the values 0 through 9 or X, meaning "10." The check digit is related to the other numbers in the ISBN by a simple formula; it is a means of identifying and preventing false or mistaken entries in computerized order systems, for example.

While an ISBN is useful when ordering a known book, the number reveals nothing

▲ The Long Room of the library of Trinity College, Dublin, Ireland. Before the information revolution of the late 20th century, libraries such as this were the main source of information for students and researchers. Each book is carefully cataloged and assigned a position in the shelving system of the library. Whereas these data would once have been stored on hand-written and manually-indexed cards, computerized systems now assist in the retrieval of books.

about a book's content. When searching for books and other publications that contain information about a given topic, it is usually necessary to browse through shelves dedicated to a given topic or to refer to a system that classifies publications by content. One of the most widely accepted of such systems is the Dewey Decimal Classification, invented in 1873 by the U.S. librarian Melvil Dewey.

The Dewey system is currently in its 21st edition, sometimes called "DDC 21," and changes have been made over time to accommodate new topics. The main part of a Dewey classification is a three-figure

number that designates the principal subject area; up to three more figures can be added after a decimal point for more detailed descriptions of subjects.

The main numbers fall into ten broad subject classes: 000–099 generalities, 100–199 philosophy, 200–299 religion, 300–399 social science, 400–499 language, 500–599 science, 600–699 technology, 700–799 arts, 800–899 literature, 900–999 history. Each of these classes comprises ten subgroups, so 000–009 is the subgroup of generalities that covers computers, for example. Each number is yet more specific—004 is data processing and computer science, for example—but can still be classified yet more explicitly by a decimal number, such as 004.019 for human-computer interaction.

It is the duty of a librarian to assign a Dewey or similar classification for each item in a library. Publications are shelved or stored according to their classification, and each item has an entry in a card index or a computer database. These systems enable readers and researchers to identify and locate material of interest to them.

example is the date format. Different keyboard operators might type "12/11/00" or "11-Dec-2000" for the same date. A sophisticated database program will identify the two entries and store them in a standard date format. Some fields require no separate data entry, since they are calculated from the values present in other fields. An example would be a monthly sales total calculated from previously entered weekly sales figures.

Spreadsheets are a means of performing routine calculations and manipulations of data. A spreadsheet usually takes the form of a grid of cells. Some cells accommodate data entry, while others contain values calculated by formulas that refer to data in other cells in the grid. Spreadsheets are particularly useful when the same types of data must be analyzed in the same way on a regular basis. First, a template spreadsheet is constructed to contain all the calculations that have to be performed. Thereafter, the data for each analysis is simply entered into the appropriate cells, and the results of the analysis appear in the formula cells. Provided enough care is taken in preparing and checking the original spreadsheet, the use of spreadsheets eliminates occasional errors that can occur and evade detection in complex manual calculations.

The contents of a spreadsheet can be ordered according to the contents of a given column in the same way that the records of a database can be ordered. In fact, the contents of a spreadsheet can be used as the starting point for a database, taking each row as a record and each column as a field. Similarly, the contents of a database can be listed as a table and used as the basis for a spreadsheet.

Word processing and presentations

Word processing started as simply a computerized version of typing, with the keyed text appearing on a screen before printing instead of being typed directly onto paper. Left-hand and right-hand margins and tab markings were set on a ruler in the screen by keying in commands or by mouse actions. With time, word-processing programs came to include formatting tools that allowed for different typefaces in different sizes and with optional bold and italic styles.

Word-processing programs now allow for highly sophisticated formatting and include subprograms that check the spelling and grammar of text in a variety of languages. Images such as company logos, photographs, and charts can be incorporated in documents, and the operator can manipulate text to flow around or within such images to produce documents that are suitable for printing or for presenting by projection onto a screen in a meeting room.

Networking

Computer networking accelerates transactions by eliminating the need for spoken or written communications. Computers can be linked by dedicated cables or by telephone lines using modems or digital signal generators. Over small distances, computers and peripheral devices such as printers and scanners can communicate through radio-frequency signals or infrared light signals.

Company networks frequently have at their core a central data-management system that contains information on stock, sales, and deliveries for the whole company. Such systems help coordinate such activities as raw material orders, manufacturing orders, and stock control.

The impact of networking on established work patterns is enormous. Many clerical workers now work from home using the Internet to provide their network link, for example. Even manufacturing companies can become "virtual" by combining a network of home-working executives with contracted manufacturing units.

Networking has the potential to improve the quality of life by reducing the number of work-related journeys made and the time spent traveling. On the other hand, withdrawal from the social environment of a workplace can make homeworkers feel isolated and has spawned the emergence of social support groups that bring together homeworkers in related professions.

▲ Libraries are key users of the latest information technology systems. Barcode scanners can be used to record details of books being taken out or returned in a database. The data can be accessed from terminals all over the building so that the librarian need not hunt through card indexes to find a particular book but simply key in an ISBN number or enter key words to call up a list of relevant titles. University libraries were among the first to make use of the development of the Internet as a means of sharing research journals and other library resources.

SEE ALSO: BOOKBINDING • COMPUTER • COMPUTER NETWORK • DATA STORAGE • INTEGRATED CIRCUIT • INTERNET

Ink

◄ The manufacture of pen ink. Distilled water, dyes, solvents, stabilizers, and preservatives are mixed in 250-gallon (900 l) batches using a high-speed agitator for half an hour at a cold temperature. Samples are taken from each batch and tested in the laboratory for color density, acidity, conductance, and blotting properties.

Although no precise date can be given for the first use of ink, some of the oldest examples are on Egyptian papyrus dating from 2500 B.C.E. and Chinese documents of around the same period. Early inks consisted of finely dispersed carbon, either lamp black or ground-up charcoal, in a water or oil base with resin or gum bonding agents. These early inks were probably formed into solid cakes or ink sticks with the liquid ink prepared immediately before writing. Such ink sticks are still commonly used by calligraphers.

From the seventh or eighth century, metal gall inks began to appear, made from galls and iron salts. Galls are growths on trees caused by insect attack and are particularly rich in tannin. The tannin from the galls reacts with the iron salts to form an iron tannate, which is a pale blue-gray color. Exposure to the air oxidizes the tannate to give a permanent black image. Later, other sources of tannin were used and the ink color intensified by using indigo—a natural blue dye.

Pen inks

Modern blue-black permanent inks as used in fountain pens are of the metal tannate type, with the addition of a blue dye to give a stronger initial color to the ink. Washable inks are basically dye solutions with the base normally being water. These inks dry by a combination of absorption into the paper surface and evaporation. They are made by dissolving the dyes in a solvent (usually water) with the addition of small amounts of stabilizers and preservatives, followed by filtration or centrifuging to remove any insoluble material. Indian or Chinese ink consists of carbon particles suspended in a solution of resin, gum, or varnish.

Fiber-tip inks

The tip of a fiber-tip pen consists of a bundle of textile fibers bound using resin with sufficient space between the fibers for ink to flow through them by capillary action. The inks are similar to normal writing inks but have a high humectant (moisturizer) content to prevent them from drying in the tip. Felt-tip markers use a felt pad to transfer ink to paper and again use similar inks, although rapid-drying solvents are often used.

Ballpoint inks

In the ballpoint pen, ink is transferred to the paper from the surface of a ball (or roller) 0.016 to 0.04 in. (0.4–1.0 mm) in diameter. Because of the small size of the ball and the space between the ball and its housing, the amount of ink delivered to the paper as the pen writes is small, and the ink has to contain a large amount of coloring matter to allow it to make a legible trace. As a comparison, the ink contained in a small ballpoint pen refill will draw a continuous line between 4,500 and 6,000 ft. (1,370–1,830 m) long, while the same volume of fountain pen ink would draw a line of just approximately 240 to 300 ft. (75–90 m) long.

To prevent the ink from drying on the ball and solid matter from jamming it, the ink is carefully filtered and contains slow-drying solvents such as oils and gums. These inks dry by penetration into the paper and have to be specially formulated to suit the pen. Erasable ballpoint inks are latex-based and dry on writing but they do not cure fully for some time, so they can be rubbed off.

Printing inks

The requirements for modern printing inks vary, depending on the materials to be printed on, which include plastics, papers, cards, and metals. The main printing processes are letterpress, in which raised surfaces carry the ink; gravure, in which the ink collects in recesses in the printing surface; lithography, where parts of the flat printing surface are treated so that ink will not adhere to them; and silkscreen, which is basically a stencil process.

Every printing ink has to meet certain basic requirements—it has to be laid down in a thin, even layer that will adhere to the surface; it should keep its shape when being transferred; and when in place, it has to have the correct color.

The color is obtained from fine particles of solid pigments carried in a base that dries to hold the pigments in place. Various additives are used to modify the printing and drying characteristics of the ink, and solvents may be used to alter the viscosity and facilitate the manufacturing process. Many materials are used as pigments: black is obtained from carbon and furnace blacks, while the main opaque white pigments are titanium dioxide and zinc oxide. Colored pigments may be inorganic—such as lead chromate yellow and ultramarine blue—or organic.

Ink characteristics

Various resins, drying oils, and often solvents are used for printing inks. Jobbing inks, for printing stationery, tickets, and so on, are thick and slow drying; the vehicle is a mixture of mineral oil, resin, and litho varnish (treated linseed oil). News printing uses just mineral oil, because it is applied to more absorbent paper on much faster presses.

Rough paper requires more ink than smooth paper. Colored ink will not cover as much volume as black ink—the coverage varies with the color. There are so many shades of colored ink that no satisfactory method of classifying them has been devised; matching must be done visually or by using a spectroscope or a colorimeter.

Inks used in gravure processes must not be too tacky, because the machinery wipes the plates clean and the wiping action must not pull the ink out of the recesses; the ink must also have enough body to fill the recesses completely. It must not react with traces of the acids used in etching, and the finely ground pigments should be soft so that the copper cylinder is not scratched. Inks used in

lithographic processes must not be soluble in water, or they will bleed onto the nonprinted area.

Most printing inks dry partly by penetration and partly by reaction of an oil or synthetic resin with oxygen, but there are many variations. Heat-set inks are often used in high-speed presses; these solidify when heated and are made with solvents that are volatile at high temperatures. Some contain polyvinyl chloride (PVC). Cold-set inks are applied at a relatively high temperature and dry when they cool. Steam-set inks dry by precipitation, and instead of drying oils, the vehicle is a glycol solvent and a resin, which is insoluble in water. On absorbing water, the pigment and resin precipitate and set simply by keeping the press room humid. Other drying processes include ultraviolet curing of resin vehicles.

Special inks

Metallic inks have particles of metal suspended in them; they are used for printing on metals and packaging. Sometimes inks are made deliberately magnetic, for printing banknotes, checks and business forms that are sorted or read by machinery. Fluorescent inks are designed to be bright, and can be coated to prolong the brightness. Inks used for food packaging have to have low odor levels, and the pigments have to be nontoxic. Scratch-n-sniff inks have a scent or essential oil encapsulated in microspheres 10 to 30 microns in diameter. They are small enough and strong enough to withstand lithographic printing processes but can be ruptured by a fingernail.

▲ A machine for testing the color density of ballpoint pen inks. The ink must be tested in an actual ballpoint device for accurate density, since only a small amount gets past the ball housing.

SEE ALSO: ANILINE AND AZO DYES • DYEING PROCESS • LITHOGRAPHY • PEN • PRINTING

Index